THE AMERICAN PORCH

THE
AMERICAN
PORCH

AN INFORMAL HISTORY
OF AN INFORMAL PLACE

Michael Dolan

OPEN ( ) ROAD
INTEGRATED MEDIA
NEW YORK

Copyright © 2002 by Michael Dolan

ISBN: 978-1-5040-9048-3

This edition published in 2024 by Open Road Integrated Media, Inc.
180 Maiden Lane
New York, NY 10038
www.openroadmedia.com

For Eileen and Marty

CONTENTS

FOREWORD

This old porch is just a long time
Of waiting and forgetting
And remembering the coming back
And not crying about the leaving
And remembering the falling down
And the laughter of the curse of luck
From all of those sons-of-bitches
Who said we'd never get back up
— *"This Old Porch," by Robert Earl Keen and Lyle Lovett, 1985*

One of the torturous joys of reporting is the process of exchanging what you think for what you know. When I started work on this book in the mid–1990s, I thought I was onto something as American as a greenback dollar. (The porch at Monticello appears on the back of the nickel and the pre-1976 two-dollar bill; next time you have a wad of simoleons, flip over a five-, ten-, twenty-, or hundred-dollar bill and see what you see.) Through my research, however, I wound up knowing that the porch represents the fruits of many nations and many cultures, each infusing the next with its flavor to create an American institution, one whose small-r republican, small-d democratic openness embodies so much of what I love about our country.

On the morning of September 11, 2001, though, I thought I'd erred in devoting so much time and energy to an emblem of an open society. Since just after 7:00 I'd been in my basement office. Many writers work to music or radio or television; I need silence. So when, after a couple of hours at the computer keyboard, I came upstairs to shower and shave, I had no idea what was occurring up in Manhattan and down at the Pentagon, a few miles south of my house. I only turned on the television to catch a few minutes of a videotaped movie as I dressed.

What I caught, of course, wasn't a videotaped movie. It was what we all saw, live or in endless replay. After watching those awful things over and over I thought that in their aftermath America might change so drastically as to render the phrase "open society" obsolete, along with the symbols that evoked it. And for a while it did look as if things were going that way—as if, in the rush to justice and vengeance, we might become as closed to life as those who'd attacked us.

But then folks started to emerge from their despair. They began to step into and through their grief, began to make tentative gestures of hope, to signal that they realized we'd been hurt terribly. They were signaling to say they knew many things might never be the same, but also to say some things were still the same and always would be.

You started to see flags—not just on vehicle aerials and lapels and flying twenty-four/seven over car dealerships and the other places where they flutter in times of bluster and braggadocio, but on houses, and nowhere more often on houses than on houses with front porches. Hang me for a scoundrel, but there is something about an American flag on a front porch that speaks even to my sharply circumscribed sense of patriotism.

For me, a flag hanging on a porch isn't the same as the fist-pounding love-it-or-leave-it jingoism that gripped our country in the late sixties. Nor is it anything like the tricolor commerciality in which the Super Bowl and other entertainments drape themselves, masquerading as heritage while trying to pick our pockets. It isn't even the brokenhearted defiance I felt watching those fire-fighters raise Old Glory on the charnel mound at Ground Zero.

A flag on a porch says to me, this is home. This is where we live. It's a place you ought to see, where different kinds of people try to get along. Some days we do a terrible job of that and some days we halfway succeed, but mainly we keep on trying, we keep on keeping on, and that's because on the whole it's a good way to live, a good place to live. Come sit with us; maybe you'll see what we mean.

As I thought about this, I realized I hadn't been wrong to study the American porch. I'd learned why a bit of cloth on a railing touches me so profoundly. I'd seen how the porch itself came to figure in my pursuit of happiness and maybe in yours, too.

I hope, if you make your way through this yard sale of history and happenstance that I've assembled, you feel the same.

—Michael Dolan,
Washington, D.C.,
May 2002

THE AMERICAN PORCH

We had to destroy the porch in order to save it, not only because it was falling apart, but because it was a butt-ugly travesty of what it had once been.

INTRODUCTION

MY PORCH AND WELCOME TO IT

The American porch, like the American nation, acquired its style and its substance from antecedents around the world. As with the nation, whose structure and significance we can trace across oceans and eons, so too with the porch, whose roots reach deep into the intertwined history of architecture and human experience.

But origin is one thing; originality is another.

For the United States to come into being, Americans had to leap beyond what had occurred before in community, in government, in politics, and in statesmanship. The porch has made that same leap, evoking its architectural ancestors and at the same time becoming something uniquely American.

This uniqueness lies not only in the once-immense popularity of the porch but also in the way that changing tastes, shifting mores, and technological advances would lead Americans, a notoriously fickle people, to hold the porch in such familiarity for so long that eventually, they would have little choice but to let that affection curdle into contempt.

After more than a hundred years of inordinate fondness, Americans at the middle of the twentieth century discarded the porch as old-fashioned, obsolete, and valueless—until a blend of conservation and revival began to restore it to a place of honor and utility. The porch will never be what it once was, but neither will it vanish. Instead, after 150 years of yawing from ubiquity to rejection, the porch will hold its place as a standard element of domestic American architecture, and we will all be the better for that.

I started to see the porch in historical terms when I acquired one of my own. You could say my porch started to talk to me.

My front porch speaks with a strong and persuasive American accent, in the vernacular architectural language of the nation of which I am a citizen, the city where I was born, and the neighborhood I inhabit. Like any tongue, this language mixes the classical and the popular, the formal and the colloquial, the sacred and the profane. And, like any language, it mutates, a process of which my porch is emblematic.

I live in Washington, D.C. (formally, the District of Columbia), which exists for many people as a vivid figment of the imagination—intrigue-ridden, peopled by villains and heroes, and obsessed with matters of state, issues of national security, and lurid scandals. These notions have basis in fact, but, like any set of stereotypes, they ignore the larger, more complicated reality. If folks could see past the Washington of the mind to the real city, they'd think more kindly of it.

One window into the real Washington is my neighborhood. It's called Palisades. Palisades occupies the city's westernmost corner, adjacent to a magnificent valley created by the Potomac River. The neighborhood's name comes from the bluffs that look out onto the valley, where the Chesapeake & Ohio Canal runs parallel to the Potomac. Behind these bluffs spreads a narrow plain, a vestige of the ancient riverbed. Palisades, which sits on that plain, began as a working-class streetcar suburb in the early twentieth century. Its stock of vintage bungalows, cottages, and four-squares has survived largely intact; we joke that if you were to shake an American awake in the middle of the night and ask what a neighborhood looks like, you'd get a picture-perfect description of Palisades. If you've used National Airport (yeah, yeah, I know—the official name is "Reagan National," but as a D.C. native I'll never call it that), you've probably flown over my house—gray roof, two chimney pots, just inside the city line, eighth in from the waterworks. Let me know when you're landing; I'll lean off the porch and wave.

Our property is fairly typical. The lot is fifty by a hundred feet, bounded front and back by sidewalk and alley. Our house—a bargain-basement bungalow— has a footprint of twenty-five by thirty-six, set streetward. The porch sits eighteen feet from the sidewalk, and rises three feet off the ground. You reach it on wide stone steps hemmed by wooden banisters. Eight feet deep and twenty-five feet wide, the porch features a glider, four chairs, a couple of benches, and a plywood coffin (fully functional, yes, but until I really need it, a storage bin for Halloween props and garden tools). Even with all that stuff, we have plenty of elbow room—the record for occupancy is thirty adults and a few toddlers.

Our porch has a shed-style roof that rides on four columns that are white, square, and tapered slightly base to crown. The railings, also white, sit high at thirty-six inches. The floor is a deep green. The wall at the back of the porch is the siding that covers the house exterior, a double-ogee clapboard in a mellow yellow that agrees nicely with the porch floor and trim. The varnished pine ceiling reflects a warm, honeyed light. Porches up and down the block have roughly the same setback; they form a grid of receding rectangles. In summer, that grid fills with foliage; in winter, bare branches allow the long view.

We use our porch a lot. As early as February, the afternoon sun sustains the drinking of a quick cup of coffee on the front steps. True porch season opens in April and lasts through October, but even as late as December, we can indulge in guitar playing, reading, exchanges with passing neighbors, and, best of all, the taking of glider-based naps. (A glider is a contraption that suggests a sofa suspended on leaf springs so that to sit on it is to float, swaying slightly or, if the mood strikes, swinging. Social critic Paul Fussell calls gliders "high-prole," which, given that I'm a journeyman scribbler and the son and grandson and great-grandson of bookbinders, seems fair enough.)

My porch looks as if it's been around forever, but it was built in 1994–95, and in its tale lie this book's beginnings.

The truth is, we had to destroy the porch in order to save it, not only because it was falling apart, but because it was a butt-ugly travesty of what it had once been. I know how nice the original porch was; I've seen photos. Neighborhood legend holds that the porch and the house were the work of ship's carpenters who spent years of weekends building the place until one partner sold out. (It could be true—tax records show the house as dating to 1926, but not occupied before the thirties.) The other carpenter moved into the house with his wife. In 1934, goes the story, he fell down the stairs, broke his neck, and died. Two years later, his widow sold out to Douglas and Lila Lynch—by all accounts, quintessential Palisades residents. Lila, a Texan, was renowned as sweet and saintly. Doug, a brick mason, had been born and raised nearby, in a house alongside the C&O Canal; his first job was leading mules along its towpath. He and Lila had three kids.

In autumn 1980, Eileen and I encountered the house and the Lynch family at an estate sale. (We'd come looking for wicker furniture, but it had been sold.) Lila was dead, waked not long before in the living room. Doug, who'd had a stroke, sat slumped in an aged wing chair, slugging whiskey from a water glass. His middle-aged children were discussing how to price the house.

"A hundred and twenty-five thousand," somebody said.

I looked around and thought, who would take this piece of shit for free, never mind pay for it?

The kitchen, vestibule, and stairs were carpeted with Day-Glo green-and-orange indoor-outdoor in an eye-scalding fleur-de-lis pattern. The dining room floor bore evidence of canine incontinence. The bathroom smelled like the small mammal building at the zoo. In the kitchen, the Formica walls were spattered with pancake batter and grease, and the Plexiglas drop ceiling had a rancid yellow tinge. The cellar was a warren of musty, low-ceilinged rooms.

And the porch? Well, the porch was just sad.

For starters, it had been wrapped in jalousies, hand-cranked cascades of narrow glass panes that, in theory, you can open or close, with metal screens behind to keep out the bugs. On the Lynch porch, half the cranks were broken or missing. The grimy jalousies and cheaply paneled interior maintained a permanent twilight that made it possible to ignore the spongy floor, paint-blistered ceiling, and general air of morbid depression. And that was the inside. From the street, the porch's curb appeal was less than zero; it looked like a punched eye, bruised and squinty. Of course, nine months later, when I found out exactly who would pay money for that piece of shit—not the asking price, but no minor sum, either—the porch was way down the list of my worries.

As Eileen and I plowed into what would be a twelve-year renovation, the porch alternated between warehouse and R&R zone. When we had a project going, the porch filled with whatever we needed to get out of the house—refrigerator, bathtub, toilet—and whatever construction supplies pertained. When the work went into remission, we'd haul a sofa and chairs out there in a parody of a living room.

We had no security worries. The jalousies were filthy. (At first we tried to keep them clean, but it was like painting the Golden Gate Bridge; as soon as you finished you had to start over, and the hell with that.) Factor in the rotating array of lumber, Sheetrock, insulation, and the rest—at one point, while we were having the floors sanded, every radiator we owned was out there—and you had a porch that projected an aura that said, "Don't bother. There's nothing worth stealing."

Some people remember the eighties as the Age of Reagan; I recall the Era of Endless Toil. As Eileen and I took walls down, our house showed us its bones, some like new, some rotten. We found wasp nests, a 1939 penny postcard urging Lila Lynch to advance her career by enrolling at the Stenotype Institute of Washington, marbles, Korean War–era newspapers wadded to support plaster patches, a 1941 Liberty half-dollar, the skeleton of a bird that had gotten into the space between the bedroom and stairwell walls and starved to death standing up, stones still in its passway and a pile of dried guano between its desiccated claws. On windy nights, the house moved like a boat at anchor. During the winter, we could smell fresh, cold air wafting through the cracks.

When we had a project going, the porch filled with whatever we needed to get out of the house.

Demolition is cheap; all it takes is time, stamina, and the skin off your knuckles. What piles up the bills is construction. When we'd run out of money, we'd smash apart a hunk of house, meanwhile amassing a war chest with which to resume battle, hand-to-hand and room-to-room. It was during these lulls that we made the porch a semi-habitable, moldering constant—always needing attention, never getting it. Often, the electrical outlets there served the rest of the house, through orange extension cords that snaked over windowsills and across the threshold to the interior. Every spring, at either end of the porch, redheaded finches would squeeze into the space between jalousie and screen to nest. The adults would produce chittering broods that would fatten into fledglings, learn to fly, and return a year later, right about the time I'd be scraping away the detritus of the previous year's tenants. As we acquired better furniture, we'd demote pieces from living room to porch status—another reason to love the jalousies, which camouflaged the comfortable but trashy panorama.

But even at its sleaziest the porch was inviting. Eileen and I would sprawl on whatever sofa was decaying there and wait for a breeze. Once, during a sudden storm, a sodden jogger materialized before our lightning-blasted eyes. We tried to get her to take a towel, but she insisted on keeping watch for her friends. A car drove up, there was another flash, and she was gone, leaving only wet footprints.

The porch was a place of industry, too. During the several years that I freelanced as a music critic for a local daily, a 1955-vintage IBM typewriter stood at the far corner. I'd return from a show, often after midnight, my clothes reeking of cigarette smoke, to hammer out a review; if you're old enough to recall the thwack of keys on platen and the clatter of an electric carriage, you know the neighbors always knew when I was working. I hope nobody noticed I was typing in my underwear.

Like hostages experiencing Stockholm syndrome, Eileen and I identified with our hulk of a home, especially the porch. At an art show opening, we separately noted a hand-tinted photo of a wrecked house. On the wraparound porch sprawled a worn-out mattress. "Just like our place!" we each thought. The picture, entitled "My Summer Vacation," hangs in our living room. When our son, Marty, was an infant, the porch made a fine playpen. Spilled milk? Hah! Splattered tempera? Big deal. Crayon marks? So what—it was only the porch, for God's sake.

Marty, in fact, inspired the porch's resurrection. One Sunday morning, I took him with me to an estate sale. He toddled ahead into the house and vanished. I followed, obviously looking panicked. "Florida room," the clerk said, pointing to a doorway. I found Marty rocking away in a porch glider from the forties that sported several dozen coats of hand-slathered paint, the topmost a pale yellow as filthy as the frazzled seat cushions on which my son was bouncing. "Let's get it!" Marty said.

I don't want you to think I indulge my child's every whim, but a ten-spot later, the glider was en route to our house, where its rattiness resonated with the rattiness of the porch to create a Platonic ideal of rattiness that I managed to overlook until Eileen issued an ultimatum: fix it up, or throw it out. Make it nice, or do without.

Discarding the mildewed slipcovers, I took the glider frame to be sand-blasted and then painted a lush, deep green. Next came new cushions and covers. Eventually, that ten-dollar glider cost about six hundred bucks, but it looked great—so great we could no longer ignore the moldy, sag-floored, misbegotten porch where the renewed glider gleamed like an orchid on a dung heap.

But we couldn't destroy the porch until we could afford to replace it; the jalousies and paneling and wobbly floor and grungy ceiling got a reprieve. During the two years it took to save the ten thousand dollars we figured we could spend, I broke my right thighbone in a bicycle wreck; it took me six months to learn to walk again. When I wasn't torturing myself with crutches, trying to climb the steep brick steps Doug Lynch had built, I was on the glider, pondering and sketching as I tried to decipher what the porch wanted to be, since it clearly didn't want to be the piece of junk it was. I developed a simple design, two feet deeper than what we had.

Finally we amassed the ten grand. A contractor who couldn't do the job for that sum suggested that instead of building a new porch foundation, we use the one we had. We could cantilever new joists over it since the eaves were deep enough. To do the job, we hired an amiable North Carolinian named Jim.

Jim and I went over my amateur sketches. Our next-door neighbors' porches have half-pillars made of cast concrete, topped by short wooden columns; I wanted ours to fit in, but with full columns. Jim concurred. Original porch railings in Palisades rarely sit higher than thirty inches, permitting porch occupants and passersby to have face time if they desire. Jim explained that the safety code now required thirty-six-inch railings, which would block those views—but I'm tall, and I like to lean on porch railings, so three-footers were fine. Instead of painting the ceiling, we'd stain and seal it, which would increase the amount of ambient light. Eileen and I argued over whether to install screens until Jim spec'd out a doorway that would permit us to go either way at any time. And Jim had ideas of his own. He brought samples of Tennessee sandstone for the steps. Sold. He suggested the steps rise seven inches over a twelve-inch run. Yes. Put electrical outlets here and there, and set a ceiling fan there. Jim, you da man.

We were ready. But Jim had a bigger job than ours on his calendar, so he sent us his second-stringers. Tommy and Harry were pure-strain good old boys, beery of gut, unfiltered of smoking product, unconcerned with the finer details of nearly everything. I steeled myself for a long autumn.

But the first days went well. In the miraculous way that demolition has of whisking away your worries, the jalousies and their frames and rusty screens flew into the back of a stake-bed truck, along with the paint-encrusted porch ceiling. To prepare for the day when we'd have no alternative, we started using the rear doorways, only the first of many dramatic changes. With the jalousies no longer there to refract it, light streamed onto the porch and into the living room.

Using a circular saw, Tommy ripped open the floor. He and Harry peeled back the boards and found that instead of installing joists every sixteen or twenty inches, some genius had spaced them every three feet. At the entryway, the joists were even farther apart. No wonder that, when crossing the porch, we'd felt as if our heels were about to go through the floor. Our heels *were* about to go through the floor.

The work and the workers were unrelentingly loud, but the noise was musical, the sound of work I didn't have to do. Anyone who's lived on-site through a renovation—especially if they've done as much of the work as Eileen and I did—knows what I mean. After twelve years of chewed-up hands, screwed-up knees, bruises, blisters, abrasions, grit-encrusted eyelids, a nose full of gray-green construction boogers (when you can write your initials on the wall with what you've scraped out of your snotlocker, well, my friend, then you're *really* renovating), I was in a clean, well-lighted place, listening to other people bang on things with hammers. It seemed almost too easy.

It was.

The end of the demolition phase meant the start of construction, and starting construction meant keeping a closer eye on Tommy and Harry. Keeping a closer eye on Tommy and Harry was not a happy experience for any of us. They'd gotten away with too much sloppy work for too many unconscious clients. I'd done too much of my own work to let it pass. I can put up with my own incompetence. But don't take my money and jack me around—that's when I reach for my metaphorical revolver.

Jim had pegged the job at six weeks. The sentence involving the phrase "six weeks" ripples off a contractor's tongue like the first bars of the national anthem: "Ih-if things all go riiiiiiiight, it should taaake us siiiiiix weeeeeeks...." Of course, in an honest universe the following lines would be, "... but we knooow that won't beeeee, so-oh whooooo am I kiiiiiiddiiiiing? It will take us two months, it will take us three years, you will come to believe that we'll neh-ever leave...."

There were weather delays, equipment delays, lumber delivery delays. And there were crew-free days—mysterious interludes when I'd be upstairs in my office and realize things had gotten quiet. Too quiet. I'd go downstairs and edge out onto a joist. I'd tiptoe to the battered brick steps, look around, and see . . . nobody. Next day, or the day after that, Tommy and Harry would be back, smoking and banging on nails, Harry moving with sheepish care, Tommy grab-assing around, no explanations, no apologies.

The fellows finally finished the floor as Thanksgiving was closing in. Washington doesn't get that cold, but it gets cold enough. Jim found inside work. Tommy and Harry vanished, probably hibernating.

But at least we could clamber up the half-demolished steps and use the front door again. And, as the winter solstice neared, I noticed a new feature. In mid-December, the sun sets directly across from our house, behind a ridge in Virginia. The sight always looked dramatic from the yard, but now we could see it from the porch and from inside the house. A sunbeam would shoot into the porch and through the upper sashes of the living-room windows, casting a shadow of the ceiling fan on the far wall—a brief but startling flourish, like the green flash off Key West or holy hour at Stonehenge. The light show didn't make up for the delays, but it reminded us that things were getting better, even though, from then until March, the project went into suspended animation.

Around the same time that the redheaded finches returned from wherever redheaded finches winter over, Harry and Tommy showed up. The finches found their customary jalousies gone. They fluttered around for a couple of days before deciding the top side of a beam was the spot for a nest. Tommy and Harry simply picked up where they'd left off, moving like just-awakened bears.

The porch was far from finished, but it had undergone dramatic improvement. Jim himself had set the railings and balusters, and they looked gorgeous. The roof joists were irregular enough that I wondered if Tommy was up to the task of installing the ceiling boards evenly and tightly. Again, Jim stepped in, knocking the first courses into place and attaching them with a power nailer.

Tommy took over, swearing he'd keep the line straight and the fit close. And he did, right up to the afternoon I came down for a break. As I was standing behind him in the doorway, Tommy reached for a board and held it up to its intended spot, right where my gaze would fall every time I walked onto the porch. The board had a long, jagged crack in it.

"Awww, this'll be fahn, Hahhy," Tommy said, not realizing I was behind him. "Put a lil' sawdust an' glue innair, look great. Never know a diffrence."

"Tommy," I said in as low a voice as I could manage.

He turned around.

"I'd know the difference," I said. "And it would look terrible. Don't put that board up there."

This time there was no affable excusatory growl. Tommy looked at me, looked at the board, and put it down. "All right, Mike," he said in a completely normal voice. He selected a straight, perfect piece of wood, handed it to me for a second check, and banged it into place.

After that, with the exception of a few minor—well, actually, there were more than a few and they were more than minor, but that's another set of stories—bollixes, the porch was done, in time for summer and much glider-powered pondering of porches and their almost magnetic attraction to the American psyche.

Of course, as in any construction project, this one was flawed. At times I spy the one misaligned column face, or the persistent hump at the middle of the floor, and wish things had gone differently.

But if they had, I might have taken a path other than the one that led to this book, which began when I sat in the restored glider on the newly finished porch and wondered, why do I like this place so much?

It certainly wasn't nostalgia for the homes of my childhood and adolescence, which had taken place in the classic trio of post—World War II suburban architecture: brick colonial, Cape Cod, and ranch. The only one with a porch had been the colonial, to which my parents had appended a second-story bedroom whose supporting pillars framed a screened back porch. The lone front porch I remembered from my youth was the one at my grandparents' house in northeast D.C., where I'd spent many a summer afternoon rocking on the glider.

Glider. Hmmmm. There was one connection.

Then there was the front porch on the house my first wife and I had rented in southern Maryland; the deerflies made it impossible to sit out there, but I vividly recalled how the pillars framed a view of the St. Mary's River. Soon after that we ditched country life to buy a badly remodeled Victorian in the D.C. suburbs. When our starter marriage disintegrated, I got the house, which was too much of a mess to try to sell. She got the pickup truck. Many an evening and weekend, as I struggled to renovate the place, I wished I'd gotten the truck. That house was a dump, but it did have a semi-grand front porch. My neighborhood was the sort of place where, when you chained a bicycle to the porch railing, one of your neighbors would regard that gesture as an invitation to use bolt cutters to liberate your ten-speed.

The porch wasn't much use in the relaxation department, either. I'd be lying out there, exhausted from installing insulation or hauling Sheetrock, trying in vain to catch some z's. Meanwhile, across the street, members of the extended and fractious Brown family would be washing a couple of vintage Cadillacs to the sleep-shattering tune of "One Nation under a Groove" booming and zooming at maximum volume from the cars' radios. After six months of grunt labor, I finally sold the house at a modest profit and moved into a series of apartments, none of which satisfied my soul.

Not until Eileen and I had gotten married and bought the ramshackle house in Palisades did I feel myself again at ease, and never did I feel more at ease than as I sat on the porch I'd designed. I decided I had to figure out the source of that sense of comfort, which seemed to stem from my collection of tangential porch recollections and a glossary of images from television, the movies, books, pictures, and songs.

I thought about the Taylors' porch in Mayberry, the porches in John Ford's movies and John Steinbeck's novels, the porches on a thousand reproductions of Currier & Ives prints and Walker Evans photos, the front porch Bruce Springsteen sent Mary dancing across as the radio played Roy Orbison singing for the lonely.

And I realized that the porch in my head, against which I measured all other porches, had emerged less from firsthand experience than through a complicated set of cultural transmissions. I began to test my memory against reality. What started as a point of passing curiosity evolved into a research project and then a personal journey through aspects of history and society, American and otherwise, that I never imagined would have any link to a subject as seemingly simple as the front porch of my house.

When I was a reporter, I used to joke that every assignment, no matter how obscure or narrow, was a keyhole that offered a view onto a universe.

Until I wrote this book, I didn't know how right I was.

My porch looks as if it's been around forever, but it was built in
1994–95, and in its tale lie this book's beginnings.

As Greek architecture evolved, different forms were codified into a system
that ordered column sizes and decorations down to the last detail.

CHAPTER ONE

AS AMERICAN AS ANCIENT GREECE . . .
AND IMPERIAL ROME

The first dwelling might have begun as a stand of saplings deep in some forest. Clearing the center of the grove and bending a ring of living crowns to form a bower, our architectural ancestors would have worked to deflect the elements by intertwining the branches and chinking the gaps with twigs, leaves, moss, and bark, in time improving on that covering with thatched grasses, skins, and crude planks, replacing the living trunks with columns of hewn wood—and voila: *casa prima.*

But the first porch? It came far earlier.

Imagine a slope overlooking a valley. Some distance up the hillside gapes a cave mouth. By accident of orogeny or erosion, a stone slab hangs over the patch of ground at the opening, protecting it and whatever might lurk there. In winter, the cave attracts creatures seeking a den in which to mate and suckle and endure the cold; in summer, the cavern depths offer relief from the heat, predators, floods, and fires. Repeated for eons, these patterns litter the passage with nesting material, shreds of hide and hair, bone fragments, dried feces, crusted gore.

Eventually, the summer day comes that our prehistoric antecedents see animals crouched at the cave entrance, enjoying the chilled air that flows from it. The hominids investigate, and soon they colonize. In the shadow of the stone, they're safe to scan the landscape for herds, lone targets, and competitors. They can defend themselves or retreat into the darkness behind.

The location invites return visits; from it, occupants observe the cycles of sun and night and season with less fear and more comprehension. During a storm, lightning sets a log afire; an enterprising hominid hauls the smoldering wood to the cave to study the mysteries of flame and tinder. This leads to the hearth, to cooking, and to the torch that illuminates deeper explorations. Stains left by feeding animals inspire the dipping of a finger into a puddle of blood, and on fire-lit cave walls, paintings take shape.

Backs guarded by the earth and faces set to gaze upon their dangerous world from a spot dry and defensible, the cave's inhabitants encounter the universe. Here unfold possibilities: respite from the wild and its brutish existence, a place of sustenance, rest, and procreation, a setting in which to weave the web of ritual precedent to culture. The focal point of this humble domicile is its protected entry, the point at which the life inside meets the outer world.

The idea of home took shape, in the fullness of time transmitted from the found setting to the built, from the nomadic existence to the stable, from the settlement to the village to the town to the city. Here, in the zone that linked the privacy of the cave to the public realm of forest and field, the first tendrils of community wove themselves into the human nervous system. Those tendrils took root and, thousands of generations later, blossomed into an understanding of where you live and how you live, so implicit that the question of why you live that way hardly ever comes up. As historian and architect R.D. Dripps has noted, one font of human society was the selection of a fixed place from which to view life.

"People exist securely in their world because its order begins with themselves and radiates outward," Dripps writes. "What they know of this world is measured from this place. As the distance from the center increases and its influence diminishes, the domain over which this center must continue to preside needs to be increasingly secure."

That center can't exist without a boundary between safety and danger—or, as on the porch, between the inside and the out. This is not as easy as it might seem. Even the thinnest such edge has an in side and an out side, an up side and a down side, undefined until a human figure straddles it. And even then, there's no shortage of ambiguity.

One man's entry is another's exit; the door that opens in welcome can as easily be slammed in rejection. To know where you stand on the porch, you have to know where you stand with the occupants of the house. Just so, the occupants have the opportunity to stand on the porch and see where they stand in the world. In antiquity, that world was natural, boundless and unmediated—until humans began to build and to realize that the sight of a landscape framed by structure affirmed their coexistence with nature.

The power of architecture grows from that realization. In few places was that power wielded as adroitly as by the Greeks, who set their temples just so, aiming to integrate society and landscape. Temple designers represented the resident deity with a statue at the back of a simple room called a *naos* or *cella*. At the center of this room stood an altar, facing out from the *naos* toward the door. The outside entry was a space covered by a projecting roof held up by a line of columns. Early temples had one of these structures—a *pronao*—only at their entrances, though later a fake *pronao* at the rear enhanced symmetry.

No roofs extended at the sides of early temples, but by 600 B.C.E., the *naos* was surrounded on all four sides by a line of columns holding up a roof—the peristyle, beneath which might stand statues of lesser gods, a place where worshippers could leave offerings. Peristyles began to appear in Greece in the late seventh and early sixth centuries B.C.E. So did *stoas*, which were shallow, wide structures—essentially a roof held up by a line of columns. "It is impossible to determine which came first in Greece, the peristyle or the stoa, and a common source is generally assumed for both," writes Robin Francis Rhodes in *Architecture and Meaning on the Athenian Acropolis*. Rhodes suggests that both may have come from Egypt, where such arrangements had become commonplace by the time the Greeks adopted them.

Sensitive to the *genius loci*, the Greeks, like many early peoples, located their houses of worship on hilltops and in river valleys—places with a supernatural charge, close to the spirit world, where they felt they had the gods' ears. Using a process akin to feng shui, priests and priestesses chose the sites for sacred buildings by walking across and praying over the holy ground onto which the structures would gaze.

Greek town planning also integrated man into his built environment. A key element in a Greek city of any note was the stoa. A stoa could be a part of another building or a structure on its own, as simple as a lean-to or as formal as the open-sided hall of a large temple, but it was always a roof supported by a line of columns. When a stoa's stone roof was too heavy, builders added columns inside the perimeter, so that the effect was of a grove of closely placed stone trunks. As Greek regional architecture grew more sophisticated, different types of columns developed—Doric, Ionian, Corinthian—and were eventually codified into a system that ordered column sizes and decorations down to the last detail.

Originally built onto temples, the stoa moved into daily life, acquiring worldly functions—some elevated, some not. Stoae provided shelter from the elements and space for markets; they served as courthouses and city halls and classrooms. A particular stoa in Athens achieved fame as the birthplace of a long-lived school of philosophy.

The core of ancient Athens was the *agora*, or civic center—the ancestor of the town square. Around its edges stood several stoae, imposing facades that helped set the agora's boundaries. One was the *stoa poikile*, or Painted Porch, which had been decorated by Polygnotus, whom the *Oxford Classical Dictionary* calls "the first great painter." Thirty years after the Greek victory on the plain of Marathon repulsed the Persians and propelled Greece toward its classical era, the Athenians hired Polygnotus and other artists to decorate the wall behind the stoa with images commemorating the battle and its heroes, such as Miltiades, who led the hoplites to victory. The general's portrait and the scenes from his triumph were still visible almost two centuries later, in 300 B.C.E., when Zeno of Citium began to teach in the stoa.

Though it made him famous, pedagogy wasn't what Zeno had had in mind when he left Syria for Athens. He'd meant to get rich, and for a time he succeeded. He became a merchant. His fortunes soared until he lost several cargoes at sea, and his business went under. Times that try men's souls can change their lives; after tasting the sweet and the sour, Zeno became a philosopher, and he started to lecture on the Painted Porch.

For a variety of reasons, Greece was in political tumult. Zeno, who knew a thing or two about turmoil, thought he had a system of belief that would put the disorder into perspective. He told his students that virtue grows from knowledge, that the philosopher tries to live in harmony with reason, and that the only good is to be virtuous—in contrast to the only evil, which is to lack virtue. Pain and pleasure are to be endured equally and are not to be regarded as real. Fixed on the polar star of virtue, a philosopher could walk through the world without yielding to its blandishments or succumbing to its brickbats. It all sounded good, but Zeno needed a name for his school of thought. He looked around the Painted Porch, considering the heroes of Marathon depicted there. They had lived as he thought men should, and here they were immortalized on the walls of the stoa.

Stoicism, he said to himself. That was what he would call his philosophy, and its adherents would call themselves Stoics.

Philosophies came and went, but Stoicism enjoyed an unusually long shelf life. Not only did the Stoic school outlive its founder and the Greek republic and empire; it survived intact and vibrant long enough to influence Roman thinkers like Cato, Cicero, Seneca, Epictetus, and Marcus Aurelius. Etymologically speaking, Stoicism even outlasted Rome, begetting the English word for one who exhibits forbearance.

Philosophy was only one of the disciplines the descendants of Romulus and Remus borrowed from the Greeks. They also adopted a Greek method of organizing the smaller holdings of peasant farmers into large farms. Presaging the plantations of the Mediterranean and the New World, these aggregations were rural city-states, where cadres of slaves worked the land, built the housing, maintained the tools and structures, and kept the books.

The Romans called their factory farms *latifundia*. Owners lived in town but maintained homes, called *villae*, on their properties. A villa was a compound: residence, stables, workshops, granaries, and slave quarters organized around a courtyard. The latifundine technique survived the end of slavery in Rome, as independent farmers called *coloni* adapted its methods to their purposes.

The Romans had a use for almost everything Greek, especially the architecture. Like *nouveaux riches* lusting for the patina of old money, the Romans draped their new civilization in the earlier society's finery, notably its sophisticated building designs. Greek architects had written at length about proportion, the use of columns, and other topics—and if interested Romans wanted to see firsthand what the books described, they could sail east to examine what remained of the real thing. One touch that appealed strongly to the new rulers of the known world was the stoa. It became a staple of Roman civic architecture, installed along main streets in cities and appended to temples and government buildings.

But for the Romans it wasn't enough to appropriate something Greek; to claim it, they had to name it. They often employed the lexicon of the legions that had carried the Roman rubric far and wide, in the process creating a flexible and evocative vocabulary.

When relabeling the stoa, wordsmiths chose a term from siege warfare, a favored Roman tactic. Sieges could last months, even years, with victory going to the strategist able to muster greater forbearance—to the more stoic warrior, as it were. Defenders usually held the high ground, abetted by elevation and gravity. Attacking legionaries had to push forward beneath a hail of rocks, spears, dead animals, and whatever else the enemy might hurl. To protect their troops, Roman engineers devised simple overhead shields, lightweight assemblages of roof and columns that soldiers could hump forward as the siege line advanced.

The Romans draped their new civilization in Greek finery, notably the older society's sophisticated building designs.

Perhaps because it helped legionaries carry (in Latin, *porto*) themselves and their weapons to the front, the army called this structure a *porticus*. During its expansion, Rome was almost always at war somewhere, with troops and commanders constantly traveling between the capital and the fighting at the frontier. Some veteran fresh from battle must have marveled at the elegant, columned pediment that was becoming all the rage in Rome, and in a moment of clarity saw through the glimmer of architectural fashion to the crude but effective shelter he and his comrades had used in combat.

And so the humble shed that had served so well in war lent its name in peacetime to the Greek structure that had inspired Stoicism. Latin is as slang-ridden as any language, and eventually the ablative form, *portico*, became the term for the airy, light-filled enclosures that graced the main streets of Roman towns, providing covered ways for shop-goers and pedestrians, as well as the more formal arrangements of pediments and pillars designed for the entrances of temples and government buildings. In its latter use the portico came to embody the power of the gods and the authority of the state, revealed to citizens through stone and plaster. Beneath that roof and among those columns flowed currents of awe-inspiring strength, whether secular or religious.

(Long after Rome had had its day, with Latin fading from use and English beginning to blossom, portico begat "porch." However, for hundreds of years the ecclesiastical inflection that originated in pagan worship persisted. As late as the seventeenth century, Europeans understood "porch" to mean a recessed entry to a church.)

17

The portico was significant enough a fixture in Roman life to figure in the writings of Marcus Vitruvius Pollio, who came into note around the time of Christ. During the reign of Augustus Caesar, Vitruvius catalogued what Romans knew of architecture and engineering and codified that knowledge into ten books he called *De architectura*. A military engineer and architect, Vitruvius was no armchair expert. He'd seen at least one of his designs built: a basilica, or town hall, at Fanum, an Umbrian crossroads town on the Metaurus River. In his middle years, however, Vitruvius turned from practicing architecture to writing about it: how to make bricks, when to cut timber, what wood to use for which application, which stone to quarry, how thick to build a city wall (wide enough at the top for armed men to pass one another without interference), how far apart to locate the towers on that wall for defensibility (no farther that an archer can shoot an arrow), and how to keep those towers from crumbling under siege (make them round or polygonal, to deflect missiles). He explains how to design the entry to a temple or government building, how to sink pilings to build a harbor, and how to pump, transport, and store water. He tells you how to lay out your *villa rustica* down to the last detail of the *latifundium*. He's the man with the plan, as well as a complex cosmogony that embraces astrology and astronomy. He goes long on the Greek orders and their proper uses, as well as on those who devised them. In fact, he sprinkles his text with references to the Greeks whose homework he copied, an oblique slam at his countrymen's place in the architectural firmament. The only Roman building Vitruvius mentions is his own basilica at Fanum.

Among the most compelling parts of *De architectura* are those that deal with the house, both in legend and in practicality. Vitruvius traces what he calls "the origins of the dwelling house" to a fire caused by the friction of tree limbs rubbing together. That fire, he says, at first frightened the people living nearby, but then drew them to its warmth and light. In gathering at the flames, men realized they could use their voices to speak with one another, and to give names to objects. So they started to converse, and soon came to understand their capacity for community: "They began in that first assembly to construct shelters. Some made them of green boughs; others dug caves in mountainsides, and some, in imitations of the nests of swallows and the way they built, made refuges out of mud and twigs. Next, by observing the shelters of others and adding new details to their own inceptions, they constructed better and better kinds of huts as time wore on."

On matters of house construction, Vitruvius is at his best, writing cleanly and succinctly of matters he obviously knows very well. He comes at the topic from every angle: climate, site, foundation, exposure, use and interplay of rooms, proportion, and symmetry. He reminds readers that an architectural drawing is not necessarily to be trusted; prospective clients need to visit the location and see how the house is going to fit into the landscape. Particular rooms get particular prescriptions: "Dining rooms ought to be twice as long as they are wide. . . .

Winter dining rooms and bathrooms should have a southwestern exposure, for the reason that they need the evening light, and also because the setting sun, facing them in all its splendor but with abated heat, lends a gentler warmth to that quarter in the evening." Vitruvius also urges designers to face summer dining rooms and painters' studios north, for ventilation and constancy of light.

To Vitruvius, good architecture meant order, arrangement, eurhythmy, symmetry, propriety, and economy. A structure that rang those gongs automatically achieved the goals of durability, convenience, and beauty. *Primus inter pares* were symmetry and balance, achieved by adjusting a design to its site in ways that enhanced the building but not at cost to its grace. But Vitruvius was no mere style queen. No matter how well a design might work and look, an architect who couldn't make customers happy wasn't going to get any commissions, so Vitruvius urged architects to design with clients' status in mind. "Those who do business in country produce must have stalls and shops in their entrance courts, with crypts, granaries, storerooms, and so forth in their houses, constructed more for the purpose of keeping the produce in good condition than for ornamental beauty," he writes in Book VI. "For capitalists and farmers of the revenue, somewhat comfortable and showy apartments must be constructed, secure against robbery; for advocates and public speakers, handsomer and more roomy, to accommodate meetings; for men of rank who, from holding offices and magistracies, have social obligations to their fellow-citizens, lofty entrance courts in regal style, and most spacious atriums and peristyles, with plantations and walks of some extent in them, appropriate to their dignity. They need also libraries, picture galleries, and basilicas, finished in a style similar to that of great public buildings, since public councils as well as private law suits and hearings before arbitrators are very often held in the houses of such men.

"If, therefore, houses are planned on these principles to suit different classes of persons, as prescribed in my first book, under the subject of Propriety, there will be no room for criticism; for they will be arranged with convenience and perfection to suit every purpose. The rules on these points will hold not only for houses in town, but also for those in the country, except that in town atriums are usually next to the front door, while in country seats peristyles come first, and then atriums surrounded by paved colonnades opening upon palaestrae and walks."

Other Romans probably wrote of architecture, but their works faded away and were lost. Vitruvius and *De architectura* survived, making the transition from scrolls to codices, still providing guidance even as the empire was disintegrating, half a millennium after the old architect died. Perhaps this popularity, combined with wide distribution, was what ensured that when the lights went out on Europe for the first time, a few book-hoarding monks would treasure, if not read, the works of Vitruvius. Whatever the reason, from the onset of the Dark Ages through the medieval era, copies of the old Roman's chronicle lay nestled on the bookshelves of monasteries, waiting to be rediscovered.

At the first floor of a Venetian house, a loggia permitted easy debarkation, with access to the storage areas at the back and the stairs to the offices a flight up.

Chapter Two

LOGGIA LOGIC, RENAISSANCE ROOTS

The Rome that Vitruvius and *De architectura* outlived was a long time dying. But the empire's demise sprinkled Europe with the seeds of cultures that would adopt and adapt Rome's classical architecture—including the portico, whose form would remain remarkably intact but whose character and use would see dramatic change.

Rome spent centuries sliding from dominance to disorder, from pagan to Christian, and from unity to a sundered society whose two main fragments were the Holy Roman Empire, governed from Trier in what is now Germany, and an eastern branch, the Byzantine, headquartered at Constantinople, now Istanbul. Rome's eastern inheritors held on longer and stronger, but in the west, the tribes the legions had subdued quickly rose up, shattering the glory that had been Rome into splinters, factions, and vestiges.

Two such pockets were at the foot of the Dolomite range, in northern Italy, where a coastal plain spread, forested and swampy. Altinum, in imperial days a popular resort and later the capital of the region the Romans called Venezia, stood at the intersection of several key roads cut through the woods and bogs. Aquileia, nearer the coast, had been an army base. The business of government, along with private commerce such as fishing and gathering salt in the shallow Adriatic lagoons, sustained the towns until the fifth century, when Attila attacked from the north. Reducing Altinum and Aquileia to rubble, the Huns drove the inhabitants toward the sea.

However, instead of dying on the strand, the survivors fled across the lagoon, making a last stand on the islands of Torcello and Grado. Where fishermen had cast nets and salt gatherers had turned seawater into seasoning, the refugees fought their pursuers to a draw. The Huns withdrew to the shore, beginning a century of on-and-off conflict with the former landlubbers. The refugees couldn't go home, so they made a new one on Torcello and Grado. With no land to work, the exiles became sailors and merchants. By default they were citizens of the Byzantine Empire, whose protection encouraged them to probe ever farther, developing profitable and diverse routes.

Ties to Byzantium were useful, but the people of the lagoon didn't think of themselves as Byzantine subjects. The islanders showed their independence in many ways. For example, they spoke a variation of the Italian language that was developing on the mainland. Boats were still *barcas,* and the mainland was still *terra firma,* but their pronunciations were unique.

Another goad to independence was the continuing turmoil on *terra firma,* which caused the exiles to withdraw farther into the lagoon. Isolation bred a sense of nationhood. The Romans had labeled the region Venezia; the lagoon dwellers adopted the term, along with the Roman model of government, for the country they called the Serene Republic, also known as *la Serenissima.*

As her fleets grew larger and her army stronger, Venezia annexed more islands—118 in all—creating land by narrowing the watery spaces between them until they became canals, 180 of which made lace of the crescent lagoon. To construct pilings and breakwaters as well as the frames of ever-larger houses, the Venetians deforested the mainland region that had provided their name.

When the trees were gone, the landward portion of Venezia reverted to swamp, but the settlement on the lagoon, now "Venice," became a full-fledged city that sparkled with wealth. Her canals were lined with houses in which Venetians mixed life and work. A typical merchant house was brick, with a fancy stone façade. At the first floor, just above the waterline, an open pillared space called a *loggia* permitted easy debarkation, with access to the storage areas at the back and the stairs to the offices a flight up. Above the offices was the *piano signorile,* the owner's home, and above that, quarters for servants. Since Venetian houses share walls, light and air had to come through the front of the house. On residential floors, the room facing the canal was called a *portego,* from the Latin *portico*; its oversize windows reprised the pillared look of the loggia several floors below.

On the mainland, chaos reigned, except where landowners defended their families and their fiefdoms from within fortified residences. With towers to survey the surrounding flatlands, these castellated houses and their heavily armed inhabitants were the only law west of the lagoons. Venice nominally controlled the swampy area but in practice ignored it, looking east for business, especially after her troops defeated a Norman force that had had Byzantium worried. Grateful, the empire granted its new ally access to entrepôts across the empire—and no customs fees, either. With Byzantium's protection, Venice became a power in trade, reaching as far as China through such adventurous entrepreneurs as the Polo family. She also succeeded in war, contracting her fleets and battalions to fight for whoever paid the highest price and, through her arsenals and shipyards, arming the world.

By the tenth century, Venice was rich and wanting to be richer. One source of income for the cities of the day was the pilgrimage, in which devout Christians traveled to venerate the physical remains of some saint. Venice's patron saint, Theodore, wasn't a big draw, so the city fathers sent agents to Alexandria, Egypt, to steal St. Mark's body and bring it home. The gospel writer's relics were housed in a basilica named for him. Outside stretched the city's great gathering place, the Piazza San Marco. The Venetian blend of piety and practicality intensified in the eleventh century, when the Crusades began. Venice was the logical jumping-off point for the soldiers of Christ, whom the Venetians persuaded to wage war on their behalf as partial payment for using their city as a garrison and matériel depot.

Venice dealt in every imaginable commodity, from silks and pearls, to grain and spices, to fabric and slaves. (The word comes from the Venetian *schiavo*, or "Slav," referring to the human chattels captured in the East and hauled to Venice for auction on the Riva degli Schiavoni, "the dock of the slaves." The cheery greeting *ciao* originated as *Sono tuo schiavo*, meaning "I am your slave.") The Venetians didn't simply trade in slaves but owned and worked them as well. After crusaders led by Richard the Lionhearted captured Cyprus, the island became a Venetian satrapy on which slave-powered factory farms grew and refined sugar cane into the sweet granules for which rich Europeans were developing a taste.

Nourished by capital, democracy blossomed in Venice, as did appreciation for the fine things money could buy. To display their status as masters of the universe, wealthy Venetians commissioned paintings, sculptures, and schools of art. They ordered up statues, churches, and basilicas. They built fabulous houses, referred to by family name not with the formal Italian *casa* but the slangy Venetian *ca'*—Ca' Michiel, Ca' Foscari, Ca' Piovene.

Venice still depended heavily on Byzantium, whose influence presented itself architecturally in the form of radish turrets, turned columns, lacy stone-work, and, prominent in the facades of the great families' canal-front houses, the Moorish arch, with its profusion of detail and its skyward point, decorating portegos and loggias, such as those the city built in public spaces like the edges of St. Mark's Square.

These public loggias came to have a particular meaning. By tradition, the Republic conducted civic activities in the open, convening tribunals, courts, inquests, and the like, as well as certain private acts like the signing of deeds and contracts. These ceremonies took place on loggias, much as the ancient Greeks had engaged the polis on the stoa as a means of investing the citizens in the life of their city. Venetians came to associate the loggia with power, public and private.

The residential room facing the canal was called a portego, from the Latin portico; its oversized windows reprised the pillared look of the loggia several floors below.

The fifteenth century saw Venice start to lose her swagger. In 1453, when they took Constantinople, the Ottoman Turks deprived the Venetians of their exclusive grip on trade with the Far East. After this calamity, the city-state on the Adriatic would never again be what it had been. The Venetians would not be masters of, or even competitors in, the new universes of commerce and wealth that opened when Columbus landed on Hispaniola and da Gama reached India. In 1509, a pan-European alliance, the League of Cambrai, smashed the Venetian army at Agnadello, a town in the Veneto. Humbled in battle, cut off from the East and the new markets across the Atlantic, Venice became yesterday's papers, an expensive tourist trap.

But *la Serenissima* enjoyed a final brilliant turn. With the Turks dominating the Mediterranean, Venice needed a new source of grain and revenue. She looked west, to the region she had deforested and now partly owned. In a last stab at imperial expansion, Venetian troops seized all of the moist area that stretched from the Adriatic shore to the Dolomite foothills. The Republic dubbed it the Veneto (accent on the first syllable, please), and set about making it pay.

The Venetians drained huge tracts of the Veneto into arable condition, distributing them among investors willing to dig canals and ditches and plant rice, corn, and other grains. Seeing a chance to preserve their fortunes, the nobility provided capital, as well as hands-on management. As each great family had run its trading business on the Grand Canal, so would each manage its plantation in the Veneto, evolving from feudal noblemen into farmers in an agrarian revolution to rival any of its kind.

But there was a problem. The Veneto had no suitable houses, only rude castles and fortified residences left from the feudal era. People who lived in palaces all year did not expect to spend the growing season in huts or tents. They required settings that would not leave them so homesick for *la Serenissima* that they could not oversee farm work and count bushels of grain. Their summer dwellings could not impede the making of money; neither could they allow visitors to forget they were in the presence of people descended from doges, and still with means, however diminished.

At their peak, Venetians had built a rich array of ceremonies and traditions, like the pageants conducted afloat, held on the steps of churches, and orchestrated in the vast beauty of St. Mark's Square. Why exclude the new mode of life from this treatment? Each spring, gaily decorated flotillas of boats rowed by slaves hauled the great families across the lagoon to the mouth of the Brenta River. The nobles could have ridden on Roman roads, but in the process of remaking the Veneto, the Venetians made the Brenta into a canal, on whose towpaths horses pulled barcas full of nobles bound for their summer endeavors. The Venetians called this rite *villeggiatura,* the "going to the villa"; the term survives as Italian slang for taking a holiday.

Although she was riding for a fall, Venice temporarily enjoyed the momentum of history and capital that transformed the Veneto from miasmic bog into bread-basket and its residences from miniature fortresses into peaceable homes. With the Republic guaranteeing their community's safety, citizens could build houses that welcomed the world instead of deflecting it—a trend that would produce an architecture of invitation and grace that synthesized Venetian and classical design. Eventually, the Veneto would be dotted with houses whose form influenced the porch as it evolved in America.

However, in its fundamental character, the American porch would not emerge from Renaissance Italy but from precolonial Africa.

A redraft of a 17th century woodcut by Franz Post shows a Dutch planter (at left), watching servants prepare food at an overseer's house on a plantation in Brazil.

CHAPTER THREE

OUT OF AFRICA . . .

As diminished trade capacity was forcing Venetian merchants and mercenaries to become farmers, a legacy of their glory days was revising the world economy. Long irked by the Venetians' access to the Far East's silks, spices, and other choice goods—a lock guaranteed by the Byzantine Empire—rival nations were searching for their own avenues to the East.

Early in the 1400s, probing for a seaward route to India and China, Prince Henry of Portugal began sending ships along Africa's Atlantic coast. Others followed. On exploratory trips that carried them farther and farther south, European explorers realized equatorial Africans lived quite differently from folks in the northern latitudes—so differently that in some cases, such as building design, white men had no precise labels for what they saw.

The visitors were seeing structures time-tested to enhance life and minimize discomfort in a tropical climate. Dwellings often featured an exterior space that functioned like a room but was open on three sides, with the house front serving as the back wall. Shade came from a roof supported by poles. During the day, when interiors became ovenlike, these semipublic areas provided comparative comfort in which to prepare food, mind children, sleep, chat with neighbors, and conduct business. Like the house itself, this open living space was elevated several feet to fend off the biting, stinging insects that crawled and flew along the ground.

There was nothing like this back home in England or France or Portugal or Holland; there, you were either inside or outside, with nothing between. Lacking words with which to tag these structures where life played out as if before an audience, Europeans reached for the language of the theater. "These houses resemble, pretty much, our mountebanks stages in Europe," wrote an English traveler. "The front is open, and the floor has a jutting-out of five or six foot broad, where the Negros, laid on mats, pass the day with their wives and family."

Deprived by climate, temperament, and habit of the impulse or the need to be outside but under a roof, Europeans had had no experience with dwellings that permitted, even encouraged, the living of life outside and inside at the same time. But the design's logic was clear to those whose fair skin the equatorial sun quickly roasted.

Besides its relentless sun, Africa imperiled northerners with diseases borne by mosquitoes, tsetse flies, and other parasites. This environment deflected some Europeans, but the Portuguese took to it with gusto. All along the African coast, whether as sailors jumping ship or as merchants opening trading posts, the Portuguese took up residence, acquiring African mistresses and wives. The result was a miscegenated society they called *crioulo*. (The formal translation is "native" but *crioulo*, or *criollo*, or Creole, means a blend of cultures.) In the patois that rose like steam from this cultural stew, the inside/outside rooms of African houses came to be called *al-painters* (perhaps from *alpendre*, to hang, because the structures "hung" from houses or because it was easy to hang things on their railings and beams).

But white men didn't come to Africa for the architecture. They came to get rich, whether by trading in peppercorns or in people. Since time immemorial, Europeans had been enslaving one another and anyone else who got in the way; remember the Slavs who gave a name to Riva degli Schiavoni? Africans, too, had long made a practice of capturing and trading one another. On both continents, most slaves were prisoners of war, human booty sold to enrich victorious warriors. Now the two cultures of kidnap merged, and the synthesis was exploitation that gradually acquired an immense and invidious scale.

The history of slaving and colonialism between the fifteenth and the eighteenth centuries suggests a play-by-play of a hellbound World Wrestling Federation gang-match pitting the great nations of Europe against one another, with periodic time-outs to stomp the indigenous peoples of Africa and the Americas:

"Portugal has Holland in an LAPD-style death-lock, but the wily Dutchmen slip the grip and take down their opponent! Oooooh, the Portagee are really riled now— they're maneuvering for a double suplex! On the other side of the ring, France and England have double-teamed Spain. The Spaniards look as if they're about to throw in the towel, but suddenly they pull off a stupendous Ferdinand Flip! Spain lands right on top of the hapless Arawak, crushing them like insects, then bounces back to Benin to pick up another hundred thousand cane-cutters! D'oh! Portugal seems to have forged a partnership with Spain, and they have the Hollanders on the ropes, but what's going on? Ladies and gentlemen, the French are setting themselves on fire and rolling across on the canvas in an auto-da-fé of stupendous proportion! It's unbelievable. . . ."

You get my drift. I'd love little better than to recount the bouillabaisse of double- and triple-cross that marked the slave trade and colonial-era realpolitik, but that's another book, if not a library. The thing to bear in mind is that, when all those Europeans kidnapped all those Africans and exported them to the New World, the commodities in the coffles and the barracoons included the vernacular architectural concepts of precolonial Africa, most notably the porch.

The architectural progression within the Atlantic Progression occurred as follows, and I beg all serious historians to forgive me the sin of *reductio ad absurdum* condensation.

From a series of popes, who, fearing Islam's burgeoning strength, required only that the captives be baptized, the Portuguese won the right to exploit West Africans, cargoes of whom began to arrive in Portugal in 1444. In the 1480s, knowing that the slave-driven sugar refineries the Venetians ran on Cyprus were under threat from the Ottoman Turks, the Portuguese got sugar cane to grow on islands in the Gulf of Guinea near the African shore. They set up their own plantations, stocking them with captive Africans whose first task was to build housing for themselves. Though no vestiges remain, the surmise is that these slaves built what they knew: houses elevated from the ground, with open roofed spaces at the front.

Not only the Dutch, but the English and the French were watching the Portuguese sugar experiment in Africa with great interest, as well as what Spain was up to in the New World, where Christopher Columbus's 1492 landing on the island he named Hispaniola had unfurled immense possibilities. Along with finding gold and silver, Columbus had found the Arawak, indigenes who called their homeland Haiti. They lived in gable-fronted huts, roofed in palm fronds and often open-sided. These *bohios,* as the Arawak referred to them, had an arrangement similar to the *alpainter* where people could conduct their lives in the shade and in semipublic.

But Columbus didn't come to the New World for the architecture. Once he got his bearings, he proposed to ship thousands of the people he'd decided were "Indians" back to Spain as slaves; three or four thousand a year would keep him in sails and salt pork. That optimism faded when the great explorer put the Arawak to work mining gold. He realized the Indians wouldn't labor like draft animals and that instead, facing the prospect of life in captivity, they lay down and died. A few years on, his son, Diego, by now governor of Hispaniola, griped in a letter to King Ferdinand that enslaved Indians lacked the stamina "to break the rocks in which the gold was found." Irritated, the king authorized shipment of Africans—"the best and strongest available," he said—straightaway to Hispaniola. The gold the Africans mined there and in Cuba fueled Spain's forays into Mexico, Peru, and North America.

The Spanish repeated the pattern Portuguese slave-masters had set. As soon as Africans who'd survived the Atlantic passage staggered onto the dock, overseers herded them to plantations and conveyed that they should erect dwellings. "Each African family builds its house," wrote an observer of slave quarters in the Caribbean in the early years. "A circular space is cleaned and forms the center of a group of houses. We don't know if the compounds are grouped by ethnicity. The master doesn't intervene except to reduce the number of houses per compound and to forbid that the women's houses be set apart. Except for that, the slaves could arrange their huts more or less as they wanted."

Seeking new opportunities, the Portuguese crossed the Atlantic to colonize the northeast shoulder of Brazil, where they started cane crops. A sugar-refining industry bloomed around what became the town of Pernambuco (now Recife). The workers were enslaved Indians, at least until dysentery and influenza killed them off. Those who didn't die simply wouldn't work, so Portugal opened a pipeline from Africa. By the year 1600, 50,000 slaves, nearly all from Congo or Angola, had arrived. The Brazilian climate being so redolent of lost homelands, early slave dwellings had an African theme—houses raised on platforms with roofed exterior spaces, arrayed in circular fashion. Overseers adopted the design, which became a fixture on sugar plantations. As early as the 1640s, itinerant artists like Franz Post and Albert Eckholt were making drawings and paintings that showed porches on slave quarters, planters' houses, and workshops.

I learned about Post and Eckholt from Jay Edwards, a professor at Louisiana State University. Edwards, a folklorist, is a prominent figure in material culture, as he and his colleagues call the study of human history conducted through the examination of what humans make and how they use those implements.

"We know from the instructions sent by plantation owners from England and from France to their managers in the West Indies that in the early days Africans were permitted to build their own buildings," Edwards said. "That was the first job they were given when they arrived off the slave ships, and were purchased by a planter: 'Go build your own house.' There were very few instructions in the first two centuries about how to build those houses, and until 1700 or so, they just built African villages."

In early colonial life, practicality trumped provenance. Whether in the Caribbean or North America, colonists were willing to embrace whatever worked. "If you could build a house that worked better than the traditional European house, or if you could cook food, or whatever it was, that worked better, if you knew how to grow crops Europeans didn't know how to grow, the planters did not care," Edwards said. "They had no compunction against adopting African culture. That's where shotgun houses came from, and that's where houses with porches came from, and where houses raised up off the ground came from—all these ideas we can associate with Africa," Edwards said. "The outside kitchen is another African idea. Europeans cooked inside; Africans all cooked outside."

Europeans weren't necessarily happy to embrace Africanisms, but ignorance can be a useful thing. "If they didn't happen to know that a full-length gallery was an African idea, then they would overlook that," Edwards said. "It was okay."

In a 1989 article that fills an issue of the journal *Material Culture*, Edwards traces the process that brought the porch to America. He closes his exhaustive piece with a clinical consideration of seven possible sources for the porch: European neoclassicism, gallery structures of Western Europe, West African vernacular architecture, Brazilian influences, Italo-Hispanic villas and palaces, military construction, and North American Creole architecture. One by one, Edwards explicates and dissects the argument for each. As a standard, he looks to see to what extent each hypothesis demonstrates the existence of a "cultural hearth area."

For folklorists, hearth areas are the zones that kindle a cultural phenomenon, ranked by their relative warmth. In primary hearths, a phenomenon is at its hottest and most intense, the point of origin. On what might be termed the Edwards Scale of Porchiosity, a primary hearth area is one in which full-length or encircling porches were indigenous, fully developed, and in widespread use prior to significant contact with foreign cultures. Secondary hearths had some indigenous porchlike structures, but they were not as fully developed. Tertiary hearths showed creolization, or the blending of designs previously separate. A quaternary hearth was a place that imported, used, and improvised on designs from tertiary zones.

That grid automatically knocks out Brazil and North America, to which the porch was imported. For Edwards's money, that leaves only two primary hearth areas for the porch: West Africa and eastern India, with Africa way in the lead. As Edwards writes at the conclusion of his article, "The indigenous West African Hearth appears to have exerted profound early influence on American porch traditions as a result of the transportation of so many persons from that area into Brazil and the West Indies in the seventeenth and eighteenth centuries."

When I talked with him, Edwards explained how he'd reached his conclusions. "One of the keys to learning about how the porch becomes translated into an American architectural phenomenon is to study the architecture of these Creoles from 1550 or before, all the way down the African coast. They were the power brokers and culture brokers who set the standards for coastal architecture," he said. "One way of understanding the porch is to understand the social functions of the porch, comparing the way the Africans used the porch—as a daytime living room—with the way it was done in the West Indies. The functions were precisely the same."

He contrasted this parallel with the pre-African patterns of European domestic architecture, whose few porchlike structures did not appear across the gamut of classes and were not social places. "They were certainly not on poor people's houses, and they did not use those spaces as open-air living rooms," Edwards said. "It was not considered a living room at all. So here you have an African idea that is being transported."

The Creole culture that began on the West African coast intensified once the Portuguese brought slaves to Brazil, where European design sensibilities tangled more deeply with those of Africans.

When they could, Africans in the New World fled their captors. In Brazil, the runaways founded remote upland communities they called *quilombos*. In Jamaica and other Spanish colonies, escaped slaves were dubbed "Maroons," from *cimarron*, for "untamed." In these settlements, removed from European ideas of building and living, renegade Africans and their descendants built hybrid houses that mixed details from Africa with those seen in the Arawak *bohio*. Contemporary artists' drawings of these houses show many having full-width porches.

In 1624, the Dutch invaded Brazil, defeating the Portuguese and taking over the sugar mills and the growing slave population. "Without blacks there is no Pernambuco," a priest there wrote.

Up north, France and England were challenging Spain for mastery of the Caribbean. Besides claiming Martinique, St. Lucia, Guadeloupe, Grenada, and several smaller islands, France insinuated herself onto western Hispaniola, where French freebooters landing for provisions saw locals preserve meat by double-smoking it over green-wood fires, a method the natives called "buccaning"; Frenchmen who learned the skill dubbed themselves *buca-niers*, soon corrupted into "buccaneers." (Seeing the African-influenced sheltering facades that the Portuguese built, French sailors were reminded of a similar protected space beneath the overhanging second stories of Norman peasant huts—in French, *la gallerie*. The term stuck, eventually anglicized into "gallery.")

The English acquired Barbados, Bermuda, Nevis, Antigua, and Montserrat, meanwhile establishing colonies in North America: Massachusetts, Maryland, Virginia, and Carolina. These were hardscrabble operations, mostly, embodied by Barbados, an island of tobacco growers and their slaves. On Barbados, whites outnumbered Blacks two to one and farmers worked small spreads at lean profits, often achieved only by proprietors toiling alongside slaves and living only marginally better.

When the Portuguese came back at the Dutch, finally retaking Brazil in 1654, a few thousand Dutchmen fled north with their sugar-making skills, their slaves, and their African-inflected architectural sensibility. Lacking any other haven, the exiles put in at Barbados. "The Dutch losing Brazil, many Dutch and Jews repairing to Barbados began then planting and making of sugar," wrote a contemporary chronicler. "Likewise, the Dutch, being engaged on the coast of Guinea . . . for Negro slaves, having lost Brasille, not knowing where to vent them, they trusted them to Barbados."

The Brazilian contingent's arrival changed life in the Caribbean. Barbadians had been growing sugar, but in dribs and drabs. The Dutch knew, and the English soon learned, that real profits on the sweet stuff demanded large farms and armies of slaves. Within two decades, Barbados had 80,000 Blacks.

The Caribbean became the new Africa. Between 1675 and 1700, English slavers shipped 175,000 slaves to the archipelago.

Not counting the slaves, the losers in this expansion were the Spanish, who kept Cuba and Puerto Rico but lost half of Hispaniola to the French and all of Jamaica to the English.

"When the English conquer Jamaica in 1655, they describe the houses they find, and they describe them as having front porches, and having a particular plan, which we now call the Spanish Colonial Plan, or the Italo-ethno-Spanish Plan," said Jay Edwards. "This design was symmetrical, with a big square or rectangular room in the middle, elongated by two smaller rooms along either side, which we call gabinete rooms. Behind those two smaller rooms, the open loggia faces the back, with a full gallery across the front. And that was really the basic small farmer's colonial architecture in the Spanish Caribbean."

On Hispaniola, the Spanish left farmhouses that the French took over. "Those early plans, with the full-length porches, already were in place by 1650; we don't know how much earlier it might have been there," Edwards said. "Then this other tradition, from the Dutch, came up into the Caribbean islands—the one in which the farmhouse was surrounded with open galleries. Now you had two porch-bearing traditions, both from places that imported lots and lots of African slaves. What we don't know, what we haven't documented, is the interplay of Africans with Europeans in those first two centuries of plantation life, and how the Africans may have influenced the Europeans to adopt the full-length galleries. We don't know what exactly the process was. Nobody that we've found so far described that process. But after that two-century period was over, the galleries were everywhere."

Caribbean fields filled with sugar cane. The planters who owned them built houses that looked like those they'd seen in Barbados, with that charming place at the front beneath whose roof you could relax in the company of your friends and neighbors after a day's work, and, eventually, when capitalism's flywheel began to roll in earnest, spend the day with your friends and neighbors watching your Negroes do your work for you. The accommodations were on the rough side—log beams and slabwood floors—but most pleasant. What to call it?

There were so many names. The French said *gallerie,* the Portuguese and Spanish, *veranda,* a term imported from India. But the English, who had an admirable string of holdings from Barbados to Jamaica to the Carolinas, Virginia, Maryland, and Massachusetts, employed an unexpected turn of phrase.

As sugar made Barbados and Jamaica ever more important, traffic between them and London increased dramatically. The city's tonier residents had grown curious about the colonies, venturing across the Atlantic to visit. Barbadians and Jamaicans, in the manner of colonists everywhere, struggled to emulate the motherland in costume and carriage and colloquial slang.

Some Londoner, ushered onto the veranda at the front of a plantation house, remarked that it reminded him of the latest rage at home, a new development owned by the Earl of Bedford. Laid out in a square shape, which no one had ever been done before in London, it was called Covent Garden, after the Earl's own garden, whose wall marked the south side of the square. The west side featured the gateways to St. Paul's, as well as a couple of houses. Along the north and east sides were town houses, packed cheek by jowl but with an interesting fillip.

Instead of building the ground floor right out to the limit, the architect, Inigo Jones, had carved a protected passageway—clever boy, he knew the London weather—through which pedestrians could stroll past the fronts of the shops that filled the ground floor. The structures above the walkway rode on columns and arches that made an elegant frame through which to view the bustle of the square—much as the plantation gallerie or whatever they called it framed the lovely scene of slaves making their owners rich.

The most marvelous thing was that Jones, who'd traveled extensively, had brought the concept back from, of all places, Italy. He'd tried to persuade his countrymen to call his project by the Italian word, *piazza,* which to Italians meant the entirety of the town square. But the English brain couldn't wrap itself around that concept. Instead, Londoners doggedly insisted on calling the covered walkways "piazzas." A year after Covent Garden went up, Britain took Jamaica, and soon travelers were remarking on how closely the open-air rooms there resembled the piazzas back in London.

That was it. In an instant, Jamaicans and Barbadians, besotted with the idea of seeming anything like Londoners, had dropped "gallerie" and "veranda" in favor of "piazza." The locution quickly traveled the capillary stream to Charleston—the main slave port for the Carolina colonies—and to Boston, up in Massachusetts. In each of those places, the structure that was becoming so popular across the Caribbean and the coast of mainland North America quickly came to be known as a "piazza."

But Inigo Jones hadn't invented the piazza; he'd only adapted what he'd seen in Italy. And what he'd seen in Italy was part of a much larger shift in architecture and society that would exert tremendous influence on the American porch.

A *baranda* provided outside shelter for the occupants of the house proper, called *banggalo*, from the root *bangla*, meaning "of Bengal."

Chapter Four

...OR WAS IT OUT OF INDIA?

I wish I could say that the origins of the porch and of so much of the language we use in regard to it are indisputably clear. But they're not.

In fact, those origins are tough to winkle out, being tangled and simultaneous, transmogrified and transposed, crosshatched with traces of cultures passing through one another from continent to continent, until the route to the extremely logical destination of the American porch seems too complicated ever to be made straight.

Consider "veranda," used in many parts of the world and by anglophile Yanks to refer to the porch. "Veranda" (sometimes with an "h" at its end) has an exotic sound—not for nothing is it the name of a fancy shelter magazine—and with good reason. "Veranda" comes from the exotic East, specifically India.

Repeating the role they'd played in Africa as the scouting party for the rest of Europe, the Portuguese reached the Bengal coast in the early 1500s. As they established business connections and living arrangements in a climate that closely resembled that of West Africa, Portuguese explorers either introduced the African structure they'd dubbed the *alpainter,* or they encountered a version already in use by the Bengali.

The indigenes called the design—often part of a house made of reeds or mud and set behind walls, for privacy—*baranda,* meaning "outside space under a roof held up by poles."

Baranda/veranda: get it?

But there's a hitch.

Hindi and Portuguese share linguistic roots; in both tongues, *vara* means "pole." The Portuguese, well-acquainted with the African structure, could have brought the term and not the architectural element. Or they could have introduced the structure and embraced the name given it by the Bengali. Or they simply could have accepted the Bengali word for the homegrown structure. In any event, *baranda* became "veranda," quickly transmitted via the trade pipeline to Portugal and its holdings in Africa and Brazil. From there, the word vaulted to the Caribbean, where fellow Iberians from Spain adopted it.

Etymology aside, a *baranda* provided outside shelter for the occupants of the house proper, called *banggalo,* from the root *bangla,* meaning "of Bengal."

Bangla was also what the Indians called the portable bamboo shelters that trading parties carried with them as they traveled Bengal. Early visitors' journals often mention "bunguloues," as well as "Bangales," "Bangalaer," "bungalo," "bungelo," and "bungelow."

Banggalo/bungalow: get it?

Not so fast, my friend.

After illuminating the route to India, the Portuguese were followed by the Dutch, Danes, Swedes, French, and British, each represented by a private trading entity, such as the British East India Company. As in the Caribbean and North America, England's ultimate competitor was France, whom she gradually elbowed aside, acquiring control of the subcontinent. But long before that, the English had begun to adopt words like hookah, bazaar, curry, and punch—spicy terms that migrated from India, with its wealth of new experiences, including life in a banggalo with a baranda, or, as the English came to say, a bungalow with a veranda.

The Moghuls who ruled India fended off European influence until 1707, when Emperor Aurangzeb died, triggering his empire's decline and collapse. By the 1750s, with the Moghuls in disarray, England and France were jousting for the Indian subcontinent. England won in 1757, a victory saluted onstage in a London farce whose script mentioned the "bunglo."

After losing North America as an outlet, English ambition and ambitious Englishmen would turn to India. Soldiers and bureaucrats poured into the country, stationed at redoubts blending the functions of frontier fort and trading post. As their predecessors had, new arrivals noticed how well the thick-walled, verandaed banggalo suited its setting. By the early 1800s, English colonials had made it their own, building what they called "bungalows," first as hostels and temporary quarters in rural regions, then later as permanent residences at cantonments like the "hill stations" of the Northern Territories. Bungalows were for Europeans only, a gesture that fitted India's and Britain's caste-conscious societies; why on earth would one wish to speak of one's place in the world when one's residence could do the speaking for one?

The English kept many elements of the banggalo: the single story, the mud walls (now of sun-dried brick and plastered with mud or mortar), the thatched roof (sometimes tiled to deflect the sun), and the veranda. The imperialist bungalow was bigger than its indigenous ancestor—some were 7,000 feet square—and sat on a parapet. It had windows, through which flowed veranda-cooled breezes. Verandas could be as deep as fifteen feet, to keep rain from pelting and melting the walls and to provide space for masters to entertain and for servants to sleep and work. Their main purpose was air circulation, an effect enhanced with punkahs—bamboo or fabric fans waved by shifts of servants— as well as roller blinds and screens. But the key to comfort was elbowroom.

A bungalow needed space, preferably several acres. In India, with its crowded villages and towns, that requirement was another badge of empire, one that would exert a strong appeal for stylish Americans.

Nearly half a millennium after his death, Andrea Palladio's name and presence are everywhere in his adopted hometown of Vicenza.

Chapter Five

. . . OR WAS IT OUT OF ITALY?

When, in 1630, Inigo Jones designed his piazza at Covent Garden, he was doing more than providing an accidental name for the airy structures being built across the Caribbean and along the North American coast. Jones was creating the first town square in London, as well as advancing an extraordinary phase in architecture that had begun in Italy.

The lodestar of this movement, which occurred in parallel to the waves of exploration and exploitation that brought the porch to the New World, was Andrea Palladio, who had a career so influential he became an adjective.

But "Palladio" wasn't even the real name of the man whose style begat the term "Palladian." He was born Andrea di Pietro della Gondola in 1508 in Padua, a university town on the southern edge of the Veneto, the name Venetians had given to the swampy region west of their lagoon.

His mother's name was Marta. His father, Pietro, was a miller. In 1521, thirteen-year-old Andrea was apprenticed to a stone carver. He took to the craft, but not the master, and soon moved north to Vicenza, the Veneto's hub city, where he joined the Guild of Masons and Stone Carvers. The region was booming, with the Venetians building villas around the countryside for summer use as well as year-round houses in Vicenza. Demand for artisans was such that a fellow who reached for a higher rung could grab it, if he had the skills and the stones. Based on his skill as a carver, Andrea became a contractor, and he started reading up on building design.

In those credentialless days, any builder could represent himself as an architect. By 1534, when he got married, that's what Andrea della Gondola was doing. He claimed as his muse good old Vitruvius, whom he'd encountered in the writings of Leon Battista Alberti and Sebastiano Serlio, two of the previous generation of Italian architects. Battista and Serlio had translated versions of *De architectura*, on which they based their own theories of design. Alberti, who loved symmetry and doted on proper proportion, developed mathematical equations for relating elements of a building to one another; Serlio invented a striking style of triple window that eventually was named for him. The logic of Alberti's equations in particular appealed to Andrea, but he wanted to drink at the source, so he read Vitruvius in Latin, absorbing the Roman's adjurations about beauty, durability, and convenience.

The mid-1500s were a good time to be a good architect in the Veneto. A new kind of residence was emerging, and it required a new sensibility. Across Europe, feudalism was fading, to be replaced by state rule, and with it the need for the fortified houses from which individual lords had ruled their fiefs. The evolution occurred in microcosm in Northern Italy as Venice began to recover from its defeat by the League of Cambrai. The loss convinced the Venetians they couldn't rely on individual nobles to protect her holdings on *terra firma*. After regaining control of the Veneto, the Republic set about changing the relationship between landowners and government—a shift that also would alter the region's dwellings, as I learned from Antonio Foscari, a noted architectural historian who explained the shift to me while I was visiting Italy on a research trip. The professor has no small standing to interpret Palladian architecture, its context, and its impact; one of his ancestors commissioned Palladio to design and build a villa that Professor Foscari now owns.

"Venice realized the feudal noblemen could not guarantee the Republic's safety, and ordered the destruction of all castles in the Veneto, the professor told me. The edict outraged the barons and counts. Centuries of combative existence had taught them that the only way to live was behind high walls, with bowmen and snipers manning towers from which to spot and repel enemies. Some landowners rebelled; the Venetians came down hard. To drive home the point that fortified dwellings were history, government forces destroyed the rebels' castles.

Now landowners really needed new houses, as well as a new way of designing them. "The mainland aristocracy, especially in Vicenza, had to find a form that would represent them publicly in the new social, cultural, physical, and architectural context," Professor Foscari said. Enter Giangiorgio Trissino, a Vicentine count whose brother had led the revolt against Venice and whose house was among those the Venetians flattened.

A fan of classical architecture, Trissino realized that if he rebuilt in the old mode, the goon squad would be back with its manual of politically correct design and its battering ram. So he devised a neoclassical form that was almost defiant in its blend of the banned and the blessed.

"Trissino built a house in Cricoli with two towers, on the verge of illegality, as if to defy the Republic's prohibition," the professor explained. "But between the two towers was a loggia, a real quotation from the Roman experience. Of course there had been porticoes and similar open spaces in earlier times, but now the loggia had a new significance."

Trissino's loggia invoked long-standing tradition in Venice, where the use of loggias as courts had made the structures symbols of justice—an image recurring in the Veneto as the Republic reasserted its dominion. "Venice had a tradition of respecting the pre-existing rights and ancient charters and statutes of the cities she took over," Professor Foscari said. "Rulings were made by *a pretore,* or magistrate. The *pretore's* judgment took place in public, on a loggia, in the manner of an ancient king administering justice under an oak tree. So in the minds of citizens, the loggia on a public building came to be understood as an official place where authority, especially the authority of justice, was exercised."

Trissino's loggia straddled a fine and contentious line. At either side, his house had proud towers of the sort the Venetians had been demolishing, but he literally linked those towers with Venice's very own icon of justice, built in the style of the Romans, whom the Venetians revered. The canny count was telling the Republic, "All right. You win. No more castles, no more keeps. No more crenelations, portcullises, moats, glaces. But fellas—that means you have to maintain the peace." The slyly witty Vicentines relished the inside joke of the conquerors' style flipped back at them like a genially bit thumb, and Trissino's loggia began a trend.

"The nobleman who followed Trissino's lesson used a new 'language' and new symbols," Professor Foscari said. "The language was no more that of strength, of weapons, of swords, of armor—he was adopting the language of letters and arts. And among the new symbols was the loggia. He was declaring publicly that he accepted the change in his political role; that he was resigning from the exercise of strength and violence, willing to go unprotected and leave it to the state to take care of the territory's defense."

As Trissino was building his villa, the stonecutter Andrea della Gondola was hired for the project. The count and the carver met; they got on famously, with the erudite older man becoming mentor to the younger. When Trissino learned della Gondola had ambitions to be a designer, he offered encouragement, as well as a new moniker. In the nicknaming style of the day, Trissino dubbed his new pal "Andrea Palladio," a nod to Pallas Athene, goddess of wisdom, and to the Palladium, a sacred image of the goddess whose protection assured the safety of Athens and later Rome. Andrea's first design, executed in 1537 for the Godi family outside Lonedo, strongly resembled Trissino's villa, with a loggia connecting towers at either front corner. The project was a success, and so was born Andrea Palladio the architect.

Trissino took Palladio to Rome, where Andrea refined his instincts and skills by making drawings, measuring ruins, and examining neoclassical buildings from the previous century. He went to Rome understanding intellectually what Vitruvius meant by durability, convenience, and beauty; he returned with a vivid comprehension that drove him to merge ancient aesthetic and modern method.

Success in architecture depends in no small part on the ability to penetrate to and explicate clients' desires. Bearing in mind their high-rise houses on the canals that had warehouses at the lower floors and dwellings upstairs, the noble families farming the Veneto wanted an architect who could give them residences that doubled as granaries, with sophisticated living spaces and great capacity to store the corn that brought the cash that paid for the plantations that supported the country houses that Venice built.

Palladio showed himself to be that architect, designing dwellings both functional and elegant. He hewed to the Vitruvian line on symmetry and balance. He applied Alberti's precision in calculating space and proportion. And he didn't forget his working-class roots. Using the stonemason's trick of sheathing rough brick with a sublime and durable veneer of stucco, he delivered his villas on time and within budget—for an aspiring architect, no less a feat then than now.

Commissions rained down. Andrea's designs began to dot the Veneto and the avenues and squares of Vicenza, where, along with building houses, he renovated the seat of regional government, the Basilica, by stacking loggias on three sides, mirroring on *terra firma* the-wave-washed look of Venice. Loggias and colonnades also suggested ways in which Andrea could set his villa designs apart.

Despite the decree against castles, villas in the Veneto still had an air of the fortified farmhouse. They didn't greet visitors so much as put them through a process of grudging admission, as in Palladio's plan for the Godi house. With those towers on either side, perhaps harboring sentries, only someone sure he was welcome would have come up that steep hill and climbed the steps to the loggia.

But the *Pax Venetiana* was calming the countryside. It was time to cast off the architecture of fear, which Andrea did by giving more prominence to the loggia. His early designs resembled those along the Grand Canal. They were democratically open to the public (well, those portions of the public that the owner's people let through the gates, anyway) while being recessed into the body of the house, and they were designed to appeal to owners who, whatever the true state of their affairs, saw themselves as powerful. Palladio took care to deliver loggias that preserved, even promoted, those self-images. At the house Palladio built for the Poiana family, for example, the entire loggia is a marketing tool.

Like many powerful Venetians, generations of Poianas had been soldiers, until Venice lost at Agnadello. That defeat, and the lure of equally profitable and less perilous opportunities in the Veneto's fields, persuaded Boniface Poiana to swap his saber and cuirass for the plough. He bought land on which to establish a rice plantation.

Boniface Poiana wasn't just changing jobs. He'd also married into another important Venetian clan, the Da Portos. With his country house, Poiana wanted to signal his new station in life and celebrate his past. This made him a perfect client for Andrea Palladio, as well as a prime example of what was happening in the Veneto. Until the Pax Venetiana, the lands of the Poiana plantation had spent a millennium as battlefields; just across the road from where Boniface meant to build his villa, ruins of a feudal-era castle stood beside shards of a Roman fort.

Despite this martial history, the warrior-turned-farmer and the stonecutter-turned-architect assumed the future would bring peace. Palladio designed a house for Poiana that was compact and plain, its exterior unornamented save for a pair of statues alongside the entry stair, and oculi, or round windows, above the loggia, which, in the new style, was recessed but open and utterly indefensible.

Luigi di Tomassi, who took me on a tour of the house, teaches Italian and history at the local high school. He grew up in Poiana Maggiore. He's been coming to the villa all his life, to play in its park as a child and later to enjoy pageants that used the villa as a set. As we walked toward the house, Luigi explained the roles it and its loggia had played in Boniface Poiana's—indeed, Venice's—self-transformation.

First, he pointed out ruins on the other side of the road, which represented a way of life gone by. "The Venetians who were investing in the Veneto knew the old structures were no longer suitable," Luigi said. "They needed a new kind of house. Palladio satisfied that need by going back to an ancient tradition and infusing it with new meaning."

The tradition to which Palladio and his clients looked was Rome's, which provided the neoclassical form in which the Venetians shaped their modern designs. Boniface Poiana and cohort imagined themselves to be the New Romans; having tamed an unruly world, they meant to cultivate a profitable garden. Like any parvenu worth his freshly minted coinage, Poiana wanted to make a statement: a dwelling of good proportion to house his family and business, store his grain, and advertise his position in life. Palladio delivered the goods. Villa Poiana ranks among his least ornate designs, but the details still convey his client's view of himself and his world, starting with the staircase— long, wide steps that make the trip to the loggia a slow, stately one.

"The staircase mediates between the inside and the outside. It also connects the land to the *piano nobile*, where the landowner lives," Luigi said as we walked up the steps. "The owner usually welcomed guests from the top of the stairs, looking at them from above. The Venetians considered it a munificent gesture for the owner to welcome guests at the bottom of the stairs and climb with them."

Whether he walked them up the stairs or watched them from above, Boniface Poiana would have been ushering guests not into a stately manse but a working farmhouse. At harvest time, the forecourt would have been spread with corn or wheat that, once dried, would be bagged and hauled up two flights of stairs for storage in the attics over either wing. The rooms below the granaries have vaulted ceilings, a fixture in most of Palladio's villas. It's easy to imagine the house at the center of a constellation of managers and farmhands, with all the attendant beasts of field and birds of barnyard: chickens, pigs, and a new species brought back from America, *il turchio*—the turkey.

But that apparent simplicity had a complicated subtext. Luigi explained the bold, though wordless, narration that unfolds on the loggia. Even dulled by the centuries, its frescoed walls and ceiling present a story line obvious to sixteenth century eyes reading for details of the status life: references to Boniface's military career, his wife's family, Roman deities, and, on a shelf above the doorway to the interior, a slightly larger-than-life bust of Poiana himself.

"The loggia was a real marketing operation," Luigi said. "Boniface Poiana was saying, 'This is me. See the bust over the door? That's my image of myself. This is my story. This is my fortune. This is my family.'"

Once Poiana's neighbors got an eyeful of his new place, with its capacious granaries and its self-advertising loggia, you could almost hear the great Venetian families exclaim, like a chorus of dot.com millionaires pondering Chez Gates, "Now, *that's* architecture!"

But Palladio (by now a one-name personage) was soon taking the loggia in an even grander direction. Recalling how Vitruvius had described the use of columns in a Roman portico, Andrea conceived of a loggia that projected from the body of a house, with graceful pillars supporting a pediment, as on a Roman temple. Alberti had urged that architects not put porticoes on residences, but Palladio decided to break new ground. "I have made the frontispiece in the fore-front in all the fabricks for villa's, and also in some for the city, in which are the principal gates; because such frontispieces shew the entrance of the house, and add very much to the grandeur and magnificence of the work," he wrote. "Besides, the fore-part being thus made more eminent than the rest, is very commodious for placing the ensigns or arms of the owners. . . ." Andrea's clientele, never shy about promoting themselves or invoking their real or imagined Roman heritage, leaped for the lure. Their villas had to have projecting loggias, on which to greet guests, bask in the sunset, or watch the workers tend the fields.

In designing his loggias, Palladio displayed a prescient under-standing of the architectural dictum, "Form follows function."

Projecting portico, pediment, columns—all merged with Palladio's trademark symmetrical stairs and wings to become a look, a signature, a movement. Andrea had found the flow. He translated Caesar's *Commentaries,* wrote the first reliable guide to Roman antiquities, illustrated an edition of Vitruvius, and, in the gesture that crowned his career, published his own treatise. *Il Quattro Libri dell' Architettura* (The Four Books of Architecture) was a manifesto of the principles that had brought him success, a work that would be the font of his immortality.

But while his credits multiplied in the Veneto and in Vicenza, Palladio couldn't break into Venice itself except in small ways: here a refectory, there a cloister. Then a client, Marcantonio Barbero, for whom he'd designed a villa at Maser, acquired power in the city. Barbero arranged for Andrea to design the Church of the Redeemer, which led to a commission for the Church of San Giorgio Maggiore, across St. Mark's Basin from the doge's palace and soon a symbol worldwide of Venice. He built churches named for Santa Lucia and Santa Maria della Prezentatione. Though he enjoyed his success in Venice, Palladio kept his home in Vicenza, where, on August 9, 1580, he died.

But Palladio's influence would spread across Europe as architects and designers came to the Veneto to see what he had wrought, and translations of *The Four Books* took the word to other cultures. Of Andrea's innovations, none saw more extensive adoption than that projecting portico, which became a staple of stately houses, first in England, and then, once there was the money for it, in the New World.

Among the villas Palladio designed in the Veneto, many still stand. Some still belong to the families that commissioned them; others have changed hands. A few owners keep their villas to themselves. Others make their houses pay, renting them for weddings and conferences, installing restaurants in outbuildings and gift shops in cellars, charging for tours. Local governments own villas, using them for offices; at the Villa Thiene in the town of the same name, administrators working on the third floor type beneath lovingly cleaned and sealed Palladian beams. Other jurisdictions run Palladian houses as historic sites, as Poiana Maggiore does with Villa Poiana Maggiore. The Villa Saraceno belongs to England's Landmark Trust, which rents it in season for ten thousand dollars a week, a price that includes sunsets flowing like warm butter onto the loggia and, for rainy days, a below-ground Palladian Ping-Pong room. Since the 1980s, Atlantans Carl and Sally Gable have owned Villa Cornaro in Piombino Dese, restoring it and preserving touches like the graffiti scribbled on the wall of one loggia by an owner wielding a chip of brick to mark the birth of a son in 1609. Some of Palladio's houses are in ruins behind cyclone fencing, some are in homely disrepair, others are as crisp and neat as if Andrea himself just finished the punch-out list. At Easter 2001, I crisscrossed the Veneto, visiting these extraordinary houses to see both how people lived in them when they were new and how folks use them now. In the process, I came to understand how Palladio's loggias and porticoes did—and did not—exert an influence on the American porch.

VILLA CHIERICATI-RIGO

As you drive into Vancimuglio from Venice on the two-lane blacktop of the Via Nazionale, you see on your left Villa Chiericati-Rigo, recognizable by its great projecting portico, which suggests the U.S. Supreme Court building as country house. The grandeur was no accident—the Chiericati family were mainstays of Vicentine society—but it had long since faded nearly 400 years later, when a man named Rigo bought the place to farm rice on the surrounding land. Now his son, Pietro, who was born and baptized in the house, lives there in the company of a few large dogs. He remembers when World War II came to the Veneto. "The partisans, the Germans, the Americans, they all came here," Mr. Rigo said, pointing to the stone figures at either side of the portico stairs. "There are still bullet marks on those statues."

Mr. Rigo is an earthy, practical man, more inclined to view his house as home than historical artifact. "I don't know why architects are interested in those decorations," he told me. "Two years ago I wanted to change the floor on the loggia, but my surveyor forbade me. 'You'll spoil it,' he said. But in my opinion it ought to be changed."

He doesn't open his property to the public, but the public still comes seeking admission. Mr. Rigo complains about the stream of Palladio-worshipping pilgrims, who are mostly young and mostly from Germany and England, though the demographic also includes architects and other adults, but I think he secretly enjoys the attention being paid his house, and, by association, him.

"They come on their bicycles, ask if they can camp here, if they can stay overnight," he said. "They stay for hours, studying the columns and decoration. I don't care for them myself, but I see that people admire them. Most of all they appreciate the loggia, because there are not many villas with an extended loggia like this. I think the people who come to see my house understand architecture."

As we were speaking we stepped out onto the loggia, much worn but still elegant, and I could see why it attracts Palladio's admirers. The elevation, the light, the long view—even with a town grown up across the road, the perspective is pleasing.

Mr. Rigo likes the loggia, too, especially as a place for an afternoon meal. Among his fondest memories of his father are those of the old man using the portico as a sort of plein-air office. "He spent his last years out here," the farmer said. "These days you have to work until you give up the ghost, but in those days landowners and farmers didn't work after sixty. He'd stay on the loggia and give orders. He used to talk to the foreman where we're standing. He'd ask, 'What have you done? What have you not done?'"

The loggia serves son as it did father; Pietro Rigo is no more retired at seventy-three than his dad at sixty. "It's a useful place for me," he said. "In a few weeks, these rice fields will be flooded. The water has to be ten centimeters deep. At dawn, I look at the mirror of water on the rice fields. From here, I can tell where there's not enough water, where there's too much, whether the workers have done a good job. I'd like to enjoy it more, sit here in peace, with nothing to do. But the workers arrive, and I have to give orders."

We stood in silence, looking across the fields to the highway. Though the spring air was cool, it promised summer pleasures. In the gloaming, the traffic had begun to thin. "It's a beautiful spot, a good place from which to see the world. The portico is wonderful in summer," Mr. Rigo said. "I like the evenings the best. When you come back from the field, and you are tired, you just sit on the loggia with a newspaper, and it is cool, as cool as if you were in the mountains. You don't even need a swing, just an easy chair. I feel quiet, relaxed. I live in a paradise. It's cold now, but when we place some vases, with flowers around, it's wonderful. You go up the stairs among the flowers, and it's cool and nice, except for a few mosquitoes. Then it's time to go to bed, and I loose my dogs."

VILLA PIOVENE

At Lonedo, a glance up a steep hillside travels the arc of Andrea Palladio's career as a designer of villas. Separated by a few hundred yards stand Villa Godi-Malinverni and Villa Piovene Porto Godi Pigafetta. The former was Palladio's first villa; the latter, his last. The older house is downhill; the newer house, begun several years after Palladio died, rides high and grand, surrounded with thick walls topped by coils of barbed wire that make it seem more fortress than residence, a theme that intensifies when you knock on a door cut into the black metal entry gate. The door is so tiny that to enter you have to duck your head while lifting your feet. I rang the bell and shivered in the shadow of the mossy battlement.

Originally, I was to interview Countess Caterina Piovene, the last person to carry that fine old name. Her line stretches back to an ancestor who came to northern Italy in the service of Otto of Brunswick. That was at the end of the twelfth century. The family ranks have included writers, architects, and sailors, and the Piovene figure in Venetian history; annotators of prints illustrating the Grand Canal and its palaces often point out Ca' Piovene.

Normally the countess doesn't talk to reporters. But when my assistant, Nadia, called to see if we could at least schedule a tour, she identified herself in the Italian manner, by saying where she lives: ____, a village in Friulia.

"____!" the countess exclaimed. "My wet nurse came from ____! Her name was ____."

As it happens, Nadia lives down the road from ____—a small-world coincidence that snagged me an interview with the countess. It seemed too good to be true.

It was.

En route to our appointment with Countess Piovene, Nadia phoned to confirm. The countess's son said he was sorry, but his mom was ill. He offered to guide us, taking care to remind Nadia that it would cost 80,000 lire (about forty dollars— back before the arrival of the Euro one of the thrills of visiting Italy was watching banknotes flutter through your hands like flocks of pastel birds).

A speaker in the wall buzzed. Nadia answered, and with the slam of a bolt being thrown and a creak from the special-effects department, the metal door opened. Out stepped Alfonso Vergnano, the countess's son. A round, casually dressed man in his thirties, the count greeted us with fish-handed diffidence, hovering silently until I produced the requisite wad o' lire, whereupon he launched into a brusque, rote soliloquy on the intertwined histories of his family and its house.

The most interesting nugget was that Palladio's client, Battista Piovene, only hired the architect to design the main body of the house, the wings, and the projecting portico. The rest came later, some in the eighteenth century via a design by Vicenzo Muttoni, one of Palladio's spiritual heirs. As we walked around the house, which has a time-stopping view down into the valley, I fancied I could see where the master's simplicity left off and rococo extrapolation began.

I'd thought my payment would rent at least a glimpse of the interior, but noooooooo. The count explained that there were no decorations or paintings inside, so the villa wasn't open to tourists—not even the loggia, which was the whole reason I'd paid him his damned 80,000 lire.

Fortunately, a thunderstorm blew in, giving the count no choice but to grant a special dispensation and allow us to take shelter with him on the loggia. We hopped the chain with its PRIVATA sign and bolted up the stairs. The exertions slightly unravelled the count's formal demeanor. As the storm swept the valley, he reminisced about his childhood, when his father did open the villa to tourists, to the son's great discomfort. "He kept records of the numbers of visitors," the count said. "I did not like people visiting the house. I considered them strangers, people who were there to take something away. Now I see things differently; I see the tourist as an integral part of this house, and someone with whom I can share its pleasure."

He prefers visitors from other nations to his countrymen. "Italian tourists always ask the most stupid questions," he said. "Once, somebody asked me why we don't cut the grass in the English style—that is, a few centimeters high. Because Palladio thought of these lawns as meadows and fields, that's why! The Italians ask why the facades of the house are in such bad condition; they don't realize that this stone, *marmorina palladiana,* cannot be quarried again."

He gestured toward the fields below the formal gardens one of his ancestors had installed. "In the old days, they measured the property in *giornata*—a day's walk. At one time, our holdings reached to Breganze," he said. Breganze is twenty-eight kilometers—almost fifteen miles—from Lonedo. As the family has for generations, he and his mother lease their land in exchange for a share of the crops. "My family and the farmers respect each other," he said. "It's an old-fashioned arrangement. I let you live in one of my houses; you cultivate the land and give me part of the harvest."

The count said he'd left the house as a child to live in Turin and only returned in recent years. "I felt the Vicentine land calling to me," he said. "I feel relaxed here; life is more grounded in tradition. For instance, when lunch is ready, especially in summer, we have the servants ring a bell to call guests for lunch. In the evening, if the help have already gone, I ring the bell myself. Tradition is important. I'd like to see the people who own these villas keep traditions alive, and keep the proper proportions, by not doing too much business from them."

I asked if he had any special feelings for the loggia on which we stood. It wasn't particularly inviting—hard edges and cold surfaces everywhere, a few chairs and a table, shutters over the windows, the entry a pair of tall, sturdy doors that clearly saw little use. He pointed to one of the shuttered windows—his bedroom. "I enjoy the loggia every morning," he said. "I listen to the birds and enjoy the landscape. It conveys the idea of summer, but it's beautiful in all seasons. These houses are built up high, and since the loggia occupies the highest space, it provides a wonderful view."

There was a noise. The count nearly jumped out of his skin. One of the tall doors opened a crack, and out reached a small, old hand.

"It's my mother," the count said with alarm, He hurried over and, after a brief conference, invited us in. Countess Piovene was still not feeling up to an interview, but she simply had to meet Nadia from _____. The countess was petite, and walked with a cane. She ushered us into the vestibule, lit only by the open door and a dusty window high on the far wall of the big dark room. Nadia and I and my son, Marty, crowded onto a wooden banquette at a small round table. The countess and the count sat opposite. I experienced the sensation of attending a séance.

"It is a pleasure to meet you, Nadia," the countess said, apologizing for her indisposition. She'd had to undergo a procedure in which doctors insert a balloon into a blocked artery and inflate it to clear the passage so the blood can flow. What was the word in English? As she spoke she beamed at Nadia as if seeing a long-lost niece.

Suddenly I had become a spectator. Nadia was deep in conversation with the countess, now blossoming. Though Nadia was graciously declining to translate, I could tell the countess was describing her operation in excruciating detail; now and again an "angioplasty" or "defibrillator" would punctuate the lyrical stream of Italian.

My eyes adjusted to the gloom. The vestibule was crammed with stuff. To my left, I could make out a sideboard; above it hung an old sepia photo of people, no doubt long dead. Behind us, on a dusty table, lay a desiccated bouquet. Odd white shapes loomed—sheet-draped furniture, surrounding a pair of enormous industrial-looking mechanisms. It hit me: they were wine presses, each about eight feet tall, with tubs big enough for Lucy *and* Ethel.

The countess finished her medical play-by-play and began interrogating Nadia about the long-lost wet nurse. She wept. She put a hand over her heart. She made a face. She smiled bravely. Sitting beside his mother, who was growing more vibrant as she wallowed in her miseries, the count blanched, as if he was seeing the ghost of Piovene future. The scene felt like a Tennessee Williams playlet rewritten by Goldoni. Nadia wrapped it up with the countess smoothly, courteously, and definitively, securing an invitation to return during the summer and have breakfast on the loggia. Outside, the storm had passed, and we made our escape, passing cages full of peacocks.

VILLA GODI-MALINVERNI

A few days later, I returned to Lonedo, this time to Palladio's first villa—the one he designed with Giangiorgio Trissino looking over his shoulder. The loggia/towers combination does evoke the feudal era, with the forward jut of the towers making the loggia seem even more deeply recessed into the building. But once you get through the gate and climb the steep staircase, the loggia is elegant and inviting. Frescoes that artist Gualtiero Padovano framed in a dazzling array of trompe l'oeil pursue the same themes as those at Villa Poiana—goddesses and farmers, Roman glories and Venetian puissance, the status, actual and aspired-to, of the Godi family, which commissioned the house in 1537—as well as more provocative concepts, like the hermaphroditic images beside the door.

The he/she figures have nipples like Bing cherries, a homage to pleasures Christian Malinverni can only imagine, since, as proprietor of Villa Godi-Malinverni, he's much too busy managing the staff, booking the events, counting the tourists, and sometimes even cutting the grass to loll about pondering perversity.

That's how it's been since Christian was a boy. His grandparents, who'd bought the place in 1950 after it had been abandoned for half a century (it was literally a pigsty, with porkers snuffling in the halls), would shoo him out of the public spaces so he wouldn't disturb visitors who'd paid to tour the restored house and grounds. Now Christian runs the estate, which draws 15,000 tourists a year, plus diners drawn by a restaurant that leases one of the outbuildings and guests at a steady stream of meetings and weddings convened in the villa—a marketing innovation Christian introduced to boost the revenues that keep the house from reverting to desuetude.

But he hews to the same line as previous generations of Malinverni; except for rare family events, the loggia at Villa Godi-Malinverni is the province of Nikon-slinging, videotaping hordes.

"I can remember one day when we closed the villa to the public and used it only for us, for my sister's wedding," Christian said. "The portico was the place where the bride and the groom met. That was the only day we enjoyed the villa for ourselves, as a family, without tourists—something very, very special."

The loggia figures in Christian's life mainly as a signpost that he's arrived from Milan, where he lives half the year. As he steers his Audi around that last, steep bend, he's waiting to see those beckoning arches. "I look for the staircase and the loggia," he said. "When the lights are switched on in the evening, it has a warm look."

Standing at the railing, Christian gestured across the hills to the spot where a clear day ends in a burst of light. "During the summer, the sun is out until nine or ten o'clock in the evening, and it sets just in front of the villa," Christian Malinverni said. "The colors are bright and red and very intense. It's something wonderful to be drinking an aperitif and sitting on the loggia to have dinner when that happens, as it has for me two or three times."

THE CONTESSAS

At the villas I'd seen so far, I'd met people who, as inheritors or latter-day purchasers or conservators, had had to submit to the realities that argue for opening these houses to the public. Christian Malinverni had put it succinctly: stop the flow of tourist-borne lire, and the house dies. But here and there I'd encountered vestiges of the private life: the family Piovene's policy of limited touristic incursions, Christian's memory of his sister's wedding day. Another house I visited occupied a band deep in the spectrum of privacy. Besides being discreet, except insofar as they agreed to talk with me, its owners, whose family has had the villa since the seventeenth century, are gracious, bearers of a noble name known in Venice before the Serene Republic became a world power. And that is as close as I am going to come in identifying them.

Their house stands near the Dolomites, which catch and hold warm, moist air from the Adriatic, rendering the local microclimate mild. Palm and olive trees flourish, as do the traditional Veneto crops of grapes and grain. The day I was there, in early spring, the villa's fields were in bud, and a furze of green showed on the vineyards marching west.

I parked in an outer courtyard that could have been a location for a European movie set in any century before the twentieth—a square of hard-beaten dirt, bare save for a bricked area on which a toddler played a game involving many sticks, with an old lady clad in black watching him from the sparse shade of a spindly tree. Among the late-model sedans stowed along the square were tantalizing anachronisms: medieval-looking farm tools, wooden wagon-wheels, and an immaculate black-and-maroon motorcycle with sidecar—a Ural, the Russian knockoff of the BMWs German troops drove during World War II. At the far side of the courtyard a sign reading PRIVATA hung on a wooden palisade. You could practically hear the director saying, "Cue the contessa."

A section of the wooden wall swung open, revealing the contessa, tall and tan, slim and dark-haired. She moved warily until Nadia and I introduced ourselves, then ushered us through the gate to a loggia that obviously saw regular use. The furniture was worn but welcoming: rattan chairs and sofa, low coffee table, benches, and, just below a window opening from the kitchen, a scrubbed pine table. The furniture was strewn with the tools of life: fashion magazines, a young rider's hardhat; at the doorway, a well-used boot scraper. The stucco on the walls was the color of crème brûlée.

The contessa explained that she lives in a nearby city—her four sisters and their families live farther away—but visits the villa every day, as she has since her father died two years ago. "He was the one who took care of everything," she said. "The house was his passion, his life. After he died, the family decided I would continue as he had. It's the reference point for all the family, but the deeper reason is that it's a way to feel closer to my father. Here at the villa, I feel his presence."

A caretaker does the heavy lifting in the vineyard, which produces Merlot, Cabernet, Pinot Grigio, and Riesling, with the spoilage used to make rich, dark vinegar. Tenant farmers raise wheat, corn, and soybeans. Summers and holidays, her sisters and mother join her at the villa. In fact, she said, her mom and two of her sisters, with their children, would be arriving soon. I said the setting, especially the outer courtyard, had a cinematic feel. "Yes, we once had an adventure with a film production company that wanted to use the villa as a set," the contessa said. "They said they would replace everything as it had been, but they did not, and in fact things were broken. So we don't have those adventures any more." She smiled sadly.

She has happier memories of life on the loggia. "When we were children a horse-drawn carriage was stored under the arcade. My sisters and I loved to play hide-and-seek in it and use it as a playhouse," the contessa said. "Now we have breakfast here, and during the summer we often have dinner here. We don't use any part of the house as much as we do the loggia, in winter as well as summer. This is my refuge, my nest. I feel good here, as if I have always lived here. I feel the presence of my family and of my father. Everything starts from here."

A deep feeling came upon her, and she fell silent. Just then a swirl of happy noise erupted in the outer courtyard. A pack of children entered: nieces and nephews, plus a young friend. Then a second contingent of three women, each of an aristocratic beauty consonant with the contessa's. Her mother and sisters smiled and said hello. The contessa suggested we repair to the loggia.

Our hostesses rued the accommodations, particularly the absence of upholstery—the season was too young for cushions—but the rattan was comfortable enough, and the hospitality all-embracing. Wine, plates of cheese, and toasted bread sailed through the kitchen window. The loggia was what I had come to think of as Palladian, with its ceiling more than twenty feet high, its length and breadth and depth an approximation of the Golden Section so pleasing to the human eye and spirit.

The sun warmed us as we sat eating Asiago cheese on slices of *bruschetta* and drinking wine pressed from grapes grown across the road. We talked of life in the city, and of life at the villa, and of how those lives differ from and refract one another. The other sisters agreed that the villa, and in particular its loggia, is their family's heart, a place at which they restore the fabric frayed by everyday existence. Hours passed. The weather shifted from sunny to stormy to sunny again, driving the children inside, then drawing them out again. More cheese, more wine, more richly inflected conversation. Another of the sisters agreed to sit for a formal interview, and the others vanished inside. Before we could talk I needed to use the facilities. The contessa led me inside, through a passageway decorated with many artifacts, including an antique frame holding portraits of several distinguished heads wearing the one-horned hats distinctive to the men who ruled Venice in its heyday. I pointed at the picture.

"Ah, yes. *I Dogi*, our ancestors," the contessa said. "The toilet is around the corner."

Back on the loggia, she and I settled into chairs. I explained that her sister had told me some family history, particularly of the loggia, but I wanted to hear more.

"This is the place where we welcome people," the second contessa said. "We live on it according to the seasons. At certain hours during the summer, you cannot sit here; the portico faces south, and gets very hot and sunny—we put up awnings so we can enjoy it. It's our sitting room; in the evening, there's a nice breeze. Sometimes we have dinner here. When we were children, the loggia was essential because we could stay outside, but be protected from danger."

In all seasons, and all circumstances, the loggia has been central to the family's life. Four of the five sisters are married; their wedding celebrations? On the loggia. Once England's Queen Mum passed through town with her entourage and her Bentley; where did the family entertain her? On the loggia.

As the sisters enjoyed the loggia in childhood, they enjoy it now as parents. Rain, snow, and hail, the loggia is always there, offering room for adults and room for children. "It repeats itself," the contessa said. "The generations live together with enjoyment and without inconvenience."

With the sisters grown and scattered, the villa and its loggias have assumed more importance. "Each of us lives her own life in the city, works there, has her own family," the contessa told me. "This is the place where we reconnect. The loggia has a very important role; it reflects the spirit of the house, and the season, and the time of day. In winter, when I come out here in the morning, it is cold, and I do not come very willingly. At other times, the sun is here, and I sit with a book as if I were in a room, with its intimate, cozy atmosphere. Some hours of the day, there is a to and fro of people—workers cutting the grass, the children. The family meets here and then parts again."

I asked about their emphasis on privacy. "We are very jealous about our home, because we live in it, and it has belonged to our family for generations. So when people ask us to come and visit the villa inside, we say, no, it is not open to the public, although we do let academics and scholars in. We're happy they want to deepen their understanding," the contessa said, adding that family opinion has not been monolithic on the matter. "My mother prefers to leave the villa closed, but my father liked to open it, so others could enjoy it. Sometimes we live one way, sometimes the other."

I wondered aloud about Andrea Palladio's intent in designing houses like these, with their blend of urbanity and country living, of privacy and public encounter, of Venetians coming to terms with life on the land. "Venetians are very solar people—smiling, pleasure-seeking. They're not irritable. Palladio perceived this, and his villas and their porticoes are testimony to the Venetian character. Certainly, Palladio thought of the sun, and the moon as well," the contessa said. "There's a beautiful view of the moon from the loggia. And these houses owe their radiance to the sun, because the porticoes and loggias collect its warmth."

It was raining again. A woman's voice called through the window. The contessa answered in the affirmative.

"Come into the kitchen," she said, standing up. "We will have something to eat."

At Villa Pisani-Bonetti, the loggia, once a place of public
encounter, has become a private zone of reflection.

VILLA PISANI-BONETTI

For Venetians, one of the Veneto's attractions was its bogginess. *Terra* that wasn't
sufficiently *firma* put off dry-landers, but not people accustomed to dealing
with water. And when the Pisani family was building a villa outside Bagnolo di
Lonigo, they had a lot of water to deal with. "Bagnolo" comes from *bagnare,* to
soak or to bathe, and that's what the surrounding landscape did, as the River Gua
regularly flooded acres of rice fields.

A tributary of the Brenta, the Gua is silted in, but once it served Bagnolo like
a watery spur line; in the 1500s, farm owners like the Pisani family could reach
the town from Venice via barge, the route preferred over traveling by carriage on
dust-ridden roads. When the family hired Palladio to build a villa for them on
Via Risaie ("Rice-Fields Street"), he sited it so his clients and their guests could
travel either way. He placed the outbuildings and a greensward behind the villa,
whose recessed loggia opened onto the river where a dock welcomed waterborne visitors. On the far shore was a ferry landing, the terminus of a roadway
down which landbound visitors could ride.

Villa Pisani marked a variation on the theme Palladio had explored at nearby
Poiana Maggiore. The house had the strict proportions, stark but pleasing lines,
scant ornamentation, and interior frescoes of the myth of Phaeton, but with a
key distinction: the sun. Villa Poiana faces west; Villa Pisani, east. Catching the
morning light full in its rectangular face, Villa Pisani's recessed loggia is bright.
However, it no longer is the semipublic place that it once was.

The Venetians thought their canals and ditches could tame the river, but the
Gua—from the Old Italian *guai,* meaning "disasters"—proved uncooperative,
often flooding. Like many agricultural towns, Bagnolo had always had the aura
of an island rising among seas of grain; when the Gua overran its banks, the

town had a shoreline as well. To cope, townsmen raised the roads on mounds of earth, and finally, after one flood too many, levees rose along the Gua, and atop the levees thick, high walls, the better to curb the wayward river.

The expenses in labor and lire were huge; so was the aesthetic cost. In exchange for dry feet, the Pisanis traded away the panoramic perspective from their loggia. It was as if fate had spun the house on its axis and made the loggia into a back porch, albeit a back porch of elegant splendor, decorated now with modern dining tables and chairs and a pair of waist-high church bells that gleam black against the Vicentine marble. "Those are the bells of Bagnolo, the ones the Pisani family gave the church," said Manuela Bedeschi Bonetti, who with her husband has owned the house since 1999. "The church gave them back to the family when the parish decided to install an automatic carillon."

The floods of the 1700s dramatically altered the loggia's character. "Until then, the loggia here had a public function. The loggia was the place from which the family could observe its property. People could recognize the villa from the loggia, from the main façade," Mrs. Bonetti said. "Whether you were navigating the river or approaching on land, you could see the house and the loggia, which represented the family."

It was midmorning, and the walls that contain the rebellious Gua were casting deep shadows on the grass beyond the loggia steps. The scene was as quiet as the grave. I asked how it might have looked when the house was new.

"On the far side of the river, there was a long avenue, perpendicular to the villa. You could see the villa from kilometers away; it was the reference point for all that went on around here," Mrs. Bonetti said. "There would have been a certain amount of animation and bustle, but remember—these were summer houses. The heat led to a slower rhythm. Life had a different cadence. The owners came from Venice, navigating along the Gua. A boat needed time and a certain rhythm to ascend the river. Those who came by carriage on the roads traveled according to that rhythm. Everyone, workers as well as owners, spoke the Venetian dialect, which is a very soft and musical language, even softer and more musical than Italian. I sometimes feel as if I can still hear it. This languid, rhythmic language also affected the cadence of life. The loggia was where the Pisani family lived. They were visible to everybody, to all the people who crossed the river, to those who worked in the rice fields, who unloaded goods from the dock in front of the loggia. This changed when the villa was closed off by the wall, and the loggia became a private thing."

But the new owners also value the unanticipated benefit conferred centuries ago when the loggia lost its public aspect. "This side has turned into a very discreet place. The afternoon and late morning are the best times to sit here, but you can enjoy the loggia every single moment of the day," said Mrs. Bonetti. "We live on it in a very intimate way. We have the feeling of being outside in the garden, in the open air, and at the same time we feel protected. This space is very bright, very serene. The air is pleasant. One feels the breeze, the sensation of being isolated from the world. The light is so warm, because the stones reflect it. You experience both the small and large dimensions of the house. We like to sail, and that is how the loggia feels—like a little sailing trip that takes you away from daily life."

VILLA FOSCARI

My last Palladian loggia might be one of the best known. Villa Foscari stands a few miles from the mouth of the Brenta, a great dark structure rising alongside the muddy stream. Its loggia is a tribute to the floods of yesteryear, standing more than twenty feet above the ground, flanked by mature trees that give the house tremendous canal-side appeal. Usually the villa bustles with tourists, but I'd arranged to meet owner Antonio Foscari on a quiet weekday morning, when the grounds wore a cloak of grace and quiet. I climbed the stairs leading to the loggia, with its elevation and its setting seeming very much like a stage—which turned out to be appropriate, because when Professor Foscari arrived, he was ready to deliver an oration.

Besides owning a magnificent piece of architectural history, Antonio Foscari is an architectural historian. A vigorous, handsome man of a certain age whose wardrobe finds the balance between academic tweediness and aristocratic panache, the professor leads a bifurcate professional life. He teaches and researches architectural history, specifically the impact of events in fifteenth-century Venice and environs on the Italian Renaissance. He oversees restorations of historic structures and designs new buildings. "It is laborious," he told me. "But I cannot give up either, because I like to construct buildings and I like to understand a building's origins."

In terms of understanding Villa Foscari's origins, the professor enjoys certain advantages. He is a scion of *the* Foscari, who had long been a power in Venice when his ancestors commissioned Palladio to build them a country house in 1555. Then in the prime of his designing life, the architect had expanded his vision of the ideal house, and he built Villa Foscari proud and tall, nearly five stories, its *piano nobile* safely elevated above the floodplain and its façade a neoclassical temple embodying all Palladio had learned from Vitruvius, Alberti, Serlio, Trissino, and from experience. Standing alongside the Brenta less than half a day's journey from Venice, the house afforded its occupants the passing show of barcas and barges. Proximity to town didn't cramp the plantation; contemporary prints illustrate a farm as bustling as any farther inland.

The villa remained a key part of the Foscari holdings until the nineteenth century, when the Republic fell and many families abandoned their villas, retreating from modernity as their forebears had fled into the lagoon. Villa Foscari became a hulk, albeit one with a desolate grandeur and its own legend, of a woman who lived there. Locals called her *la malcontenta*, "the unhappy one," and the name stuck to the house.

La Malcontenta remained in ruins until 1925, when financier Albert Clinton

Landsberg and his wife bought and restored the villa. Their stewardship lasted until Mussolini's Italy, mimicking Hitler's Germany, passed anti-Semitic statutes, and the Landsbergs left for safer regions. Meanwhile, Antonio Foscari's father, who had a soft spot for the house that should have been his, had moved his family from Venice to a villa nearby. Father and son began bicycling past La Malcontenta, to monitor its condition and discourage vandalism. These patrols introduced the younger Foscari to the intricacies of Palladio's design, setting him on a course for a career in architecture. After World War II, the Landsbergs returned, grateful to the Foscari family for looking after their villa.

"When Bertie came back to Italy, he used to invite me to his house. I'd have breakfast with him and his wife, Dorothy, on this loggia. I still saw the house as a great mystery, as very different from other houses," the professor said, pointing to metal fixtures mounted head-high on the pillars. "He used to keep sails out here that were tied to those rings, which originally were meant to hold lights."

Landsberg had a sense of history and of humor. Once, while entertaining an English government delegation at breakfast, he included young Foscari on the guest list. "Randolph Churchill was there, and many other ministers, whose names I don't remember," the professor said. "When lunch was about to be served, Bertie said, 'The Lord of the House, my friend, my young friend . . .' and left me alone with his guests, but not before he leaned down and said to me, 'After all, this is *your* home.' I stayed there to preside at the English cabinet's lunch. They continued speaking in English; I only understood a little. It was a fantastic scene, as sometimes happens when you're a child, and in a way it expresses the good fortune that characterized my encounters with this place."

From the Landsbergs the house passed into the hands of an English lord named Philmore, who also befriended the young Italian. In the 1970s the Foscari family reacquired the villa, and now it belongs to the professor, who works to ensure that on some level the grand house retains a lived-in feeling.

"My attitude toward the house, rather than being that of 'owner,' is more that of a person who loves architecture and tries to appreciate the importance of a historic place of this quality, and who wants to keep it accessible to people, so that they also can enjoy it," Professor Foscari said. "The fact of my being an architect, a historian of architecture, carrying the name I do, my father's presence, and meeting Bert Landsberg and Lord Philmore, are the roots of my relationship to this building."

For the interview, the professor and I settled on the loggia, into chairs whose design dates to the days when the house was being built. He reminded me of the loggia's place in Venetian history, as well as the societal shifts that defined life in the Veneto of the sixteenth century. "A house with a portico was completely different from the ancient houses of the *signori,* the noblemen, which had been fortified houses," the professor said. "A house with a portico is an indefensible house; it is an open house. It implies that the State, and in particular the Republic of Venice, maintains the territory's defense."

Defending the Veneto meant making it habitable and profitable, and that meant a campaign to control water that was no less ambitious than the one that had wrested Venice from the sea. "The separation of the land from the water in the Veneto was almost like a divine event, a sort of continuity of Genesis," Professor Foscari said.

Under the eye and at the hand of warrior-businessmen like Boniface Poiana, the region blossomed. The discovery of the New World had sapped the Republic's power, but it brought Venice corn, potatoes, tomatoes, and other new crops that boosted soil fertility, improving farmers' output and encouraging people to move to the Veneto. "This was the first agrarian revolution in the modern world, and it was an agrarian revolution in the deepest sense," the professor explained. "With it, feudal culture was over; public and private joined forces, and their cooperation produced wealth—and, according to Adam Smith, wealth originated by farming is the best kind of wealth. The Venetians, who had been denied access to the New World, compensated by discovering on the mainland their own new world. They imported American crops and 'discovered' the land, agriculture, and agrarian production."

It was in this context that Andrea Palladio came into his own. Through it, the young architect created the open-faced farmhouses of the Veneto that embodied a new way of living. "In a generation or two, feudal noblemen turned into farmers. Their cultural background and social role changed. In the span of Palladio's life, the first small houses of the Vicentine noblemen, with their loggias, turned into farms," the professor said. "In the seventeenth century, there was a strong political relationship between the Veneto and the Dutch. Through them and Englishmen like Inigo Jones, the English encountered this agrarian revolution and the Palladian architecture that represented it. The English needed a form suitable to indicate their own lords' new social role, so they imported the agrarian revolution and its image, which started the great English agrarian movement that would be the motor, the spring of the capitalistic accumulation of wealth which nourished the Industrial Revolution."

Thanks to vestigial memories of high school Latin, I had managed to digest most of this even without benefit of translation. But the professor wasn't through making connections, and he meant to take Palladianism across the Atlantic. "The physiocratic culture that arose with the English agrarian revolution was brought to America," he said. "We must remember that President Jefferson, who built his villa at Monticello according to a Palladian model, was a Physiocrat. He was convinced America had to be and remain an agrarian continent, with no contamination by the dangerous industrial process. Washington, D.C., is the ideal capital of an agrarian territory. What happened was that a culture—the physiocratic culture, an agrarian revolution, and an architectural style—were transferred from one place to another, and I believe we can better understand the migration of these models as a matter of the migration of great cultural and political phenomena."

The professor sat back in his Renaissance-style chair and smiled, then announced that he unfortunately had to go. I was welcome to enjoy the loggia as long as I wished. With a handshake and a *"Ciao!"* he was down the stairs and around the corner.

So this was it. Last interview, last day in the Veneto, last villa, last loggia. I walked out to the edge of the Brenta and framed the house in my camera's viewfinder. I thought of the lives this house and others like it had contained and defined: owners, farmers, servants, guests, tourists, historians. The generations of Foscari for whom it had been a refuge and a headquarters, the decades when only the rumor of *la malcontenta* lived here. Albert Landsberg's restoration. Young Antonio Foscari bicycling the grounds, puzzled at his father's love for a house he didn't own.

As I was about to squeeze the shutter, the front door opened and Professor Foscari stepped out. He crossed the loggia, descended the steps, and strode to a place on the wall. He had something shiny in his hand. I cranked the zoom lens. It was a pair of scissors, blade open. The professor was using the point to extirpate weeds that had taken root in the mortar at the foundation of his house.

My immersion course in the Palladian loggia showed me much about how that form had taken shape and how it had become a mainstay of Renaissance architecture and culture. No one could have been more accommodating than my hosts in the Veneto, who proved again and again that the region's hospitality—and its loggias' beauty and comfort—are as advertised. But even as I reveled in the company and the context, I saw a sharp difference between life on the loggia and life on the porch.

Palladio had designed for a time when houses were moving out of the role of fortress, with walls and castellations and stout doors and gun-ports, and into the role of dwelling. But just as the society of the Veneto only reached a certain point on the path to the modern, Palladio's villas only got partway to hominess. Their loggias offered a highly qualified welcome, but the walls and gates built more than four hundred years ago to protect Palladio's clients still protect his clients' inheritors, many of whom have seen fit to improve on brick and iron with ribbon wire and electrical security systems, expressing a tradition of wariness that has mellowed but not disappeared.

Andrea Palladio popularized the shape that the American porch would take, but his loggias weren't places in which the public and the private met. Rather, they were—and are—places that mark the convergence of the private and the somewhat less private; elegant zones of encounter, but zones where the known encounters the known. Then or now, you wouldn't sit on your Palladian loggia and expect to say hello to your neighbor unless your neighbor called from the gate and asked to come in.

For its time, Andrea Palladio's reinvention of the portico marked an extraordinary innovation. But for the Palladian loggia to evolve further, it would have to emigrate—first to England, then to America.

One of the oldest plantation houses on the East Coast, Middleburg, in the Low Country of South Carolina, exemplifies the synergy of Caribbean and neoclassical styles.

Chapter Six

FROM THE OLD WORLD TO THE NEW

As Palladianism was spreading across Europe, it found a particularly enthusiastic, if climatically inopportune, home in clammy England—hardly the place for loggias premised on fair weather and balmy summers. It wasn't the first time the form had gone awry. Palladio himself thought the Romans had had porticoes on their villas before putting them on temples and public buildings.

"His knowledge of temples and public buildings led him to believe, quite erroneously, that the ancients 'very probably took the idea and the reason from private buildings; that is, from houses,' and he therefore designed all his villas with an impressive entrance portico," writes architectural historian Peter Murray. "This, in the strong sunshine of Italy, has much to recommend it, but it should be remembered that many English and American country-houses have enormous, inconvenient, and draughty porticoes simply because Palladio misinterpreted ancient architecture: yet the spell of his own works was so strong on all English architects of the eighteenth century that they copied this feature irrespective of its impracticability in a northern climate."

Nonetheless, the 1716 English edition of *The Four Books of Architecture* spawned a Palladian movement. Inigo Jones laid the groundwork with his piazza at Covent Garden and the Queen's House at Greenwich. Christopher Wren delighted clients with his economical, serene country houses. Colen Campbell incised the rules of Palladian engagement in his book *Vitruvius Brittanicus*, invoking the Roman as well as Palladio and touching a philosophical nerve.

England was buzzing with protorepublican sentiment, embodied by the Whigs, who went head-over-heels for Palladian style's clean lines and demure ornamentation. They saw the look as an inheritance from republican Rome, and as egalitarian—well, as egalitarian as it got in the England of that day. Whigs also embraced Palladio's construct of the country house as a site of contemplation and restoration, untainted by the city's venom and venality.

The cousins in the colonies took careful note. With its references to the Greeks' democratic ideals and Rome's republican ambitions, as well as the Venetians' mercantile muscle, the neoclassical mode spoke to the New World's slave-owning, soil-tilling strivers in the same exuberant tones that had entranced the Veneto's agrarian grandees. The Palladian way also provided a stylish means of adding a European gloss to the rudiments of colonial life.

As Palladio's signature loggia was becoming fashionable in England, the less classical structure known variously as the piazza, the gallerie, and the veranda was insinuating itself into the vernacular architecture of the Caribbean and North America. Apropos of its name, vernacular architecture is slangy—it comes from the street, or, as might be better said of colonial times, from the road and the river and the sea. The long trip across the Atlantic and North America's vast size shook designs and structures loose from their original contexts and encouraged fresh approaches to building and living, especially in the liminal area between inside and out. Besides the combination of the precolonial African housefront with the Arawak *bohio* that had become so popular in the Caribbean, there were other treatments. The Dutch introduced the stoop. Spanish colonists built *portals,* enclosures they'd used in Cuba and Mexico. And, as the English came to dominate North America, they brought their beloved Palladian loggias. All these elements blended into what we know as the porch through a process folklorists call "creolization," an intermingling of two or more cultural patterns that produces something new.

Architectural historians, who tend to focus on formal designs and their impact on one another, have traditionally addressed the populist porch in passing—at least until the mid-nineteenth century, when it achieved near-ubiquity. But threads of porch culture wove through the Colonial (1600–1700) and Georgian (1700–1780) periods, before becoming a bold component of the Federal (1780–1820) era.

According to historian Hugh Morrison, colonial architecture in America before 1700 was "medieval"—a rough-hewn, anachronistic stepchild of Western European Gothic. Colonists needed cheap, fast shelter, so they built what they knew: post-and-beam houses, simple and barely decorated inside or out. In the early days, residents of New England understood "porch" to mean a space inside the front door that functioned like a modern mudroom—close quarters, with the interior walls made up mostly of doors to other rooms and the stairway to the second floor. The closest that early colonial houses in the Northeast came to an exterior shelter was an overhanging second story, or "jetty," a design imported from the Old World. The jetty may have been an aesthetic touch or an effort to make the most of limited urban building space by colonizing the very air.

Down the coast, in Nieuw Amsterdam, a different entry was proliferating. Made of stone or brick, the *stoep*—Dutch for "step"—was a roofless link between doorway and street. Though municipal tradition required a building's occupants to maintain the stoep, the Dutch deemed it public territory. However, in Nieuw Amsterdam, the stoep acquired a private connotation: ". . . before each door there was an elevation, to which you could ascend by some steps from the street," an observer wrote. "It resembled a small balcony, and had some benches on both sides on which the people sat in the evenings, in order to enjoy the fresh air, and have the pleasure of viewing those who passed it."

South of Nieuw Amsterdam, near the convergence of what would become New Jersey, Delaware, and Pennsylvania, Sweden had a toehold. The Swedes' lasting gift to colonial architecture, the log cabin, solved two problems; trees felled to clear farmland also provided building materials. However, concerned more with defense than decor, the Swedes only extended their cabins' roofs far enough to deflect water.

At first, colonial architecture in the region from Virginia to Carolina was as mean and drab as its northern counterpart. But the South was another country whose very nature spurred new directions in building and society.

Early Southern houses, even those of wealthier colonists, were plain and simple, though on some houses in Maryland and Virginia the porch, previously an interior room, was extended outward. However, it remained closed, except for ventilation openings high on the side walls. "The eighteenth-century porch was not dissimilar in size and shape to the porches built onto seventeenth-century English houses," writes Henry Glassie in *Folk Housing in Middle Virginia*. "The British porch is usually enclosed, whereas the porch in Virginia is open (a skeletal representation of the British prototype), but they functioned similarly as sheltered extensions of the entrance."

Given the Southern weather, it was inevitable that someone would put a roof over exterior space. An early example was the "dog-run" or "possum-trot" cabin, in which builders erected two square structures—usually no more than twenty-four feet on a side (longer logs were too heavy to move)—a few yards apart. A single roof over cabins and gap created a shady breezeway used to store gear and cure skins, as well as cool the cabin interiors. The family dogs could loll there. (And if they didn't, possums were likely to be rummaging around; hence the structure's two names.)

The South's climate, topography, and soil encouraged cultivation of commodity crops like indigo, rice, and tobacco, profitable only when worked on vast acreages. To create farms of the scale needed, England's rulers granted their allies tracts of land with which to enrich themselves, by selling it, leasing it, or working it themselves. The resulting enterprises resembled the plantations of the Veneto; in like spirit, owners lived on their farms but kept houses in town, to the extent that there were towns in the distinctly unurban South, which, like the Veneto, had a lattice of rivers that linked plantation owners not only to one another but to the world. Many plantations had deep-water docks, reducing the impetus toward city building. Besides facilitating shipment of goods in and out, ease of transport attuned plantation dwellers to fashions in adjoining locales, as well as the more distant cities of the Caribbean and Europe. Their situation also fostered a culture tinged with feudal mores. "Compared to New England, [the South] was a land without towns and villages," writes Morrison. "With its one-crop economy, huge land holdings, and the introduction of slave labor, the South was destined to develop an aristocratic society and an aristocratic architecture."

Noting how well the Caribbean's slave-driven farms worked, planters in the South adopted that business structure. They also admired the pleasing practicality of Caribbean architecture, still being influenced by battalions of slaves with memories and sometimes firsthand experience of African vernacular forms. Many new arrivals, white and Black, came via the South's main outpost of urbanity, the Carolina port of Charleston. Early settlers there made do with wooden dwellings until they could afford brick townhouses—tall, narrow, and ell-shaped—like those in English cities. But in the Carolina summer, brick houses became ovens; Charlestonians sweltered until the Caribbean provided a solution: the single and double piazza, easily added after the fact.

(As sister ports, closely allied in commerce and culture, Charleston and Boston shared many trends. "Piazza," both word and structure, quickly migrated north. Boston painter John Singleton Copley extolled the joys of what he spelled as "peazer" and "Peaza," describing it as "... very beautiful and convenient ... so cool in sumer [sic] and Winter break off the storms so much I think I should not be able to live an house without." Bostonians and other New Englanders still say "piazza" when they mean porch; in some parts of the region, "piazza" also means the tent of mosquito netting placed around a picnic table. And to the north, Canadians speaking of what Americans call porches say either "piazza" or "veranda.")

What worked in town also worked in the country. Planters took the piazza back to their farms. To catch the breeze and discourage the bugs, residents of the soggy, boggy Low Country in Carolina raised their houses and piazzas off the ground—another echo of the African model. Adding piazzas fore and aft made houses more comfortable and, in a culture that prized status, more stylish, especially as English Palladianism began to make itself known.

The taste for the porch spread west. Describing the architecture of Natchez, in the Mississippi territory, Fortescue Cumming writes, "I was much struck with the similarity of Natchez to many of the smaller West India towns, particularly St. Johns Antigua, though not near so large as it. The houses all with balconies and piazzas—some merchants' stores—several little shops kept by free mulattoes, and French and Spanish Creoles. . . ."

Along with piazzas and porches, colonial America had other kindred structures. In French-ruled Louisiana, the big architectural influence was the Caribbean island of Saint-Domingue. There, the slave population came largely from Congo and Niger, where the basic house was a series of corridorless rooms with a gable-ended porch at the front. Builders in Saint-Domingue had adopted and improved on the style; most houses there had a *gallerie,* often enclosing a house on all sides, and that became the standard in Louisiana, especially the port of New Orleans. To catch the breezes on sultry Saint-Domingue, builders elevated houses. So did New Orleans contractors, but they had a more urgent reason: floods, frequent and heavy. Buildings and their galleries went onto brick piers, sometimes eight feet high. This functional gesture became a regional fashion. Even when there was no risk of flood, planters stood their houses on piers, often stacking four- and two-sided galleries atop one another. As in England's southern colonies, water was the vector that carried the virus of style. The gallerie rode the Mississippi and its tributaries into the continent's heartland.

To the west, the Spanish were adopting and adapting techniques and materials native to their colony of New Mexico. The Indians there built with adobe, a mixture of sand, clay, straw, and sometimes manure pressed into blocks, stacked into walls, and plastered over with mud. As roof beams, Native Americans used peeled logs. Called *vigas,* these round rafters extended beyond the outside wall; to create shade, a building's inhabitants piled branches and leaves onto them. Spanish colonists introduced the *portal,* a recessed arcade at the front of a house (when built facing an interior courtyard, this feature was called a *corredor*). The portal was part passageway, part outside living space. Over time, the portal acquired aspects of the viga-shaded area that Indians used. It became deeper, with room for furniture.

But the main locale of evolving colonial architecture was the East, where the English boxed out the French and Spanish, gradually dominating the Atlantic coast. In the colonies as at home, the prevailing style was the one named for the three Georges who occupied the English throne in the eighteenth century. Designers of the Georgian era (1700–1780) could be stuffy, but there's no denying that the period's architects, along with pattern-book authors like James Gibbs and Batty Langley, knew their customers. The people who hired architects and devoured pattern books were status-savvy strivers. On their behalf, Georgian design cast the house as tall, proud, and symmetrical, an advertisement for its owner's wealth and taste—the same favor Palladio had done for his clients in the Veneto. But the Georgians, who lacked the Venetian tendency to associate the loggia with authority, eschewed it. They made rooms larger, and they built more of them; a decent home was no longer one room deep, but two. The old cramped "porch" expanded to hold guests, family members, and servants or slaves. To lend these larger interiors maximum drama, Georgian façades were flat, entered through beautiful doorways covered only by small pediments. That doorway was synecdoche for the whole Georgian look: rich in detail, subtly variegated, and almost perversely simple.

Georgian forms were adopted quickly by colonial fashionistas. But the style of no-style that is folk architecture remained popular with owner-builders, carpenters, and contractors. They put up what worked, and what worked was a front porch, even if its roof rode on a peeled trunk or a crudely adzed pillar. Such porches might extend from the house or be built into it, in the manner of the West Indies and the Carolinas. And often a porch was added after a dwelling was completed, as in Charleston.

But the beauty of the porch was its adaptability. It could be crude and rustic or sophisticated and dapper. With the hard start-up years behind them and their investments starting to pay off, plantation owners began to imagine themselves as lords of a new culture. Of course, the first thing new money wants is to look and smell like old money—in this case, old European money. House façades and porches began to gleam with fresh paint, crisp trim, grand columns. No more would planters throw up outbuildings at random or as utility dictated, or let slaves arrange their own quarters in a style that suggested a transplanted African village.

"Now you had to be purely European—and not only European, but European nobility," folklorist and porch chronicler Jay Edwards said. "You had to be an aristocrat. Planters were now sufficiently wealthy that they could purchase European landscape and architectural theory. They began to lay out their plantations as grand estates, like the villas and the chateaus back in Europe, with *allees* of trees. They put the slave quarters in the back like little peasant villages, but lining them up and making the rows all neat, with roof angles matching one another and so forth, a totally European idea—not an African idea at all."

However, a distinctly African sensibility was loose, and nothing could erase it. African architecture survived, sometimes in Maroon communities, where defiant ex-slaves clung to their remembered and imagined roots, as well as on remote, small-scale coffee plantations whose owners couldn't afford or stomach the fashion for extravagant veneers. Towns in the vicinity of such pockets inevitably felt their influence. The African porch also stayed in the mainstream—in disguise, camouflaged by colonial decorative impulses. Whether out of embarrassment at or ignorance of its origins, estate owners troweled on the trappings of neoclassicism until the porch looked as if it had flown straight across the Atlantic from Andrea Palladio's drawing table instead of coming from Africa to Brazil to the Caribbean.

From the Caribbean, it was a very short hop to the coast of North America, where the gallerie or veranda became a standard part of French and English military architecture, taking enthusiastic root. "The French and English military were picking it up and using it, putting open galleries on their buildings," Jay Edwards said. "The oldest gallery building I've been able to find evidence of in North America dates to 1702. It's in the port of Mobile, Alabama, where there's a French building with a full-length open-front gallery, akin to the Spanish plan in all ways save one. The Spanish liked that long rectangular room, the *salle*, or *sala*, but the French didn't; their traditional reception room was exactly square. So the French modified the floor plan a little to suit their architectural psychology, but they kept all this Creole stuff that had been added to the outside of the house—gabinetes and loggia. Once that design was established, it survived right up to the present. It's been going on for five hundred years in this hemisphere."

By the 1750s, classicism had returned to fashion in England, and the portico's popularity rebounded. The trend was duly followed in America, where another mode of cultural transmission was at work: war, this time between British and colonial forces and the French and their Indian allies. During expeditions into French-held regions, a young American officer named George Washington, who'd visited porch-happy Barbados in 1751 and had inherited a Virginia plantation house he wanted to expand, might have seen a gallerie or two that stuck in his memory.

The French and Indian War also sped the plough of independence. You could read the early and middle Georgian periods and their buttoned-up housefronts as a final assertion of Old World reserve in colonial architecture. Centuries of conflict and close quarters had taught Europe the wisdom of living behind barriers. Even the Veneto's loggias welcomed only those who were allowed past the high walls—and what was the Georgian façade but a graceful wall, to be penetrated only by those with proper credentials?

But in America life was different. Colonial cities were crowded, sure, but in the country, especially in the South, folks had to depend on one another. The traveler at your door on a miserable night could be the fellow to whose house another storm might send you. And it got lonely on the plantation, with no fresh faces or personalities to enliven the talk at breakfast or supper. So in the households of the region there evolved a culture of hospitality, and what displayed hospitality—as well as power and style—better than a portico? And if one portico, why not two?

Georgian designers in the southern colonies adapted the loggia. Doorways that hadn't had roofs acquired them, whether by extending the roof from the house or subsuming the entry into the structure. A dwelling might have a single portico or, in echo of Palladio and those ingenious piazzas in the Caribbean or the galleries of Louisiana, one atop the other. Drayton Hall, in South Carolina, half-copied the master's Villa Cornaro at Piombino Dese, with a projecting double portico. But Drayton Hall was not only early; it was unusual, in that it was built all of a piece. Most plantation houses took shape gradually, as owners acquired the resources in cash and slave labor to do the work. Whether the owner didn't want tradesmen and laborers wearing out what would be his home's most visible part or because he decided after the fact that style demanded or economics permitted that his house have a front porch, the portico or piazza or gallerie was often the last element built.

In fact, many a colonial homeowner never quite stopped building his house, continuing to tinker interminably with it. That persistence—some might say, idiosyncrasy—sometimes caused the construction of great houses to go on for years, even decades, as occurred at two of the most famous, and famously porch-equipped, homes in the young United States of America: Mount Vernon and Monticello.

Washington designed his piazza not so much as a display of puissance as a personal space, although he made sure it would be visible from the Potomac.

CHAPTER SEVEN

GEORGE'S PIAZZA AND
TOM'S PORTICO

When it came to designing and constructing homes for themselves and their families, George Washington and Thomas Jefferson were utterly different and yet soul mates. The diverging ways in which these men outfitted their houses jelled styles still vibrant in America's building habits.

Both approached home design from an aristocratic angle, being removed only by geography from the experience and spirit of the Poianas, the Cornaros, and the other Venetians for whom Andrea Palladio had designed villas that advertised their hospitality, nobility, and power. Like many prominent colonists of their generation, Washington and Jefferson were Palladians, albeit of drastically contrasting backgrounds and outlooks.

But neither Washington nor Jefferson had a Palladio to interpret his desires.

Instead, in addition to fomenting a rebellion and founding a nation, the two shared another experience: the designing and building (and rebuilding) of their homes, which now stand as character studies in wood and stone. "Those who construct their own shelter replicate themselves, at their deepest and most significant level, in their houses," writes Jack McLaughlin in *Jefferson and Monticello: The Biography of a Builder*. "They are what they build."

If that's so—and, speaking as one who has torn a house apart and put it back together to suit myself, I believe it is—then the porches at Mount Vernon and Monticello say much about their creators. Both illustrate the simplicities and complexities of the porch, as well as its intertwined debts to neoclassicism as well as to vernacular architecture.

Despite many similarities, such as their bourgeois beginnings, great ambition, revolutionary thinking, chronic debt, profound sense of history, and limited introspection, Washington and Jefferson differed greatly, and never more than in their approaches to their houses. You'd hardly call Washington mellow, for example. However, compared with the epically fussy Jefferson, he was Madison— Oscar Madison, that is—intense but eminently practical, inclined to disengagement, capable of extraordinary focus but willing to live with inconsistencies that maddened more rigid minds, like Felix Unger's, er, Thomas Jefferson's.

That duality had its embodiment in the two men's porches. At Mount Vernon, the piazza, as Washington preferred to call it, was completed in time for the aging leader to enjoy it before he died. But at Monticello, construction dragged on so long that when Jefferson finally was able to relax on its portico, he found himself facing tourist throngs, goggling as if at a dancing bear.

Being the less doctrinaire of the two amateur architects, Washington designed his piazza not so much as a display of puissance as a personal space, although he made sure it would be visible from the Potomac. Jefferson, on the other, more strictly Palladian hand, called Monticello's east porch a portico, a formal setting in which he could greet guests with elegance, grace, and the iron control he liked to maintain over his privacy, even in public.

Washington's incessant and meandering alterations bemused some acquaintances. One called his house "uncommon," the contemporaneous equivalent of saying, when confronted with a particularly odd-looking infant, "That's *some* baby." Other visitors to Mount Vernon, like German military man Friedrich von Steuben, were appalled by the proprietor's irregular execution of his concepts. "If . . . Washington were not a better general than he was an architect the affairs of America would be in very bad condition," von Steuben said, out of his former commander's earshot.

Washington was above all practical. He was not averse to style, but he wanted things to *work*. He used pattern books—at his direction, woodworker William Sears followed a design from Abraham Swan's *British Architect* to carve a panel for the wall above the dining room fireplace—but didn't genuflect to them. ". . . As time went by, Washington also showed himself to be notably more willing to strike out on his own—to ignore fashionable taste and build instead simply what pleased him," write Robert F. Dalzell, Jr., and Lee Baldwin Dalzell in *George Washington's Mount Vernon: At Home in Revolutionary America.*

Rather than toe a strict line on symmetry, for instance, Washington let the pieces of his house fit as they might. He put a proper Palladian window into the dining room's north wall, but on the west front he let doors and windows crowd one another rather than spacing them precisely. And when he built his porch, Washington eschewed the four or six heavy pillars a paleo-Palladian would have employed. Instead, he ordered eight skinny, slightly tapered square columns. The result was not only a more expansive view *from* the house but a dramatically different look *for* the house. George Washington was less intent on doing the thing right than in doing the right thing.

Mount Vernon is an example of the familiar refreshed through experimentation. Certainly the house was like an old shoe to Washington, who spent part of his youth there, returning in adulthood to rent, then inherit the property. He devoted nearly half a century—from 1754 until 1799—to expanding and renovating the house in, essentially, two near-complete rebuildings. His last big job was the piazza.

Built at the rear of the house to face the river one hundred twenty-five feet below, the porch at Mount Vernon is flat-roofed, two stories high, ninety-six feet long, and fourteen feet deep. The first American president's piazza is, by one measure, quite public: "a remarkably open space in a social as well as a physical sense," is how the Dalzells put it. Today, as during Washington's lifetime, occupants of passing watercraft can see the east front of Mount Vernon, in warm weather through gaps in the shoreline foliage or in winter through bare trees.

"Washington was trying to frame the landscape," said architectural historian Robin Dripps, author of *The First House: Myth, Paradigm, and the Task of Architecture.* "In Latrobe's *Views of America,* which consists of sketches that he made around the country, his view of Mount Vernon is quite wonderful. You see the porch as an attempt to frame the river views—to put into perspective and bring into comprehension and order this wild landscape that Mount Vernon was a part of."

Nobody knows for sure where Washington got the idea for his piazza. But antecedents existed. Here and there around Virginia, there were houses with porches, though they were more often single-story affairs closer in type to Caribbean vernacular architecture. Pattern books that included porticoes were circulating in the colonies. As a young officer during the French and Indian War, Washington had fought in districts where he might have seen French-built galleries. And though, as James Thomas Flexner writes in *Washington: The Indispensable Man,* "In all his later writings he never mentioned the journey or used a metaphor that revealed he had been in the tropics," he may have been inspired on his only trip out of North America—to Barbados, in 1751.

That September, Washington sailed south with his half-brother, Lawrence, who was very ill. Years before, fighting the Spanish in the Caribbean under Admiral Edward Vernon, Lawrence had contracted tuberculosis. The disease was gaining on him. He hoped the Barbadian air would slow or stop its advance.

The brothers arrived at Carlisle Bay, on the island's south side, in early October. Lawrence stayed longer—he would come home in the spring, dying in July—but George did spend two months on Barbados. Part of that time he was sick—a mild bout with smallpox that may have saved his life by immunizing him against an epidemic that struck during the Revolution. When he wasn't confined, however, George roamed the precincts around Bush Hill, the house overlooking Carlisle Bay where he and Lawrence were bunking. Surely the alert surveyor would have seen houses with piazzas, double- and single-storied, as well as more modest shed-roofed porches. And, being a fellow who took note of things that pleased or might prove useful to him, he would have committed them to memory. In *Architecture, Men, Women and Money,* Roger Kennedy says Washington never forgot the dual pleasures of sitting on a deep, broad Barbadian porch and seeing how it added a satisfying finish to a house façade.

Another building that may have helped beget Mount Vernon's piazza was the Redwood Library in Newport, Rhode Island, a city through which Washington passed in 1755. To lend that wooden building gravitas, architect Peter Harrison had his crews work the exterior siding to resemble cut stone, deepening the illusion by "rustication," a technique that coated wooden walls with paint to which sand had been added. Washington would use the method so effectively at Mount Vernon that much of the original siding remains in place. In the proper

Palladian mode, the library in Newport had a four-pillared portico that would have appealed to the general's neoclassical side.

Washingtons had been building on a site adjoining the Potomac since Lawrence and George's father, Augustine Washington, had bought it in 1726. Washington *pere* put up several structures on the land, originally known by its Indian name of Eppsewasson but also called "the Little Hunting Creek tract." When he inherited the property, Lawrence demolished his father's shacks and built a small house he called "Mount Vernon," in honor of his old commander. Lawrence lived there with his wife, Anne, and their children. After Lawrence died in 1752, Anne leased Mount Vernon to George for fifteen thousand pounds of tobacco a year. By 1761, Anne and her children had died, leaving the house George's property by default. He had great ambitions for it, but no sooner had he inherited Mount Vernon than his military star began to rise, in the usual and inconvenient way. War broke out—in this case, the French and Indian War, the colonial edition of the Great Game being played around the world by the European powers. Just as Washington was about to start his renovation, he had to take to the battlefield. It was a pattern he would repeat during the Revolution and modify in peacetime with absences to serve as president.

Being a leader of men and later the father of his country didn't make it any easier to get work done. If you've renovated a house, you're bound to nod in sad recognition at the stuttering progress of Mount Vernon's construction. Washington had to cope with a series of wayward carpenters, not only hired tradesmen but their indentured servants and slaves, as well as his own contingent of Africans, all of whom persisted in resisting his efforts, polite and irate, to make them more efficient. He even undertook a time-and-motion study to show how they could and should be working smarter and harder, but his threats and pleas were to no avail. Sounding like anyone who has ever tried to get a house built or rebuilt, Washington wrote of "the slothfulness of my Carpenters," observing that "there is not to be found so idle a set of Rascals." He often warned his overseers away from liquor, but without much success. His slaves ran rampant. "Mount Vernon was a whirlpool of anarchy where all managerial efforts hardly sufficed to keep the confusion from overflowing the banks," writes James Flexner.

(The one bright spot in Washington's experience as a general contractor may have been John Ariss, an architect active in the area at the time; in *The Mansions of Virginia: 1700–1776*, Thomas Tileston Waterman ties Ariss to the designs for Mount Vernon.)

Despite all the difficulties, though, the work eventually did get done. Ever the compartmentalizer, Washington was able to use Mount Vernon as a distraction from combat. For instance, during 1777, the year that saw rebel fortunes at their lowest ebb, he planned and directed (by mail, yes, but still . . .) construction of the piazza. Perhaps Washington endured those terrible nights at Valley Forge by imagining himself in a rocking chair, watching the river flow, a Cincinnatan image appropriate to one who prided himself on his "republican stile of living."

When the war ended and Washington was able to return home—at least until called back to service as president in New York—the piazza was among his favorite places at Mount Vernon, and it proved a delight to his guests as well. Visitors arriving by land approached on a hilly, winding road that offered varying well-calculated perspectives on the house and its dependencies. Waterborne travelers would dock slightly downriver, then climb a steep path leading up to the south side. At the west front, unroofed steps led to an entry hall. Depending on their status, guests were shunted to interior rooms of varying intimacy. Some might be escorted to the piazza, whose shade, breezes, and spectacular views were what many visitors wanted to see even then. The general griped about the hordes that swarmed his house, often at his invitation. But he and his wife were sociable people; as was true of other great houses in Virginia and the other colonies, their home was also a place of business and politics, often conducted over dinner and during extended convivial visits.

Between 1768 and 1775, Mount Vernon hosted some two thousand visitors, many of whom stayed for days. The crowds no doubt encouraged Washington to ponder ways to make his house roomier without marring its character. The piazza provided that elbowroom, perhaps helping to moot the ancient principle about guests and fish.

Surely the piazza softened George Washington's last years, which were marked by conflict with his old allies John Adams and Tom Jefferson. One of the ailing general's final acts before an infection sent him to bed for the last time was to walk out onto the piazza and then across the lawn to mark trees for cutting.

However public a fixture it might have been, Mount Vernon's piazza also was, and is, quite private. At the end of the day, it was where the Washingtons could relax, where they could entertain old friends, and where—in spite of a lengthening history that would turn them inexorably into icons—they could be themselves. On a visit in July 1796, Benjamin Latrobe made a sketch of the piazza at dusk. In it, Washington stands looking through a spyglass toward the Potomac. Behind him are Martha, Washington's step-granddaughter, Eleanor "Nelly" Custis, Washington's secretary, Tobias Lear, and Lear's son, who sits on the flagstones looking at a small dog running toward him from the lawn.

Besides images like these, the main link between George Washington's porch and those of his countrymen may have been a factor that frustrated the president to the end of his days: a leaky roof. Simply put, Washington hadn't given the piazza's roof enough slope to shed water, and it leaked constantly. He tried every surface he could imagine, as well as some that others suggested, but he never was able to solve the water problem. It not only outlived him but nearly was the undoing of Mount Vernon's porch, and, indeed, Mount Vernon itself.

In 1858, when the Mount Vernon Ladies' Association bought the property for $200,000 and began restoring it, the mansion had fallen into near-ruin.

An 1850s photograph shows Mount Vernon to be in ragtag shape. One porch column had rotted away entirely, replaced by an old ship's mast that the Ladies replaced with a proper simulacrum of the original.

Along with saving the house, Mount Vernon's resurrection helped make its piazza an American icon as well as a near-permanent influence on residential architecture. Since then, a staff of restorers has strived to preserve everything they can. But even national shrines don't last forever.

In 1914, for instance, the piazza's flagstone floor was so far gone as to need wholesale replacement. Research showed that Washington had imported the flags from England—but where? Analysis of a bit of original flag led the Geological Museum to conclude that it had come from a quarry at St. Bees, from which the Ladies' Association ordered a stock of fifteen hundred flags for future use.

Considering the extent to which repairs have touched so much of the house, a finicky observer might conclude that Mount Vernon, at least the porch portion, is a sort of WashingtonWorld, a re-imagining of a real place that is gone forever.

I disagree.

When I sit on George Washington's porch, what matters is not that the pillars and the flagstones be original but that the view and the ambience be consistent with what Washington experienced. I believe that to be so—except, of course, for the fact that George and Martha, though they entertained mightily, didn't have tourist hordes at their backs while they sat and gazed across the Potomac.

Architectural historians still debate whether the Mount Vernon porch was truly an innovation. Dennis Pogue, director of restoration for the estate, sees that as a dead-end discussion. "The rap on the piazza is that it is the most emulated design in America. Was it original to George Washington, or was it his copy of something else? You can flog that forever," Pogue says. "It makes no difference whether he saw the design as different; he adapted it as a major design solution. What is important is the size and scale; there is no evidence of that having been done before."

Pogue sees Mount Vernon's porch as an environmental, social, and architectural feat that interlaced with the central interior passage that circulated air and light through the house. "It finished the design of Mount Vernon in a distinguished way and created an indoor/outdoor space that linked the house to the landscape. It was a place to have tea, to entertain, to cool off—and a very public display and visual cue of the house's presence on the land," he said. "The colonnades on either side take advantage of their vistas to frame views, and the piazza does the same. Washington was concerned with creating landscapes, and he built a California house before there was a California."

Unfortunately, just as Washington never explained where he got the idea for the piazza, he never described how he felt about it. It's up to each of us to try to discern what was in his mind by putting ourselves in his place.

For research purposes and sheer pleasure, I visited Mount Vernon pretty often, and in every season. At noontime on a mid-August day, when the sun is at its fiercest, the piazza is at its most welcoming. There's always a crowd. Having entered and passed through the dining room in the north wing, tourists queue up along the exterior wall of the piazza, fidgeting on the well-shaded flagstones and contained by a judiciously arranged row of Windsor chairs. They are truly Washingtonian; a 1799 audit of Washington's estate listed chairs in that style, and today's chairs are copies of one whose provenance has been traced to Washington's day.

As you wait, you sometimes see it dawn on people that they're on the first First Family's porch, and inevitably comments break out.

MAN: "Got a nice organized line here."

GROUCHY BOY: "I don't like the nice organized line."

MIDWESTERN HUSBAND: "You know, I've been reading a history that explains how, in battle, the bullets would just bounce off Washington."

MIDWESTERN WIFE: "You know, the porch really came from Africa. I don't know where I heard that, but I remember hearing it."

WOMAN 1: "It would be nice to bring your coffee out here in the morning and look at the river."

WOMAN 2: "You could screen it or glass it in and make it an enclosed porch."

When I heard that last sentiment, I cringed. But it probably wouldn't have fazed Washington. After all, this was the man who, having made a revolution and built a nation, thought it worth his time, trouble, and expense to add this porch to a house that many people had long thought completed. George Washington was a relentless renovator, and had he been born into the twentieth century instead of the eighteenth, he probably would have considered enclosing the porch at Mount Vernon. He was that kind of guy.

Now, Thomas Jefferson was a different kind of guy, so particular about so many things that aspects of his personality seem to express the overlap between the contents of American history books and those of the *Diagnostic and Statistical Manual of Mental Disorders*. Like Washington, Jefferson was a very private man with a very public existence, haunted by debt as well as a perennially decaying house and vexed by the workmen, enslaved and free, who labored reluctantly on his behalf. Washington was an architect by avocation, learning as he did, freely adapting and adopting, contenting himself with what seemed to work. Jefferson, who collected architectural portfolios the way some men collected fowling pieces, had educated himself about architecture, and he always strove to meet or exceed the models he held as his guides. "Palladio is the Bible," the notoriously irreligious thinker once told a friend. Driving himself to execute and re-execute, Jefferson held his designs and construction up to a nearly impossible ideal, always frustrated that they could not more closely approach his vision for them.

Monticello, 867 feet above Charlottesville, Virginia, is at once a tribute to Jefferson's multifaceted personality and evidence that he was, well, let's be honest: kind of wack. During the fifty-four years he spent trying to get Monticello done, as Jack McLaughlin notes, "Jefferson built one house, tore much of it down, doubled its size, and continued to alter, remodel, improve, and add to it for decades. It is a wonder that the house was ever finally completed; many thought it never would be."

Of course, during his extended construction project, Jefferson had his share of preoccupations, among them practicing law, leading Virginia's delegation to the Continental Congress, writing the Declaration of Independence, serving as his state's governor during the Revolution, drafting the fledgling nation's coinage system, writing *Notes on the State of Virginia,* and founding and planning the campus of the University of Virginia, never mind his stints as U.S. minister plenipotentiary to France and secretary of state, vice president, and president of the United States.

But in the early years Jefferson could focus on his house, whose porticoes teach us much about their creator and his influence on American architecture.

Jefferson began building in 1769, after starting to clear the top of a mountain his father had left him. The location confounded tradition; Jefferson wasn't after mundane goals like the easy transport, rich bottomland, and shallow well depths available at riverside, where most Virginians of substance built. He wanted the sublime—that grail of the Enlightenment, which sought moments of pure illumination in unmediated encounters with nature. Atop his slave-flattened peak, Jefferson could tap into the sublime as if turning on a spigot. Plus, his main man, Andrea Palladio, had endorsed putting houses on high ground (though, we must recall, the Veneto was a big bog, where the high ground was and is often a hump of landfill).

Palladio's masonly preference for brick and stone also comforted the Virginian, who once wrote that he could not imagine dwellings "more ugly, uncomfortable, and happily more perishable" than wooden houses. Monticello would be a brick house, and it would be as Jeffersonian as only Jefferson could make it. He chose as a design Plate Three of Robert Morris's *Select Architecture*—a two-story main block with symmetrical one-story wings, at the end of which dependencies extended to form a courtyard. Jefferson traced the plate, adding a four-columned portico. As owner-builders are wont to do, he kept drawing, monkeying with proportion, adding and subtracting porticoes. His formal drawings illustrate what McLaughlin calls "his kind of compulsive personality."

"Lines are executed mechanically, with rule and compass, to precise scale," McLaughlin writes. "Measurements are carried out to four or five decimal places, an absurdity in the building trades where carpenters and bricklayers are often lucky if they can keep to the inch rather than the ten-thousandth of an inch— It was as if he consciously made a distinction between mechanically accurate drawings, which were ink-and-paper maps of Palladian law, and mere sketches that were only the dance of ideas around these laws."

Like many a piece of American currency, the nickel carries a reminder of how much Thomas Jefferson valued the portico as an element of house design.

What Jefferson finally drew seems to have been a pair of double porticoes, the lower of the Doric order and the upper Ionic, one facing east and one west. (Artists have imagined what it looked like, but no images survive of the west side of the original house.) They would have been very close in look to Villa Cornaro, featured in the *Four Books* and the model for Drayton House in South Carolina. Another influence may have been the double portico on the state capitol in Williamsburg, built after a 1747 fire gutted its predecessor, which Jefferson strongly admired.

Constructed of bricks made from clay dug on-site and lumber harvested from nearby forests, the house went up gradually—very gradually. Jefferson came to live there in 1770, in the first outbuilding to get a roof. When he wed in 1772, his bride, Martha Wayles Skelton, whose first husband had died, joined him there.

The Jeffersons lived a rude form of the aristocratic life. They had an abundance of slaves. Thomas owned 52 Africans and Martha, a slave-dealer's daughter, brought another 135 to the marriage. But rough living is rough living, and the living at the far-from-finished Monticello was plenty rough.

Jefferson had trouble getting his designs executed. The first column for the east portico came out thicker than ordered. This threw the lower and upper porticoes out of line, but stonecutting cost so much that, rather than junk the oversize pillar, Jefferson tweaked his design (eventually, he had to give up on stone and instead use brick columns covered with stucco—a gesture not only economical but also properly Palladian; the master had done likewise to please ducat-pinching clients). To get the west portico into a semblance of completeness, Jefferson had the workmen substitute the trunks of tulip trees for stone, figuring to replace them at a later date. He had no idea how much later it would be.

As soon as the main building was semihabitable, the owners moved in; later, Jefferson said it was never more than half-finished. Three years into the Revolutionary War, when he became Virginia's governor, Jefferson moved his family to Williamsburg, perhaps as much for the relief as to satisfy the demands of office. Two years later, an incident occurred that added an aura of legend to one of Monticello's porches.

The Jeffersons were at home on the mountain in June 1781, when Banastre Tarleton sent troops toward Charlottesville. The British colonel meant to capture Governor Jefferson at his home and the legislature in town. And he might have, save for one Jack Jouett, who saw the English cavalry forty miles out and galloped to Monticello. After pouring the messenger some Madeira, Jefferson directed Jouett to warn the legislators, then sent his family to a neighbor's. When Jefferson finally fled, he left the house in the care of slaves Martin Hemings and Caesar. As they waited on the east portico, the men loosened floorboards. Caesar climbed down among the joists and, as Martin brought it from inside, hid the family silver. According to Jefferson family legend, Martin was handing over the last few pieces when the dragoons came thundering around the mountain. "Martin slammed the plank down as the first horsemen appeared, trapping Caesar under the porch for the three days the British troops stayed," McLaughlin writes. Tarleton, who was not the rapacious beast-man portrayed fictionally in *The Patriot*, had given orders to leave the house intact. After the dragoons departed, Caesar emerged with the silver.

In 1782, after a four-month illness, Martha Jefferson died. She had spent the preceding decade pregnant every year—a pattern that contributed to her demise. Her son, John, and four of her six children with Jefferson had died already. His wife's passing undid the supremely rational Jefferson, who sought refuge in work and then, twenty-two months later, as minister plenipotentiary to France. The appointment took him to Paris and brought him face-to-façade with a Gallically-inflected Palladianism that would shape the next edition of Monticello by illustrating for Jefferson a new approach to the unfinished house he'd left behind on his little mountain.

Among the French structures that impressed Jefferson were the Hotel de Salm, a low-lying but high-flown house between the Seine and the Rue de Bourbon; the Hotel de Langeac, which Jefferson rented for much of his five years in France; the Halle aux Bleds, a public grain market in Paris; and the Maison Carrée, a classically inflected house in Nimes. Maison Carrée had a pedimented portico. The rest had rounded entries, roofed by the front portion of domes supported by columns. The Halle aux Bleds was nothing but dome, a 130-foot expanse of wood and glass.

Jefferson transformed himself in France. He liked the way the French cooked, and he liked their wines and their employment of skylights, windows, and domes, as well as their indoor toilets. And, perhaps because he was renting a house someone had actually completed, he took to the role of host.

But while he loved living in France and traveling in Europe, Jefferson longed to return to America. Immersed in international intrigue and political infighting, often of his own creation, he itched for concrete tasks and for Monticello's familiar domesticity. He'd decided to use what the Continent had shown him to remake his half-built house.

Jefferson came home at Christmas 1789 to a Monticello far more ragged than he'd left it. The portico where Martin and Caesar had hoodwinked Tarleton's raiders was still incomplete, and now it was rotting. The dependencies—stables, laundry, kitchens—still existed only on paper. And no sooner was Jefferson back than he was named secretary of state, an appointment that called him to New York. From there, he fitfully attempted by letter to chivvy his crews to build slave quarters and manufacture stone columns for his porticoes. The former took place; the latter did not.

But Jefferson's forced absence also allowed him to solidify his plans for the new Monticello, which he wanted to enlarge and equip with a dome that would please his Francophile tastes and improve on the house's Palladian design. The houses he'd admired in France had been handsome, practical, and one-storied, with small stairwells. Besides being two-storied, Monticello was less than handsome and not yet practical. To recast it, Jefferson would have to expand it, by demolishing either the west or the east side. He opted to break out of the east side, and the rest is architectural history.

Demolition began in 1794. The roof and porticoes came down. But then work halted so Jefferson could manage his farms and organize a nail-manufacturing operation he hoped would boost his cash flow. In 1796, demolition resumed. Away with the columns, away with the front walls and windows, away with floors and staircases and interior walls and framing. It was the most exciting time in any renovation—the spasm of creative destruction that must precede rebuilding.

And, like any house-proud renovator, Jefferson invited guests to join him and his family amid the chaos. Jefferson had hoped to finish rebuilding before the cold came, but he didn't come close. In November, he was elected vice president, without having left Monticello. This might have been the first front-porch campaign, since the candidate spent much of it on the portico directing demolition work. The national capital was now Philadelphia, where he traveled that winter, beginning a twelve-year period that saw Jefferson serve out his term as veep, then as the twice-elected president.

Progress on Monticello slowed to a geological pace. In 1797, Jefferson's daughter, Maria, was married in the parlor, a ceremony set among masons' scaffolding and junk. In 1800, a roof went on—wooden shakes, not only a fire hazard but homely, and hardly the elegance Jefferson wanted to project. However, shakes were all he had. Room by room by room, the house edged toward completion. On trips home, Jefferson threw himself into supervising the work, once declining to visit Maria, who had moved nearby and was ill, on the grounds that work could not proceed if he were not on hand. His daughter Martha, who lived at Monticello with her family, bore the brunt of Jefferson's social inclinations, trying to raise four small children while managing the disorderly household.

Built and rebuilt in the course of nearly half a century of construction and reconstruction. Monticello's porticoes are the focal points of the exterior.

As Jefferson was starting his first term as president of the United States, stonemason and plasterer Richard Richardson got the job of reassembling the portico's columns, which had been reduced to a jumble of stone drums without having been marked for reassembly. Each piece tapered a bit; by measuring them, Richardson could divine the order in which to restack them. But he didn't know which round went into which column, and the first two pillars came out crooked. Jefferson—who, remember, had drawn plans to the ten-thousandth of an inch—ordered the pillars rebuilt. Again the columns came out wrong; the drums had to be rotated to match the original cuts. Richardson spent three years getting all four pillars placed. In the process he chipped them so much that the imperfections had to be filled with mortar and a layer of tan stucco applied to give the appearance of solid shafts.

As Jefferson aged, and as fame wore at him, he found in Monticello both an outlet for his compulsions and obsessions and a shield against the prying eyes of the public. He loved the sun, but he labored to keep it out of his house, and he struggled to retain his privacy. He and his family enjoyed socializing on the east and west porticoes, and he often sat alone reading on one or the other. However, he considered installing louvered blinds between the portico columns—not only for the shade, but for the barrier it would put between him and people who came up his mountain to gape; ". . . parties of men and women would sometimes approach within a dozen yards, and gaze at him point-blank until they had looked their fill, as they would have gazed at a lion in a menagerie," writes biographer Henry Randall.

Jefferson also devoted much energy to the grounds at Monticello. Unfortunately, just as the construction of the house had served as a distraction from other events in his life, the landscaping helped him ignore the continuing decline of his house and finances. Struggling to slip the noose of debt, Jefferson sold his library to the government—it became the germ of the Library of Congress—and tried holding a lottery, with Monticello and the surrounding land as the prize. It failed. He owed money not only to relatives, friends, and bankers, but to the tradesmen who had built his house and agreed to let him keep their salaries as loans. (Not that Jefferson didn't take care of his workers. Jack McLaughlin tells of how he looked out for Richard Richardson, the mason who hadn't been able to get the portico pillars straight. Seeing an obituary that mentioned a Caribbean estate waiting to be claimed by one "R. Richardson," Jefferson obtained a passport for the young man, provided a letter to verify his identity, and paid for his trip to Jamaica, where Richardson learned he'd inherited a sugar plantation.)

By 1809, when Jefferson came home from Washington for the final time, Monticello was remarkably complete, except for the perennially unfinished porticoes, which still had "temporary" wooden steps and floors. Instead of classical pillars, the west portico still featured those tulip tree trunks. Finally dispensing with the folly of worked stone, Jefferson decided to replace the trunks with columns of stuccoed brick. But he wasn't able to get the work going until 1822, when, at age seventy-nine, he hired a mason who had done much of the stone construction at the University of Virginia. A year later, the pillars were in place.

Jefferson died July 4, 1826, in debt by $100,000. Within a year his heirs had auctioned off his 300 slaves and his furniture; within two years, Monticello was on the market. But no one wanted it. Vacant and vandalized, the house Jefferson had taken fifty-four years to build stood empty until a druggist bought it with the idea of raising silkworms on the grounds. That scheme flopped, and in 1834 Uriah P. Levy, a Navy officer who greatly admired Jefferson, bought the house and 218 acres for twenty-five hundred dollars. The Levy family owned the house for ninety years, going to great lengths to preserve, protect, and defend it. During the Civil War, Confederate authorities confiscated Monticello for use as a hospital; during Reconstruction, a caretaker named Joseph Wheeler took great liberties with the house, stabling cattle in the basement and using the salon as a granary. By the time the Levy family regained control, in 1878, Monticello was a ruin, and the family resumed its efforts at preservation. In 1923, a charitable foundation bought the property from the Levys for $500,000. Since then the house has undergone a mythopoetical restoration so utter that, as Jack McLaughlin eloquently notes, today's Monticello bears only a theoretical resemblance to the rough-and-tumble place its creator knew. "Never in Jefferson's lifetime did Monticello appear the way it does today," McLaughlin writes. "Jefferson's Monticello is irretrievably lost, for the soul of the house perished with its builder."

But if Jefferson's Monticello is lost, its architectural influence continues. Look around you. Courthouses and colleges across the country emulate the look of the little mountain house. And in our capital, we salute Jefferson with a monument that harks to the loggia, the portico, and, finally, the stoa. Set among cherry trees and tidal pools, John Russell Pope's marble pantheon honors the Virginian's relentless intellect and devotion to freedom. The Jefferson Memorial completes one of five cardinal points proposed by Pierre L'Enfant for Washington's monumental core, and it recreates on an immense scale the holy porch of ancient Greece.

Located on landfill reclaimed from swamps, the memorial has more than design in common with the original Pantheon, which was a temple to Mars, the Roman god of war—as well as an architectural echo of the *stoa* that had served the Greeks so well and variously, as marketplace, a court, a schoolhouse.

That his memorial would be based on a Roman temple design itself derived from one beloved of the Greeks no doubt would have pleased Jefferson, whose architectural theories inform the look of Washington, D.C., to this day. The fourth president may have found his greatest spiritual connection with the Greeks and the concepts that underpinned their building design.

"Since Jefferson was looking at those examples, it is no surprise that some of that kind of meaning—even though it is not necessarily appropriate to the American democratic experiment—would creep into our architecture," said Robin Dripps, citing as an example the Acropolis in its role as a temple. "According to the ancient Greeks, the landscape around the Acropolis was charged, invested with the qualities of the gods and goddesses being worshipped." The Greeks sought to experience such landscapes by framing views of them while engaged in some important activity. "For example, when you come to the entrance of a temple, you see a notch in a mountain or a particular knoll," Dripps explained.

By that count, the Jefferson Memorial is a perfect setting in which to ponder the man it honors, the meaning of his life, and the landscape, now thoroughly urbanized, that he envisioned as the capital of the country he helped found. Though begun in 1938 and completed in 1943, the memorial has a timeless quality. The Jefferson statue, a nineteen-foot bronze by Rudolph Evans, looks resolutely to the northwest—not accidentally the direction in which Jefferson sent Lewis and Clark on their historic expedition—through one of the four openings in its templelike home. Excerpts from Jefferson's writings are engraved on the interior walls, overseen by a frieze bearing his creed: "I have sworn upon the altar of God eternal hostility against every form of tyranny over the mind of man."

The memorial and environs may be at their spiritually charged apogee when the Tidal Basin's cherry trees are in bloom, but I prefer to encounter them in the presence of less company—on a rotten day in deep winter, perhaps, or on a blazing summer afternoon at midweek, as I did a few years ago. Thanks to a reconstruction project, most of the Tidal Basin side was cordoned off, but if you stepped carefully you could find views such as a worshipful Greek might have seen. One put me in line to spy, through a notch in the trees at Washington's heart, the double-decker back porch of the White House, as starkly framed as if Mr. Jefferson himself had plotted the perspective.

In the fledgling nation, home design quickly became a way of establishing personal identity, often through use of pattern-book designs.

CHAPTER EIGHT

EARLY DAYS OF AN ICON

With the colonies' 1783 victory in the American Revolution, George Washington and Thomas Jefferson could stop waging war and start building a country—and, in their spare time, finish building their houses. The Founding Fathers weren't alone; everywhere in the thirteen states houses great and small were going up, their form and appearance often strongly influenced by a familiar means of transmitting architectural style: the pattern book.

Aimed at carpenters, who built most houses, as well as their potential customers, these illustrated dream books showed structures and their components in detail. Along with dimensions, pattern books provided varying degrees of instruction in taking the design from the printed page to the completed building. These guides had been around for centuries—Palladio's vaunted *Four Books* was a variation on the theme, and both Jefferson and Washington had been avid readers of English editions by such authors as Batty Langley—but latter-day advances in printing made the pattern book more of a mass-market commodity. One of the first published in the United States appeared in 1797, when Asher Benjamin brought out a compilation of methods cribbed from English pattern books. He called his assemblage *The Country Builder's Assistant,* which sold well and was followed in 1806 by *American Builder's Companion.* Benjamin's success spurred imitation, and the pattern book library grew rapidly.

One reason for this success was a scarcity of architects; another was that many pattern-book readers weren't able or willing to hire an architect, even if they could find one. As Linda Smeins explains in *Building an American Identity,* a history of pattern books, the target market for these volumes was the middle class, which even then steered American popular culture. As more publications began to appear, they, too, carried house designs; an avid reader could find plans in farmer's periodicals and general interest magazines like *Godey's Ladies' Book* and *Ladies' Home Companion,* as well as pattern book publishers' catalogues. All a householder had to do was select a design and have a local wood butcher execute it.

From their initial popularity in the early 1800s, pattern books grew into a vibrant publishing sector, especially as the Industrial Revolution brought mass-production techniques to the lumber and hardware industries. Once laboriously fabricated by hand, boards, beams, nails, and spikes became ready-made, cut to standard dimensions. From standardization emerged the "balloon" method of framing houses, which drastically sped construction time. Instead of ramming posts into the ground, joining them with rafters, and filling in the blanks with hand-hewn boards, carpenters could plan for and use manufactured components, structural as well as decorative, which even the least literate joiner could assemble into a stylish house by following the illustrations and directions in a pattern book.

High-minded onlookers, especially those with a professional interest at stake, disdained the genre. "The more entrepreneurial, and the most used, were harshly criticized by the architects who wrote from the urban perspective of the northeast," Smeins writes.

But people building pattern-book houses could have cared less about architects' Olympian ire. They wanted what they liked, and they liked what they saw and read. And what they saw and read often involved a porch—or veranda, to use the term being made popular by Britain's widely advertised reign in India. In an 1800 pattern book, author John Plaw offered designs of "ornamental cottages . . . with a viranda in the manner of an Indian bungalow." In 1818, English architect J.B. Papworth declared, "No decoration has so successfully varied the dull sameness of modern structures as the verandah." A year later, in the anglophile South, real-estate advertisements were hawking houses with verandas.

These designs sold because they were safe. "What made the arguments of the plan-book promoters most effective was that they had sensed the basic conservatism of the middle class and incorporated it into their design theories," writes historian Clifford Clark. "Thus they could insist that their new styles were appropriate for both rich and poor, and could stress that a common building vocabulary would create a sense of visual community because both ideas had already become commonplace in rural and small-town America. What is most clear is that the pattern books gave the home builder a new range of choices and alternatives in ornament and philosophical justification."

Americans also were being introduced to new wrinkles in house design through the indirect effect of their rebellion, the success of which soon spurred other uprisings. These conflicts had surprising influences on life in the United States—and life on the American porch.

In 1789, for example, revolution swept France. That spasm of Grand Guignol quickly had a bloody echo on Saint-Domingue, the Caribbean colony made rich by sugar, slaves, rum, and trade between Europe and the Americas. From there, the final infusion of African vernacular architecture would come to the United States after as tangled and multifarious a series of exercises in realpolitik as any the world has seen.

When the Bastille fell, Saint-Domingue's French-speaking population was 556,000—counting 32,000 whites, 24,000 free Blacks, and half a million slaves. The Africans of Saint-Domingue were mostly Yoruba speakers from Nigeria and Congo.

Along with its darker-skinned residents, Saint-Domingue had a light-skinned African elite, the product of rape, intermarriage, and plantation owners' taste for Black mistresses. These aristocrats, some still slaves and others *hommes du colours libres*, or free men of color, were integral to the colony's power structure.

Slave and free, African and mulatto, white and Black, all of Saint-Domingue's inhabitants knew the colony's basic unit of housing, which came in two models: the single-story *maison basse* ("low house") and the two-story *maison haute*. Both were simple structures at whose façade a gable-roofed gallerie allowed occupants to sit in the shade and catch the breeze. The gallerie recalled not only the open-sided *bohio*, home of the doomed Arawak who had greeted Columbus when he landed on Hispaniola three centuries before, but the precolonial African porch that evolved into the Portuguese *alpainter*. Behind the gallerie, with no halls or corridors separating them, flowed a formal sitting room, an informal sitting room, a bedroom, and kitchen. The houses sported an additional African touch. Instead of the sixteen-foot standard employed in Europe, they were built on a twelve-foot standard, with room measurements expanding or contracting by halves. Historian Sibyl Moholy-Nagy calls this elemental design, with its dogged adherence to African ways, "the architecture of defiance."

In 1791, emboldened by France's chaotic experiment with *liberte, egalite, et fraternite*, Saint-Domingue's slaves revolted. The ensuing war wrecked the colony's economy and established a cycle of attack, reprisal, and flight that went on for years. Seeing the bloody handwriting on the wall, planters began to flee via the Windward Strait to eastern Cuba, folding themselves, their mulatto children, slaves, and free Black comrades into the sugar economy around Santiago, which always needed new investors and field hands.

Trying to quell the revolt on Saint-Domingue, France abolished slavery there. Until that point, Spain had maintained tenuous control of eastern Hispaniola. Now the Spanish ceded Santo Domingo to France—a move sort of like assigning the deed for your burning house to a neighbor whose home is afire, too.

By 1801, Napoleon had taken command of France. After restoring slavery in other French holdings, he sent forces to do likewise on Saint-Domingue, but a Black army led by Jean-Jacques Dessalines and Henri Christophe defeated the invaders. Dessalines and Christophe declared their island a nation, called by the island's Arawak name of "Haiti." Dessalines became Emperor Jacques I. But he and his dark-skinned cohort had alienated the mulatto elite, which rebelled. In the subsequent combat, Dessalines died. Christophe succeeded him. The civil war burned on, now fought within a race rather than between the races.

Britain and France were hard at the global conflict that historians dub the Napoleonic Wars. Employing the time-tested strategy of befriending an enemy's enemy, England, eager to encourage any gesture that would discomfit the French, helped Spain retake its end of Hispaniola. In another of the era's dizzying turns of tactic, Napoleon retaliated by sending French troops into Spain, which besides declaring war on France responded by declaring all Frenchmen on Spanish soil, homeland or colonial, persona non grata—including what had become a community of 30,000 French-speakers in and around Santiago, Cuba. About to be exiled again, the expatriates looked for the nearest Francophile place. They found New Orleans, main port of the Louisiana Territory, just purchased from France by Thomas Jefferson.

"They couldn't go back to Haiti, so they went to Louisiana," said folklorist John Vlach, likening the Santiago evacuation to the Mariel boatlift of the 1970s. "In four months during the summer of 1809, nine thousand of these French-speaking expatriates showed up in New Orleans."

At the time, New Orleans was home to two whites for every Black resident, a ratio that was reversed by the influx of Haitians from Cuba. Now that the number of free Blacks approximated that of whites, the Crescent City was about to be Africanized.

The newcomers did not lack means; they'd had money enough to reach Louisiana. However, they weren't welcome. After a petition by the region's governor failed to secure federal aid in deflecting the Black immigrants, local antipathy kept them on the other side of the Mississippi River from New Orleans in a neighborhood called Algiers. But time, and the fact that the erstwhile Haitians could afford to buy land and build houses, gradually eroded resistance. In enclaves near the French Quarter, the expatriates in their thousands set about reassembling their lives yet again. The Haitians bought lots, erecting replicas of the houses they'd had at home.

But instead of adopting the terms *maison basse* and *maison haute,* their new neighbors, who were a people given to amusing themselves with wordplay, had a more vivid description. Noting the immigrant structure's lack of hallways, which meant that a load of double-ought fired into the front porch would blow straight through to the back of the joint, some droll American dubbed the Haitian dwelling the "shotgun house." The nickname stuck, and so did the design, which quickly spread across Louisiana and beyond, adding another type of porch-equipped house to the American mix.

(Around the time the Haitians were bringing the shotgun house to New Orleans, a far less grand and far more gradual infusion of a similar Caribbean house form was starting south of mainland Florida. There, fishermen, pirates, and wreck salvors from the Bahamas were settling on a rocky island called *Cayo Hueso,* or "Bone Key." The name, supposedly given by Spanish sailors who found the island littered with skeletons of Indians killed in intertribal battle, was anglicized to "Key West." The town that developed in the early nineteenth century sported shotgunnish houses—some carried intact across the 280 miles of open sea separating the key from the Bahamas—with shuttered windows, roofs pitched steeply to shed hurricane-grade rains, and wide porches. Unlike the Haitian *maison,* however, the Key West house would have to wait quite some time to have its effect on American vernacular architecture.)

As the shotgun house was insinuating itself across the South, other influences were creeping in, too. Neither the Revolution nor the War of 1812 had been enough to alienate America from Britain; everywhere in the States, style mavens were taking careful note of Britons' affinity for bungalows and verandas. The English had adopted these as the emblems of colonial presence in many settings other than their native India; in recently settled Australia, for instance, the veranda was on its way to becoming a national symbol. And when, in 1821, little Greece stood up against its Ottoman Turk overlords, that revolt resonated with Americans, whose support for democracy in the land where the very word had been coined led to a new style of building.

The Greek Revival was tantamount to an architectural cheering section for the oppressed Mediterraneans, who had to fight until 1829 to throw off the Turks. It was also the first of America's serial infatuations with particular architectural looks. With its characteristic stoa-like classical columns and its preferred paint color of white, to mimic marble, the Greek Revival scheme could be, and was, grafted onto almost any house. As the rebellious Hellenes battled on, American house façades, humble and proud, acquired the look of miniature temples. Instant porticoes became the rage even in regions mild of climate and brief of summer, regardless of whether they were stylistically appropriate to the dwellings onto which they were pasted.

The mode's august pediments and whiter-than-thou columns held a special allure for the South. Across the region, new wealth and a hardening attitude toward the outside world—specifically, toward abolitionists' increasing barrage of complaints about slavery, which had caused northern states like Vermont to outlaw the peculiar institution and, in 1808, Congress to ban importation of slaves—were changing house styles.

Absent notable exceptions like Drayton House, Monticello, and Mount Vernon, for the most of the eighteenth century, Southern porches had tended to be less than formal. Here and there, plantation owners might have added Palladian touches, but most planters lacked the cash to gussy up their houses in a serious way until the invention of the cotton gin spawned a boom market for that crop.

King Cotton handsomely rewarded its subjects, allowing them to indulge themselves in new houses and expansions of old ones, often on an exaggerated Greek Revival motif. But growing more cotton meant acquiring more Negroes to clear and plant and harvest fields, crank gins, stock warehouses and docks, and serve in the big house. As the South's slave population soared, abolitionists' attacks intensified.

Under psychological siege, Southerners stood defiant. One way of venting that defiance was in their dwellings, many of which came to mirror the collective fantasy slaveholders fostered of the region as a wayward Arthurian idyll. The South's primary visual fetishes came to include what one commentator called "white-pillared architecture."

Southern mansions began to sport porches as synecdoche. These enormous arrays of glaringly white multistory columns, which carried Palladian themes into a new realm of self-importance, evoked, depending on your outlook, either aristocratic gentility, chivalric grace, and the natural order of things—or feudalist thuggery, unspeakable cruelty, and mass psychosis.

Instead of deploying the classical orders to achieve proportion and balance, Southern architects employed the column as "a device for exhibitionism, a sectional emblem, and a symbol of paternalistic and chivalrous society, aristocratic rule, and hierarchical rigidity," write Michael W. Fazio and Patrick A. Snadon in the *Encyclopedia of Southern Culture*. In the culture of the antebellum South, nothing mattered as much as power, conveyed by size. Albert Speer would have understood.

Although the Greek Revival became as much of a staple in the South as cotton, a backlash set in barely a decade after the form had become *the* populist American architectural mode. The reaction was less against the South's version of the style than against its general debasement by huckstering pattern-book publishers, who strove to sell the look no matter how silly it looked. Like siding salesmen, they urged homeowners to slap on porticoes willy-nilly.

One eloquent critic of the trend was Andrew Jackson Downing, himself a pattern-book author but one who saw himself as a messianic theorist. Rather than presenting page upon page of plan upon plan, Downing cast himself as his own hero, able to perceive in a soffit or a spindle an entire way of life, dignified and fulfilling, that could be attained by using the correct house design.

Heir of a Hudson Valley nurseryman who died when his son was twenty-two, Downing inherited his father's business. He used his patrimony to launch a writing career. Along with a horticulture magazine that he started, Downing made his reputation with books like his 1841 *Treatise on the Theory and Practice of Landscape Gardening, Adapted to North America*.

Besides manipulating the American landscape, Downing meant to change the way Americans lived and the buildings they lived in. In matters of dwelling design, he was more of a Bill Gates than a Steve Jobs—not an innovator, but a popularizer. In 1842's *Cottage Residences* and 1850's *The Architecture of Country Houses*—the latter going through nine printings and 16,000 copies—Downing synthesized ideas from more creative architects and earlier pattern-book writers, translating them into the standards and practices of balloon framing.

The Architecture of Country Houses, for example, depended heavily on J.C. Loudon's *Encyclopaedia of Cottage, Farm, and Villa Architecture*, a large (1,138 pages, 2,039 illustrations) and widely admired text that had debuted in London in 1833. "To the nurseryman in Newburgh, New York, the immense popularity of the older English writer's works must have been highly appealing," J. Stewart Johnson writes in the introduction to a 1969 reprint of the Downing book. "Downing's book became, in a sense, a miniature Loudon, simplified, pared down, and specifically aimed at American readers."

Downing also used native sources. Many illustrations in *Country Houses* were by architect Alexander Jackson Davis, whose generosity to his friend paid dividends. By allowing Downing to use his drawings, Davis guaranteed that his work reached the wider public and that Downing, a fluid writer but ham-handed draftsman, enjoyed the coattails and imprimatur of genuine artistry.

Downing had fine timing, as evinced by his broadsides against the Greek Revival. Evolution tends toward the grotesque, and the grotesquery into which the Greek Revival had evolved offered a career-enhancing target. Downing slashed away with the deftness of a Swift or a Voltaire.

"The temple cottage is an imitation of the Temples of Theseus or Minerva, in thin pine boards, with a wonderfully fine and classical portico of wooden columns in front," Downing wrote. "The dimensions of the whole building may be twenty or thirty feet. The grand portico covers, perhaps, a third of the space and the means consumed by the whole building. It is not of the least utility, because it is too high for shade; nor is it the least satisfactory, for it is entirely destitute of truthfulness; it is only a caricature of a temple—not a beautiful cottage." Even the Greek Revival's white paint drew his fire. Too cold and distinctive, said Downing, who plumped for earth tones that wedded a house to the land. And though the movement had begun out of admiration for Greece's struggle to gain independence, Downing and other critics suggested that the Greek Revival was unpatriotic, a borrowed antiquarian vestment unworthy of a new and unique country.

As an alternative, Downing bowed toward England, endorsing the Gothic Revival, with its pitched roofs and dormers, decorative gables, and board-and-batten siding. However, he hammered hard against that form's proto-Victorian tendency toward frippery and folderol. "All ornaments which are not simple, and cannot be executed in a substantial and appropriate manner, should be at once rejected," Downing wrote. "All flimsy and meager decorations which have a pasteboard effect, are as unworthy of, and unbecoming for the house of him who understands the true beauty of a cottage, as glass breastpins or gilt-pewter spoons would be for his personal ornaments or family service of plate."

In matters of dwelling design, Andrew Jackson Downing was more of a Bill Gates than a Steve Jobs—not an innovator, but a popularizer.

Truth was what Downing sought. For him, the first hallmarks of verity in a house were windows, doors, and chimneys. But Downing also found truth on the porch, where the neighbors could see it. "Verandahs, piazzas, bay-windows, balconies, etc., are the most valuable general truths in Domestic Architecture," he wrote. "They express domestic habitation more strongly because they are chiefly confined to our own dwellings."

(Truth also depended on the suitability of house to setting. In an observation that could as easily have been written last week as in 1850, Downing declared, "There is nothing more common in some parts of the country than to see the cockneyism of three-story town houses violating the beauty and simplicity of country life.")

Downing sought honesty in materials, too. Instead of torturing it to resemble stone, let wood be wood, he urged. "To build a house of wood so exactly in imitation of stone as to lead the spectator to suppose it stone, is a paltry artifice, at variance with all truthfulness," he wrote. However, Downing made an exception for wooden verandas, which he grudgingly allowed could be sanded and painted to harmonize with a stone house to which they might be attached.

For Downing, the porch served not only as a badge of merit but a guardian of privacy and a buffer against the elements. Even more important, he said, the porch was an "expression of domestic enjoyment" and a symbol of the inhabitants' inner lives. "A much higher character is conferred on a simple cottage by a veranda than by a highly ornamented gable, because one indicates the constant means of enjoyment for the inmates—something in their daily life besides ministering to the necessities," Downing wrote. "A more ornamental verge-board shows something, the beauty of which is not so directly connected with the life of the owner of the cottage, and which is therefore less expressive, as well as less useful."

Downing tempered his enthusiasm for porches with edicts for strict adherence to proportion. He tended to equip his designs with smaller verandas, lest he tar himself with the same brush he wielded so brutally in attacking the latter Greek Revival's exaggerations of scale. However, Downing admitted that taste and utility could justify a bigger porch. In the text for an illustration of a house with a small wraparound porch that he dubbed "A Gate-Lodge in the English style," Downing wrote, "A veranda eight or nine feet broad might extend along one side of the cottage, so as to cover the two large windows of the living-room and parlor—either or both of which, extending to the floor, would give easy access to the veranda, and render it, for summer enjoyment, equal to another apartment on the same floor." But Downing couldn't resist the temptation to proselytize: "Such a veranda would be more convenient and comfortable, but not quite so harmonious and picturesque as that shown in the present elevation."

Downing's voice was stilled when he drowned on the Hudson River in 1852, but his writings lived on. They had plenty of company, sometimes dedicated to new construction and sometimes intended to help the renovator. The title of an 1855 book by Gervase Wheeler gives away the whole story: *Homes for the People in Suburb and Country; the Villa, the Mansion and the Cottage, Adapted to the American Climate and Wants. With Examples Showing How to Alter and Remodel Old Buildings. In a Series of One Hundred Original Designs.* Wheeler's hundred designs, of course, included many with porches, all characterized in lofty tones of the moral rectitude at the core of an American housing reform movement that began in the middle decades of the nineteenth century.

For all our emphasis on rugged individualism and freedom of spirit, we Americans have always been big on telling people how to live. That impulse was on prominent display among the era's housing reformers, who contended that "properly designed houses would stabilize society, attest to the moral development of the owners, meet the needs for new housing evident in the expansion of the suburbs, and help improve society at large," Clifford Clark writes in *The American Family Home 1800–1960.* "Indeed, housing and family reformers, by associating certain kinds of single-family homes with certain kinds of communities and by suggesting that any American could purchase a home, have helped reinforce the myth that all Americans are or are becoming part of the middle class."

After the pattern book, the place where readers in the first half of the nineteenth century were most likely to encounter the porch as an image associated with the American way of life was in self-help literature and, later, in fiction.

In the self-help category, porches appeared frequently among the adjurations of bluestockings with a variety of axes to grind and oxes to gore. Reformers aimed to revive Americans' spirituality, eradicate the scourge of drink, elevate ethics and morals, and set new standards for the way people lived and the dwellings they occupied. These activists gave pole positions to temperance, education, and the abolition of slavery, but domestic life was never far from nineteenth-century progressives' hearts.

"Like the abolitionists who idealized the slave in order to galvanize public opinion, the housing reformers glorified the virtues of the single-family dwelling. The house was praised as 'the quiet repository of man's fondest hopes, and the cherished sanctuary of earthly happiness,'" writes Clark. "Like the temperance advocates who condemned those who drank as sinful and morally degenerate, the housing reformers attacked poorly designed houses as inconceivably ugly, useless, and corrupting."

But the foes of whiskey and slavery simply wanted to do away with the objects of their ire and replace them with virtuous behavior. The crew pushing for better housing had in mind to impose what Clark calls "a new national family ideal" that married the American family to the American single-family home, preferably with a veranda out front. This concept proved immensely popular in the mid-nineteenth century, and still influences the way we live. If Walt Whitman were alive today, he could as easily pen the sentence he wrote in the 1840s: "A man is not a whole and complete man unless he *owns* a house and the ground it stands on."

Among the most famously literary reformers were the Beecher sisters, Catharine and Harriet. Both were writers, inclined to make the personal political, and both wrestled private satisfaction from public accomplishment and spiritual grace from the struggle for the legal tender.

Catharine Beecher's first fame came from her 1837 *Essay on Slavery and Abolitionism with Reference to the Duty of American Females*. Written after riots the August before, in which white mobs had sacked Cincinnati's Black quarter, *Essay* characterized American women as morally superior beings vouchsafed to form and guide the national character. On slavery, Beecher's views were only semi-enlightened. She wanted Negroes freed and sent back to Africa—a position that shifted radically both as she and her siblings forged individual and collective stances on the topic and as Catharine found common cause with her younger sister and fellow writer.

Harriet, who followed Catharine into the word trade, was a hard-charging hack with a gift for fast, fluent prose that quickly had the younger Beecher outpacing her older sister. In 1837, income from writing—which she pursued more as avocation than business—earned Catharine all of thirty dollars, while her sister clocked three hundred. ("I do it for the pay," was the dogged Harriet's motto.)

Eventually, Catharine regained the lead, with her 1841 *Treatise on Domestic Economy*, a compact volume on how to run a household. Earlier books in what Clifford Clark calls "the canon of domesticity" had established the models of home as refuge and family as societal stabilizer. *Treatise* took those models to the next rung; it sold well, often being bought by schools for use as a textbook. A keen marketer, Beecher updated *Treatise* annually through 1856, and it made her a heroine to women around the United States, as well as a nationally recognized expert. "Catharine's *Treatise* explained every aspect of domestic life from the building of a house to the setting of a table," writes Kathryn Kish Sklar in *Catharine Beecher: A Study in American Domesticity*. "Catharine's was the first American volume to pull all the disparate domestic employments together and to describe their functions in the American environment."

Besides guaranteeing Catharine Beecher financial independence—she and Harper & Brothers split the book's profits—*Treatise* made her the Martha Stewart and Dr. Joyce Brothers of her day. Catharine meant to use that fame as a social fulcrum. She hit the lecture circuit, advocating educational reform and urging women on in the self-sacrificing role she assigned them. Catharine also helped her ambitious sister by lending her name to Harriet's first book of fiction. And when Harriet, much the fiercer abolitionist, decided to write a novel about slavery, Catharine moved to Brunswick, Maine, caring for her sister's six children and her husband, Calvin Stowe, so Harriet could complete her project.

That project, of course, was *Uncle Tom's Cabin, or Life among the Lowly,* which Henry James termed "much less a book than a state of vision, of feeling and consciousness." James might have added that *Uncle Tom's Cabin* was also a gigantic, if unintentional, advertisement for the delights of the porch.

Literary the book wasn't, with its purple prose and steamy plot. But *Uncle Tom's Cabin* served its purpose, namely to heighten certain contradictions inherent in American life. *Uncle Tom's Cabin* cleaved the nation like the blade of a froe, hacking a bright line that forced readers to ask themselves and one another on which side they stood. The book had the subtlety of a trip hammer, the power of a locomotive running full out, and an almost intoxicating sheen of what the baptismal rite calls "the glamour of evil"—a glamour nowhere more luridly lustrous than in Harriet Beecher Stowe's repeated use of porches and verandas as settings for key scenes. Again and again, Stowe puts characters out on the porch, positioning that ordinary liminal space as a site of enormous transformation:

- Eliza greets George on the Shelbys' porch the day he sets out for Canada; later she pauses there to pet her owners' Newfoundland, Bruno, before making her doomed escape with Harry.
- Cartoonishly malign slave trader Haley preens on the porch like a vaudeville villain, just before cagey slaves Sam and Andy set him up to fall off his horse.
- Cartoonishly benign slave Uncle Tom cavorts in the St. Clare mansion courtyard to amuse a veranda-bound Eva.
- Mrs. St. Clare, on the same veranda, about to depart for church, "gorgeously dressed . . . clasping a diamond bracelet on her slender wrist."

Stowe so despises her Southern characters that she subjects them and their way of life to descriptions nearly erotic in their intensity. Describing the St. Clares' summer house on the shore of Lake Ponchartrain, Stowe sketches the decadence through which these spurious aristocrats glide: ". . . an East Indian cottage, surrounded by light verandahs of bamboo-work, and opening on all sides into gardens and pleasure-grounds. The common sitting-room opened on to a large garden, fragrant with every picturesque plant and flower of the tropics, where winding paths ran down to the very shores of the lake, whose silvery sheet of water lay there, rising and falling in the sunbeams,—a picture never for an hour the same, yet every hour more beautiful."

Later, Stowe takes out after life on the veranda at the St. Clare mansion. Meaning to excoriate the slave-owners, she italicizes the allure of their existence:

"It was Sunday afternoon. St. Clare was stretched on a bamboo lounge on the verandah, solacing himself with a cigar. Marie lay reclined on a sofa, opposite the window opening on the verandah, closely secluded, under an awning of transparent gauze, from the outrages of the mosquitos, and languidly holding in her hand an elegantly bound prayerbook. She was holding it because it was Sunday, and she imagined she had been reading it,—though, in fact, she had been only taking a succession of short naps, with it open in her hand."

The book also includes Cousin Henrique's back-porch meanness and Little Eva's death prefigured on the front veranda and brought to finality on one at the rear, with scenes in between that have saintly Uncle Tom sleeping on the porch floor so that at a moment's notice he can carry his little mistress out to catch a cooling breeze. After Eva's death—which Stowe describes from the point of view of slaves on the porch watching St. Clare watch his daughter expire— Uncle Tom falls asleep in a chair on the porch, dreaming of the freedom his creator will never allow him to have.

About the only porch in the book you wouldn't want to be caught dead on is Simon Legree's: "The house had been large and handsome. It was built in a manner common in the South; a wide verandah of two stories running round every part of the house, into which every outer door opened, the lower tier being supported by brick pillars. . . . But the place looked desolate and uncomfortable; some windows stopped up with boards, some with shattered panes, and shutters hanging by a single hinge,—all telling of coarse neglect and discomfort."

Uncle Tom's Cabin was an instant sensation. Its first day on sale, Americans bought 3,000 copies. The book's inaugural year saw it rocket through 120 editions and 300,000 copies; in time, 1.5 million copies would circulate in Great Britain and its colonies. Theatrical troupes would stage eight adaptations, six before the Civil War. *Uncle Tom's Cabin* joined Lew Wallace's Biblical epic *Ben-Hur* and Edward Bellamy's utopian fantasy *Looking Backward* as nineteenth-century America's most popular novels.

But despite the ferocity with which *Uncle Tom's Cabin* skewered slavery and all that flowed therefrom, its author couldn't help but make it sound like a really good idea to have as many porches and verandas and galleries as possible, whether as means of escape from durance vile, or to palliate the pain and guilt adhering to any who profited from trade in human chattel, or just as a great place to smoke a stogie and snooze.

With its enormous notoriety and equally enormous sales, *Uncle Tom's Cabin* not only drove the North and South closer to the breaking point over slavery, it drove home the image of the porch as a uniquely American setting.

In years to come, that image would be reinforced by a surge in romantic nostalgia for the vanishing colonial past, as well as by a flood of progressive tracts, pamphlets, and pattern books urging Americans to improve— and exhibit—the quality of their lives by living in houses with porches. But perhaps the most persuasive argument on behalf of the porch as an American icon was made all but wordlessly, in the era's only true mass medium—the lithograph.

The Currier & Ives oeuvre defined America for Americans, shaping what they were talking about when they talked about history, heritage, hearth, and home.

CHAPTER NINE

GETTING INTO PRINT

In the seventeenth and eighteenth centuries, as the porch was cementing itself into American culture, it attracted scant attention. Contemporary paintings and sketches show loggias, galleries, porches, and verandas, but only in passing; the artists and draftsmen who captured these scenes were aiming more to document than to dictate style. And only rare pictures saw wide distribution as illustrations in books, themselves rare commodities in colonial times. For the porch to become a mass media icon there had to be mass media.

The first of these was lithography. Invented in Germany in 1798, the process, named with the Greek words for "stone" and "writing," quickly became popular in the United States thanks to portable, affordable equipment and a national hunger for pictures—of news events, religious figures, landscapes, practically anything. People wanted something to put on the wall. One of the most successful and prolific lithographers of the 1830s and 1840s was Nathaniel Currier, whose lower-Manhattan establishment printed and distributed images by the million over the counter, by mail, and off peddlers' carts. Currier had an appetite for disaster; he'd made his first fortune with prints of steamboat sinkings, fires, explosions, and other catastrophes. But when Currier hired James Ives to keep his firm's books in 1852, the company took a turn for the sunny side. Ives, who was also an artist, not only brought the company's records into the modern age but suggested ways to speed printing and fulfillment. He gave off ideas like sparks. One was to make prints showing ordinary people doing ordinary things. At first, Currier resisted. Who would buy such pictures?

"Currier had not earlier regarded these tableaux as particularly salable, given his dramatic successes with catastrophe," writes Walton Rawls in *The Great Book of Currier & Ives' America*. "But James Ives was attuned to subtler vibrations in the air, correctly sensing in the discontent of harried city-dwellers a ready market for inexpensive depictions of what they imagined was a simpler, more fulfilling, more American way of life."

Currier decided to let the marketplace persuade him he could profit on happiness and light. He could and did. Prints from the *American Country Home, American Winter Scenes,* and kindred series began to decorate tenements, offices, parlors, and saloons. The new fellow had proved his mettle; in 1857, N. Currier & Co. became Currier & Ives.

For the rest of the century, the firm's oeuvre defined America for Americans, shaping what they were talking about when they talked about history, heritage, hearth, and home. Perhaps because we are a nation of people who came from someplace else—or, at some point near or far, who came from people who came from someplace else—we balance our relentless forward tilt with a tendency toward the backward glance, the longing for what might have been, the receding light at the end of the dock.

The output of Currier & Ives fit that frame precisely. As the firm was taking its new direction, America was taking new directions of its own. Colonial times and the Republic's childhood were slipping from fact into legend. Immigrants were pouring in. The era of mass production and mechanized transport had begun. The slavery debate was edging toward violence. People were leaving the manicured East for the West's open land and wild possibilities. Those who stayed behind were leaving the farm for the city or were quitting the city for a new way of life at the urban fringe. In the "suburbs," as these developments were called, promoters then, as now, ballyhooed the privacy, safety, and homogeneity awaiting those who left the mean streets and high rents for the suburbs and home ownership—a concept that would become a national ideal, along with the single-family house.

Lithographers quickly put a face on that fantasy. In the Currier & Ives inventory, the word "home" eventually appeared in more than fifty titles; only "America," at two-hundred-plus, ranked higher. In those pictures, home often included a porch, rarely stressed but almost always present—the liminal space endorsed subliminally. The "American Home" series was a perennial best-seller, thanks to variations on a theme of foregrounds showing yeoman farmers atoil in verdant fields, with the beautiful cottage, the picket fence, and the front porch, often graced by the lady of the house, in the distance. The pictures fixed in the collective consciousness a clear yet adaptable idea of what home was supposed to look like. Generally, it looked like it had a porch.

(The concept penetrated to fiction, as well. In his 1856 short-story collection *The Piazza Tales,* Herman Melville's organizing metaphor was a farmhouse in Massachusetts perfectly suited to having a porch, er, piazza, but lacking one, to the protagonist's dismay—". . . I like piazzas, as somehow combining the coziness of indoors with the freedom of outdoors, and it is so pleasant to inspect your thermometer there. . . ."—and thereby unleashing the character's imagination to wonder how best to design and build one.)

Even though they were creating fictional images, printmakers seemed to be looking into lives actually being lived. "A characteristic aspect of practically all the Currier & Ives prints of homes is their picturesque privacy amidst bucolic surroundings," writes Rawls. "One might think of them as idealized visions, but evidently they conveyed enough reality to seem attainable to certain city dwellers—some cramped in tenement rooms, yet still inspired by the American dream of success—who eagerly bought the prints . . . the houses are often unpretentious, but they bear unmistakable signs of being real homes, with extensions built on later for new kitchens and storerooms, dormers put through pitched roofs to add attic bedrooms for growing families, and decorative trellises attached to porches for climbing roses and vines. The structures are usually of simple frame construction, clapboarded, and, like most of the houses then lived in by ordinary folk, look as if they were built by local craftsmen."

This homey approach, plus consistency of style, breadth of subject matter, and relentless marketing, gave Currier & Ives a strong grip on the market. However, a large and growing country—between 1830 and 1860, the United States admitted six states and organized the rest of the subcontinent into territories; the urban population rose from 500,000 to 3.8 million—offered room for competition. Diversity of taste and markets, plus easy access to equipment and low start-up costs, caused print shops to multiply. Many sold American scenes, whether original or copies of fine art, especially as the U.S. citizenry began to realize that artifacts of its history and its legacy of wilderness stood in danger of vanishing. Just as the romantic perspective of Hudson River School painters like Thomas Cole and Frederic Edwin Church bolstered Americans' affection for the shrinking frontier, visual works on historical themes galvanized popular concern about historic sites.

By the 1850s, for example, George Washington's beloved Mount Vernon was so far gone that its demise appeared inevitable—until a group of women chartered themselves as the Mount Vernon Ladies' Association to restore and preserve the mansion. To buy it, the Ladies solicited donations and sold lithographs showing three views of the house. Mount Vernon was a near ruin; the piazza roof wore a cheesy railing and a discarded ship's mast stood in for a rotted column. However, the artwork showed the house in exquisite condition, complete with figures in period costume. The prints were big sellers.

Abetted by the Ladies' campaign, Mount Vernon vaulted into popularity, and became a media star in its own right. "The Home of Washington," an enormous 1860 painting by Louis Remy Mignot and Thomas Pritchard Rossiter, gave the First Porch star status. "Home" imagines the piazza at the end of a summer's day, perhaps in 1797, when the Marquis de Lafayette visited his aging ally to present him with a key to the liberated Bastille. Mignot and Rossiter show the Frenchman and the general hanging out. There's no other way to put it; though dressed to the postcolonial nines, the two could as easily be wearing Lacoste shirts, Dockers, and Topsiders as they shoot the breeze in the breeze. Martha Washington, seated at a table, plays cards with two nieces. On the lawn behind Lafayette, a white boy and a Black boy frolic. All about are the details of life: hoops, hats, a toy cannon, a dog, a cow.

In those days, audiences gathered in auditoriums, much as they would later flock to the cinema, to view such grand pieces of art. But fewer people saw the Brobdignagian canvas (it hangs at the Metropolitan Museum of Art, opposite Emmanuel Leutz's equally heroic "Washington Crossing the Delaware") than bought lithos of it by copy artists like Thomas Oldham Barlow. To modern eyes, the image teems with kitschiness—would George Washington really have let cows roam his yard?—but it also conveys the democratic notion that even the Father of His Country was entitled to kick back on the porch. Less famous but more moving is an oil Mignot did in advance of his collaboration with Rossiter. Painted in 1858–59, the sketch shows the piazza at Mount Vernon in real time and real decay, empty, with floor worn, columns peeling, and ceiling cracked. No wonder the Ladies wanted to adopt the place and bring it home.

Along with the heroic image of Washington entertaining Lafayette on his piazza, mid-nineteenth century American art included many images of porches. As the Blue wore down the Grey and the Confederacy began to fall, deadline artists like Thomas Nast, working for newspapers and periodicals like *Harper's Weekly* and *Frank Leslie's Illustrated Weekly*, regularly included plantation scenes in their submissions. In an engraving for *Harper's*, Nast depicted General William Sherman at the porch of a Georgia mansion, intact but awash in Federal soldiers. From the veranda, the house's female inhabitants scowl at the invader, who is raising his hat to them. Behind Sherman his troops mingle with newly freed slaves. A Black child hands a drummer boy a sunflower. No doubt an artist with Confederate leanings would have painted a different picture.

After the war, sated with images of dead soldiers stacked like cord-wood, the country struggled to regain its balance, an effort reflected in its art. An 1867 best-seller for Currier & Ives showed a young man being greeted by his family on the porch of their house; the title: "Home to Thanksgiving."

(Ever alert to opportunity, Currier & Ives were always ready to license popular images to manufacturers and advertisers, giving their pictures extraordinary reach. For example, "A Home on the Mississippi," an 1871 scene by Alfred Waud, commissioned by the U.S. government as part of a documentary program on the big river, was acquired by the printmakers. The image featured Woodland Plantation, a river pilot's house in West Point La Hache, Louisiana. After Prohibition ended, Currier & Ives licensed the picture to the makers of Southern Comfort. Since then, the house has decorated the liqueur's label, an epic achievement of subliminal salesmanship that has replicated that image billions of times.)

Winslow Homer, who'd come to public notice during the war with battle-field paintings he often rendered as engravings for *Harper's*, turned to pleasanter themes, such as the croquet fad of the late 1860s; his croquet series often featured young ladies reclining on porches. In the 1870s, Homer began portraying country life, joining painters like Edward Lamson Henry in composing scenes of ordinary people doing ordinary things on ordinary porches, maybe enjoying a moment's peaceful repose (Homer's "Girl Reading on a Porch"), calling the family to a meal (Homer's "The Dinner Horn"), or sitting down to eat it (Henry's "Country Breakfast"). The country-scenes genre, long a favorite of Americans, faded as the nation grew more urban and Impressionism took hold. Another reason the style fell from favor was excessive sentimentality, embodied by Jennie Augusta Brownscomb's 1887 work "Love's Young Dream," in which a demurely dressed and wistful young woman and her parents occupy a porch, she standing on the steps and looking longingly into the distance at an approaching rider while her father reads the Bible, her mother knits, and a kitten plays with a ball of yarn.

Besides reinforcing a sense of national identity with familiar images, artists and printmakers were contributing to a growing library of ever more elaborate pattern books. In addition, the progressive movement was continuing its efforts to persuade Americans to live right by publishing housing-related broadsides. In 1869, the Beecher sisters brought out *The American Woman's Home; or, Principles of Domestic Science: Being a Guide to the Formation and Maintenance of Economical, Healthful, Beautiful, and Christian Homes.*

This expanded version of Catharine's evergreen *Treatise* filled 500 pages and thirty-eight chapters, adding not only extensive information on practical matters like indoor toilets but also a large dose of Christian proselytizing and philosophizing. Dedicated to "The Women of America," the book was Catharine's magnum opus, trading not only on Harriet's name but her motherhood, a stripe the older sister could not claim. "It is probable that Mrs. Stowe's fame as author of *Uncle Tom's Cabin* and many other books and her practical experience as a mother of seven children led Catharine to conclude that having her sister as coauthor would enhance the reputation and sale of the book," writes Stowe-Day Foundation director Joseph S. Van Why. "Catharine was shrewdly aware that the public might question a spinster woman in her late sixties writing authoritatively on such subjects."

Will it surprise you, dear reader, to learn that *The American Woman's Home* is chockablock with pictures of porches, or that, besides touting the porch's contributions to the leisurely side of family life, the sisters Beecher find ways to put this instrument of enjoyment to work? The cover shows a Downingesque cottage, and, in the chapter setting forth the dimensions and details of "the Christian house," the sisters write, "The piazzas each side of the front projection have sliding-windows to the floor, and can, by glazed sashes, be made greenhouses in winter. In a warm climate, piazzas can be made at the back side also." Plus, as millions of readers knew from *Uncle Tom's Cabin,* on hot days you could loll around on the veranda and smoke cigars and flash your jewelry.

The English fascination with India and its vernacular architecture continued to pique Americans' curiosity. By the 1850s, "bungalow" had entered English parlance as a term for a vacation home; William Thackeray had a character build a house he dubbed "Bungalow Lodge." In his best-selling book, *Curry and Rice (on Forty Plates) or The Ingredients of Social Life at "Our" Station,* George Atkinson drew louche remittance men lounging on verandas amid hovering servants, reinforcing the idea of the bungalow as an outpost of leisure. "In the 1860s and 1870s, life in the country or hill-station bungalow was seen as a positive experience, far from the madding crowd and waited on hand and foot," writes Anthony King in *The Bungalow: The Production of a Global Culture.* "Like other facets of Indian and Anglo-Indian life, it seemed to represent something which had been lost in England, increasingly industrialized and urban, and offering an opportunity to escape from social changes which some people were beginning to deplore."

Although images of the porch had an impact, direct or indirect, on real life, one actual porch seems to have exerted a profound influence on American literature, bringing together an unlikely pair of collaborators, who after years of polite acquaintanceship were able, thanks to the peculiar nature of the porch as a place of human encounter, to achieve a new level of understanding. The porch was in upstate New York, but this subtly momentous exchange flowed from Mary Ann Cord's and Samuel Langhorne Clemens's formative experiences as southerners accustomed to porches as places between the worlds of whiteness and Blackness. Had this conversation taken place anywhere else but on a porch, it's unlikely that Cord would have been as excruciatingly honest and Twain would have been as humanely receptive to her pain.

Catharine Beecher's highly charged but highly practical writing on women's themes made her the Martha Stewart and Dr. Joyce Brothers of her day.

I heard about Cord and Clemens from Shelley Fisher Fishkin, a professor at the University of Texas at Austin and an expert on Mark Twain. "Mark Twain!" was what pilots on the Mississippi River shouted when sounding bottom, and it is, of course, the pen name by which the world knows Sam Clemens. The world scarcely knows of Mary Ann Cord at all. But with a story she told him on a porch of the house where he and his family spent their summers, she helped the author find the voice that would make him immortal.

Shelley Fisher Fishkin has forgotten more about Mark Twain than most of us will ever know. She edited the definitive collection of his work. She lectures on him around the world. Her books *Lighting Out for the Territory: Reflections on Mark Twain and American Culture* and *Was Huck Black? Mark Twain and African-American Voices* are exhilarating excursions into Twain's impact on America.

As Professor Fishkin documents in *Lighting Out,* one summer night in during that in-between time after dinner, when household roles slackened and servants stood more eye-to-eye with their employers than at any other, Mary Ann Cord had the occasion to tell Mark Twain and his family a story.

A former slave, Cord was the cook at Quarry Farm, east of Elmira, New York. The farm belonged to Twain's sister-in-law, Susan Crane. She'd inherited the property from her father, Jervis Langdon, who'd made his money in coal. An ardent abolitionist, Langdon underwrote the Elmira station of the Underground Railroad, through which some 800 fugitive slaves—including, in 1838, Frederick Douglass—had traveled to freedom.

Cord had come to Elmira from North Carolina after the Civil War. She was a woman of formidable stature, but she seemed at ease in the role of the jolly, warm-hearted Black servant who endures her white employer's good-natured jibes with peals of laughter—then, as now, a persona African-Americans find useful when dealing with folks of the Caucasian persuasion.

Clemens was formidable, too; talent and tenacity had carried him a long way since his boyhood in a slave-owning family in Hannibal, Missouri. Growing into his *nomme de plume,* he'd already scored his first critical and financial successes with *Innocents Abroad* and *Roughing It.* He had reached past the benign local-color humor of "Jim Smiley and His Jumping Frog" to the bitter anti-lynching satire "Only a Nigger." Twain was shedding his heritage; still, he fancied himself, as some southern white men still do, a fellow who knew Negroes. As they all sat around after dinner on the porch steps, he and his family liked to kid the cook, who by tradition sat lower on the steps than her employers. The porch at Quarry Farm saw a lot of use. Clemens, whose office opened onto it, made a practice of reading the first drafts of his novels and other writings to the family there.

This particular evening, Twain uttered a crack that shattered Mary Ann Cord's happy composure. He joked that in her sixty years she surely must never have had any trouble; she was too consistently happy. As if her employer had shut off a tap, Cord stopped laughing. Looking up the steps at the writer, she fixed him with a gimlet eye.

"Has I had any trouble, Mistuh Clemens?" she asked.

Cord then told the family her life story. She'd grown up in Virginia, where in slavery times she'd had a husband and seven children. At Eastertime in 1852, the woman who owned the Cords needed cash. To raise it, she put the slave family up for auction in Richmond.

The sun was going down. Cord, who'd been sitting at the foot of the porch stairs, stood up straight. Looming over the mesmerized Twains, she described how, one by one, her husband and children went on the block. Last to go was her youngest, Henry, who before his new owner hauled him off vowed to get his freedom and find his mother to buy hers. That was the last she saw of her family, Cord said; the man who bought her lived in Newbern, North Carolina, where she worked as his cook until the Union troops came. Then, through a series of startling coincidences, Henry, who'd fled to the North and become a barber in Elmira, lived up to his word and found her in Newbern.

The story poured out of Cord in a stream of hurt and anger, spontaneous yet succinct, full of emotion, riveting in detail, like the scars on Henry's wrist and forehead with which his mother confirmed his identity. When she was done, Cord nailed her boss with a closing sentence.

"Oh, no, Mister Clemens," Cord said. "I ain't had no trouble. And no joy!"

Twain sat transfixed. Like any writer worth his mercenary salt, he regarded tales told to him as raw material from which he might refine something salable. This time, though, he'd fallen into ore of much higher quality. As soon as he could, he transcribed Cord's soliloquy. (In an unpublished memoir that Professor Fishkin quotes in *Lighting Out*, Twain said he resolved "to copy it here—& not in my words but her own. I wrote them before they were cold.") He reordered the sequence and renamed Cord "Aunt Rachel," but he stayed true to her African-American dialect and the tone she'd used. He sent the text to William Dean Howells, editor of *The Atlantic Monthly*, under the title "A True Story Repeated Word for Word As I Heard It." Twain apologized for the lack of humor in the piece, offering to take a lower rate since it wasn't in his usual vein.

Howells paid his publication's premium rate for the 2,000-word piece, which ran in the November 1874 issue, marking Twain's *Atlantic* debut. The same month, the *New York Times* ran his "Sociable Jimmy," a briefer dialect article of similar tenor.

Cord's story had showed Clemens new possibilities for his writing. These included not only the power of using everyday speech but of granting independence and equality to a dialect speaker instead of setting her up as a foil for condescending derision, as the coon shows of the day did. Refusing to play Mary Ann Cord cheap, Mark Twain broke through to a new level of American writing.

In 1874, "A True Story" discomfited Twain's fans and other readers. The same is true today. It's a tough read, unleavened by the merest tweak of humor. It's pure and it's harsh and pain leaches from it like acid from a cracked battery. In those days, "nigger" was even more the household word than it once was, and without the neutralizing veneer of po-mo irony. Mary Ann Cord had let it fly with vehemence. So did Aunt Rachel, and so would Huck Finn and Jim and the other characters Twain would invent as he traveled along a path Professor Fishkin sees as having started on the Quarry Farm porch that evening.

"This event was incredibly significant, a turning point in American literature. Hearing Mary Ann Cord tell her story reconnected Clemens to the storytellers of his childhood. Her story really made him aware of the power of the vernacular voice as a compelling narrator," the professor told me in a telephone interview. "Cord's story—and the story Twain wrote—broke the frame of the traditional dialect story, in which the editorial narrator introduces and then mocks the dialect speaker. In this story, *she* mocks *him*. It was a key step along the road to writing *The Adventures of Huckleberry Finn*, which he began two years later."

Professor Fishkin said the larger and smaller setting in which Cord told her story had its own significance. "The fact that this took place on the porch is important," she said. "Neither Twain nor Cord was sufficiently inside the house that the norms of social inequality would apply. It's possible she felt more comfortable telling her story outdoors than in the house, where her position as a servant and cook would have been clearer. On the porch, her position was less defined. She rises up and towers over him and his family. In this context, the porch is a site on which some of the social stratification gives way to an exchange in which sheer storytelling ability trumps status and class lines. Twain and his family are listeners; Mary Ann Cord is the storyteller. It's such a compelling narration that he gives her full credit for being a literary artist, for having literary artistry—he wrote later that it was the 'greatest literary work to come from a mouth untutored.'"

In the 1870s, as Twain was hitting his literary stride, the country was madly building houses, still using pattern books. Before the Union and the Confederacy ever began trading shots, housing reformers and pattern book publishers had concentrated on selling readers the idea of the single-family house. After the Civil War, they applied that same intensity to the idea of the suburb as the American way of life.

The chaste look of the Gothic Revival began to fade as architects like Henry Hudson Holly, S. B. Reed, and George and Charles Palliser interwove floor plans and highly detailed specifications with streams of narrative and hyperbole (and not infrequently outright invective) that argued for a more eclectic approach to design. They reprised familiar layouts but laid on bay windows, porches, roofs, canopies, and all manner of visual detail in a rich mélange that came to be known as Queen Anne. This form's immense popularity not only helped establish the subliminal American idea of house and neighborhood, but it also helped shatter the notion that residential architecture ought to have stylistic purity.

Reed, a builder based in Corona, New York, first published his designs in *American Agriculture*, later collecting them in a volume entitled *Village & Country Residences: How to Build Them*. His catalogue ranged from a $250 cottage intended as a wing for an eventual larger house to a block of five row houses built in Bayside, Long Island, for $10,000. Unlike some other pattern-book authors, Reed in his estimates drilled down to an extraordinary level of detail: "painting, $40; carpenter's labor $IOO, incidentals $25.07 . . . [total]

$165.07," reads one line-item entry. He also reached for the stars in his predictions of suburban development ("Gas-pipes are inserted in the frame-work of the house, with connections arranged for 37 attachments. These are easily put in during construction, and even when the house is located far from any city or village having gas, there is strong probability that ere long we shall have convenient apparatus for making and supplying gas to isolated dwellers.").

Reed's rhetoric was typical of his day and of the ardor with which pattern-book authors called out to builders and their clients, and of latter-day pattern-book planners' practicality: "To a certain extent, one's dwelling is an index of his character. Any effort at building expresses the owner's ability, taste and purpose. Every industrious man, starting in life, has a right, and should be encouraged, to anticipate prosperity, as the sure reward of honest worth; and he may, with propriety, give emphasis to such anticipations in every step, and with every blow struck. His dwelling may well express the progressive character, rather than a conclusive result. Beginning a home by starting with a room or two, as present means allow, and increasing its dimensions as can be afforded, without the precarious aid of the money-lender, is honest, independent, and best provides against the ever-changing vicissitudes of life."

Like Reed, the Palliser brothers also expanded the concept of the pattern book. George, who came to Bridgeport, Connecticut, from England in 1868, was a master carpenter. For a time he owned a factory that made doors and sashes. In the early 1870s, he and brother Charles moved into land speculation and development. George realized people were eager to buy his designs, so in 1876 he brought out *Model Homes for the People, a Complete Guide to the Proper and Economical Erection of Buildings.* To make the book's twenty-five-cent price possible—other pattern books sold for as much as $IO—*Model Homes* carried twenty-two pages of advertising. It sold more than 5,000 copies and generated a lavish flow of business to Palliser & Palliser. The firm would later provide lithographed plans to build a $3,000 house for fifty cents or, for $40, detailed elevations and floor plans showing how to put up a $7,500 house. Clients wanting a custom design could fill out their answers to a sheet of questions and send it to the company; such designs cost customers two percent of construction cost, compared with the three-and-a-half percent conventional architects charged. Palliser also published books of specifications and drawings of details, with the latter selling more than 50,000 copies.

Palliser house books presented field-tested designs, each accompanied by a page of prose that might include a customer's name, job, and hometown. This meant a prospect would not simply be examining a floor plan and sketch but a floor plan and sketch for R.R. Henry's residence in Tazewell, Virginia, or Albert Trinler's place in New Albany, Indiana, or Rev. Dr. Marble's house in Newtown, Connecticut: "This house commands a particularly fine view from both side and the front, and is situated in one of the pleasantest country towns in New England, the hotels of this town being crowded during the summer months with people from the cities. . . . The sight of this house in the locality in which it is built is very refreshing, and is greatly in advance of the old styles of rural box architecture to be found there. When people see beautiful things, they very naturally covet them, and they grow discontented in the possession of ugliness. Handsome houses, other things equal, are always the most valuable. They sell quickest and for the most money. Builders who feign a blindness to beauty must come to grief."

Whether the house in question was for a laborer, a tradesman, or a surgeon, the porch was integral to the Palliser sensibility. This was brought home not only by the plates but the text, which varied by emphasis but amounted to a rolling endorsement: "The front Porch is arranged with a seat on each side, so that one may sit out of doors, and yet be in the shade, which is a very desirable feature . . . the front veranda and especially the hood over entrance is very pretty—in fact this is one of the prettily designed Cottages, which will always attract attention . . . the veranda is a pleasant feature, and is very useful besides being ornamental . . . the spacious veranda gives ample space for the occupants to enjoy nature, and at the same time be suitably protected from the glare of the sun . . . the front veranda is wide, and arranged so that a group can sit out upon it with ease . . . a front porch for everyday use, and a spacious front porch and front veranda. . . ."

The Pallisers strove for elevated tone and sophisticated content. In the 1878 *Model Homes,* an introduction entitled "Hints On Building" opens with a verse from Shakespeare's *Henry IV:* "When we mean to build/we first survey the plat, then draw the model/And, when we see the figure of the house/Then must we rate the cost of erection/Which, if we find outweighs ability/What do we then but draw anew the model/In fewer offices; or, at least desist/To build at all. . . ." The book also invokes high-brow music as a metaphor for design as part of twenty densely printed pages on the nature of architecture: "There are millions of people who derive more enjoyment from listening to a hand-organ playing a popular air, than they could possibly appreciate from hearing Beethoven's Seventh Symphony; but do we doubt for an instant that this preference is due to a lack of education or a sense of music?"

The Pallisers fought hard in the antidrab campaign that spawned Queen Anne. They began by bludgeoning Palladianism's traditional symmetry. "A close observer in travelling through the country towns and villages in almost every portion of our country, cannot fail to notice the sameness and monotony of most country residences, which are nearly all built after one order, and very frequently a large number in each village all just alike, presenting symmetrical aspects," they wrote. "This matter of symmetry is a very grave question, and one which may work well enough on large public buildings, but should have nothing to do with the design and arrangement of private dwellings. . . . Symmetry applied to private architecture is an invention that has had its day and is completely run out, except in rare cases, where old fogyism holds the sway and reigns supreme."

The brothers even invoked Roman tradition: "The ancients never troubled themselves about symmetry in their residences; the houses at Pompeii are not built with any regard to it, and the villa or country house of which Pliny has left us a full description does not give us any appearance of symmetry . . . there are too many buildings assuming the air of Grecian or Roman temples, with the aid of sham decoration that is as vulgar as false jewelry."

By arguing for professionalism in design, pattern-book outfits of the late nineteenth century also helped create the physicianly status architects now enjoy. In a passage that echoed Downing's antebellum disdain for carpenter Gothic, the Pallisers mocked "the ignorant village carpenter" who lacked an aesthetic: ". . . all he knew was what he had done before over and over, and in which the houses are made up of white boxes with green blinds. Such men as these are stumbling blocks in the way of architecture in the village and the country, and we would strongly advise any one who intends to build to let such men severely alone." Instead, the Pallisers declared, householders owed it to their families, their communities, and themselves to hire architects to build houses—not only to see that the resulting dwelling pleased the eye and satisfied every practical requirement, but also to make certain it safeguarded inhabitants' physical well-being. "The profession of an architect is closely identified with that of public health, and as sanitarians in the construction of every kind of building, whether it be a stable, private dwelling or public building, the vastness of their responsibility is at once evident," they write.

Fearing the mail-order boys would steal all their residential business, architects like Robert W. Shoppell began to counteradvertise. Designers' efforts to promote "real" architecture still used the Queen Anne model. In a before-and-after study of an expanded Greek Revival house run in *Modern Houses,* Shoppell noted that "the large front veranda is new, and with its twelve-foot-deep secluded bay, formed by the staircase hall, is a feature that is much liked; the side veranda was re-modelled to conform to the style of the other changes."

But no matter how hard the professionals tried to steer carpenters into more elegant designs, the tradesmen kept on building what they and their customers wanted. According to architect Marian Griswold van Rensselaer, it was, thanks to climate and resources, ingrained in Americans to construct fanciful houses with big porches and loads of ornamentation. "Our more freely social, more lavish, more varied and complex ways of living cannot find full and truthful expression in any colonial pattern, nor our growing love of art full and lawful satisfaction," van Rensselaer wrote, urging architects to embrace and refine the vernacular styles that people loved so much.

Ultimately, though, pattern-book publishers' influence would fade, as mass-production building took hold. Lithographers like Currier & Ives would lose their hegemony to photography. But the message about the porch would go on, muted but persuasive, transmitted subliminally through the blossoming medium of advertising. In a reaction against the increasing fussiness of Victorian design, the Arts and Crafts movement would encourage Americans to think of themselves as people of the outdoors, linked to the landscape and the seasons by the front porches—sometimes open, sometimes screened—on their newly popular bungalow-style houses. And, in the 1880s and 1890s, with a flourish echoing its classical ancestor's origins as a forum for public debate, the American porch would come to stand front and center in the political arena.

Balloon construction, combined with the easy availability of mass-produced wood-work, enabled Victorian-era builders to turn out enormously eye-pleasing forms.

CHAPTER TEN

UBIQUITY

In the summer of 1880, facing a tightly contested presidential election, the Republicans needed a gimmick.

It shouldn't have been this way. The party of Lincoln had held the White House for twelve years. Their candidate for the 1880 race, James A. Garfield, had all the credentials a candidate could want: a fatherless and impoverished childhood on a farm (he was even born in a log cabin, the last presidential nominee to wear that badge), upright adolescence and young manhood as a scholar and teacher, charter membership in the Grand Old Party, election to the Ohio legislature, combat at Shiloh and Chickamauga, and eight terms spent in the House of Representatives building a reputation as a radical Republican, on the basis of which the Ohio legislature sent him to the U.S. Senate.

But the Republicans were in disarray. Inflation-plagued incumbent Rutherford B. Hayes had declined a second term because he knew his party wouldn't give him the nod. Despite all his attributes, Garfield was a compromise choice, only picked by the bosses after thirty-five ballots couldn't swing the convention to either James G. Blaine or Ulysses S. Grant—neither of whom, it must be said, was free of taint.

The Democratic nominee, Winfield Hancock, was no match for Garfield as a politician; he'd never run for office before. However, when it came to a military record, Hancock could go toe-to-toe with the Republican, having ended the Civil War, like his opponent, as a general. And considering the ire that Hayes and Grant before him had aroused, simply being a Democrat was a big asset. With Reconstruction three years dead, the Democrats had begun to think of the former Confederacy as "the Solid South," a likely foundation from which to effect a restoration to power. Add the lingering scent of Grant's slime-spattered tenure as president, mix in the economic woes that had sunk Hayes, and it was clear why James Garfield needed whatever help he could get to win the Oval Office.

Reconstruction, charges and countercharges of corruption, and inflation had worn away the nation's patience, persuading Republican tacticians to decree a new approach. Rather than haul their candidate around the country like a tame elephant, they would keep him at home—literally. Garfield would stay in his own house on the outskirts of Mentor.

There, visibly linked to his Buckeye roots, Garfield could project the dignified and earnest image of a family man, a yeoman son of the soil, a Cincinnatus waiting for the call to serve. He endorsed the gambit. Years of working in Washington and campaigning to stay there had allowed him little time with his wife and children. He also was happy to stay at home. When he'd bought the place four years before, it had been a dilapidated farmhouse; Garfield dramatically enlarged it, wrapping the old structure in a Queen Anne–style renovation whose focal point was a vast front porch.

The boys from the GOP liked that porch. They could envision the candidate on it, speaking to crowds of his fellow Americans. But how to get those fellow Americans to Garfield? No problem—the railroads, a mainstay of the party, agreed to build a spur line from the station in Mentor proper to a spot behind the house and to provide passage at low or no cost. Visiting delegates, en masse or individually, could disembark, walk around to the porch, and cheer as Garfield uncorked a few chosen words. Even better, the Garfields had enough land at the front of the house to let the gentlemen of the press— whose publisher bosses also were staunch GOP members—observe the spectacle. There were no living accommodations, but the journalists could pitch tents.

The scenario played out perfectly. Garfield spent the summer and fall on the porch, meeting and greeting individuals and addressing enthusiastic crowds of farmers, tradesmen, veterans, and other interest groups shipped in on the temporary spur line.

One day might bring seven railcars of Germans; another, 1,880 members of the Indianapolis Lincoln Club, uniformed in long linen coats and tricornered straw hats. Once, the Jubilee Singers, from all-Black Fisk University, came to sing spirituals. "Visitors were charmed by scenes of unpretentious domesticity," writes historian Allan Peskin. "Garfield's aged mother rocking on the back porch, pitting cherries; the candidate himself perched on a window sill playing the hose on his naked sons; the entire family playing word games around the dinner table."

Garfield's performance, quickly tagged "the front-porch campaign," was duly reported by the scores of journalists camping on their allotted turf, delighted to file essentially the same story every time. They nicknamed the candidate's property "Lawnfield," a sobriquet that sticks to this day. Reporters genuinely liked Garfield, a personable fellow always willing to deliver a usable quote. Politicians had always played the family card, but Garfield literally played with his family, tossing the baseball with his sons, squirting them with the hose, and relaxing on the porch, which often found its way into the text of newspaper stories and the photos and engravings run by illustrated weeklies.

The front-porch campaign strategy worked—barely, but it worked.

In November, Garfield squeezed past Hancock, winning by 9,644 votes. However, he took 215 electoral votes to Hancock's 155, and he went to Washington the following March for a presidency both brief and tragic. On July 2, 1881, Charles Guiteau, usually described as a "disgruntled office-seeker" but in reality a lifelong Bible-banging lunatic who combined the worst aspects of John Brown and Arthur Bremer, approached the president in the capital's train station and shot him. Garfield's wounds became infected; eighty days later, he died. Republicans mourned him as a martyr, and GOP strategists never forgot the utility of the front-porch campaign.

That tumultuous sequence, with its mixture of hominess and violence, brought the United States to the apogee of the uproarious period Mark Twain called "the Gilded Age." During it, pioneers and soldiers and settlers carried the flag toward the Pacific. The South began its post-Reconstruction descent into Jim Crowism. The cities went industrial, with immigrants filling their tenements and factories. Around these urban complexes spread widening tracts of suburb. And in those suburbs, styles of single-family housing continued to evolve, all beneath the tent of a grand mode of living named for the queen who'd held the English throne since 1845.

In America as in England, the Victorians conceived and applied complex codes of behavior and symbol intended to advertise personal status while reinforcing public decorum and preserving private life, especially the life of the family. A Victorian house was a series of chambers, each with its own degree of access as well as concealment.

The most public was the front porch. The term "porch" had finally, thanks in part to the late, lamented president's widely publicized campaign strategy, gained a margin of favor over "veranda" and "gallerie." But behind the façade, there were vestibules and front parlors and back parlors, as well as front stairs and back stairs, the former for family and friends, the latter reserved for servants, who existed, like so many of the grittier aspects of Victorian life, behind a screen of assumed invisibility.

That was eminently true of the backyard, which in the latter nineteenth century was a miniature industrial zone, dotted with coal and wood piles, ash mounds, garbage heaps, stables and their animal ordure, outhouses and their human waste—not to mention, even inside the city line, the occasional chicken coop. Like the mutually exclusive worlds of the Eloi and the Morlocks that H. G. Wells would portray in *The Time Machine*, the Victorian household was separated into one place of beauty and quietude and another of rank, clangorous reality. Further down the economic chain, those worlds overlapped more closely. But even at the lower echelons, houses still presented a unified front of porches.

Whether they were shotgun shacks or mansions, houses built around the United States in the 1880s almost invariably had front as well as back porches. The rear porches, on the first floor, were for food preparation; those on the second, for sleeping.

Users of these structures became accustomed to seeing their lives refracted in what they read. What handbills and posters had been to the early 1800s, mass-circulation magazines and newspapers were to the century's later decades.

The porch began to be an object of backward-looking affection whose power was attested by that most nakedly self-interested of media, advertising. Then as now, ads aimed to sell by the most efficient means available at a particular moment. When viewed in hindsight, the settings they employed, the images, body language, and characters all constitute a visual record that shows us what the people who spent money to make and place ads thought would persuade consumers to buy.

Advertising historian James B. Twitchell says one of the elements that influence consumers is brand, which literally can mean the design burned into a heifer's hindquarters or the logo identifying the maker of a purse or pair of jeans. But for Twitchell and other advertising experts, "brand" is a more complicated matter.

"A brand is a story that can be told in many formats," Twitchell told me. "When we think of stories, we think of prose—with a beginning, a middle, and an end. But images are also stories. They tend to be logos, like the bull's-eye on the Coke can or the Nike 'swoosh.' The story exists below that level, and it's built on ads. If the brand is the story, then the ad is the individual sentence. But the porch is a brand that is built on a slew of stories that are highly evocative. They are so reminiscential, so nostalgic—and there is nothing more powerful than nostalgia. The porch has become a subverbal brand."

In fact, the porch was a subverbal brand more than a century ago. A series of ads collected by Edgar R. Jones in *Those Were the Days: A Happy Look at American Advertising, 1880–1930* shows how uses of the porch in promotional contexts mirrored its status across a fifty-year span.

An 1883 ad for the White Mountain Hammock Chair, made by the Goodell Company, touts that contraption's economy, durability, and superiority to ordinary outdoor-seating gear. The illustration shows a man and woman each enjoying a hammock chair. He lies supine beneath a tree branch from which the device hangs, reading a newspaper with his straw boater casually laid on the ground; she is demurely seated on the porch, upright in a chair suspended from a ceiling hook and reading a book, with a fan in her left hand. Their yard has a picket fence. The only other house shown is on a distant hill.

A 1905 ad extends the metaphor of leisure, showing a Gibson Girlish matron and pinafore-clad child on a luxurious porch with stone railings, spindles, and newels, multiple columns gathered at the corner, and no other houses in sight. With Daughter's blocks and picture book at her dainty feet, Mother sits in a wicker chair. She and Daughter seem a bit wary as they regard a swarthy, mustachioed man, clad in suit and tie and wearing a fedora. With one foot on the step below and one extended onto the landing, he stands and takes notes. Is he a reporter? A pollster? A policeman?

No, he's the delivery guy from the grocery store, and he's writing down what she's saying so he can assemble her order and deliver it. "After you have given the grocer's man your order for tea, sugar, flour, coffee, biscuit, breakfast food, eggs, and vegetables, add 'And a quarter's worth of Ivory Soap,'" the copy reads. "Ivory Soap is the handiest thing you can have around the house. You can use it in the bathroom, in the washroom, in every bedroom, in the kitchen, and in the laundry. There is no better soap than Ivory—none which is at once so economical, so pure, or which can be used for so many different purposes."

Ads like these worked because so many people had porches, and they used them so often. In the South, of course, the porch was the only solution for the summer. After the Cause was Lost, those proud piazzas and gorgeous galleries fell into disrepair—though, lacking cash to improve or replace them, southerners made a virtue of impecuniousness, maintaining their homes in shabby gentility as reminders of what the Yankees had done.

Not only in the South but around the country, summer unleashed critters that enveloped households in winged clouds. "Swatting insects was an impractical solution to the summer invasion of flies, mosquitoes and their kin that turned the farmhouse into a buzzing, biting bedlam. In fact, there was no solution," writes Otto Bettmann in *The Good Old Days—They Were Terrible!*

Help came in the form of a byproduct of the Civil War, a surplus of the horsehair screening material from which sieves and strainers were made. Pondering the dark, heavy stuff, some anonymous thinker realized the fine mesh passed air as easily as water, and set the material in a frame that let a window stay open while keeping out insects. Soon frames were being made large enough to protect an entire porch, and wire mesh replaced horsehair. One observer called screening "the most humane contribution the nineteenth century made to the preservation of sanity and good temper."

(Screens also increased the degree of privacy afforded occupants of porches, to the delight of courting couples who realized that once everyone else had departed for the interior of the house, they were free to sneak a smooch or even more. "Spooning," which during the Civil War had meant the practice of soldiers huddling together in the field to stay warm on cold battlefield nights, took on a more romantic association.)

Every economic stratum had its porch. The sweetest might have been the front porch on a farmhouse, with the fireflies winking and the cows lowing in the barn, and all around the quiet dark countryside. The meanest wasn't a porch at all, but the roofless, naked urban stoop—at once the most minimal of liminal spaces and the most social. If you were out on your stoop on the Lower East Side, in West Baltimore, or in downtown Philadelphia on the half-day each week that you didn't have to work, you were available for social interaction. Whoever came down the sidewalk was bound at least to acknowledge your presence—a pattern that, once set, has never faded.

Different incomes meant different forms of porch life. Working-class families sprawled across their porches seeking respite from the summer heat. Middle-class suburban ladies served one another tea. Managers and businessmen unwound from the rigors of the office, relaxing with cigars and drinks. The homes of the wealthy often paired the porch with a *porte cochère*—a voluminous shelter, tall enough for a horse-drawn carriage, that had the added benefit of making the house seem larger than it was, at a fraction of the cost.

Great public porches graced resorts like the Homestead and the Greenbrier in Virginia's blue-tinged Appalachians, Mohonk Mountain House in the Shawangunks of the Hudson Valley, and the Great Hotel on Mackinac Island in Lake Huron. These and similar establishments boasted long, deep porches—at 800 feet, the Great Hotel's was a world beater—on which guests seeking the fruits of the Gilded Age could congregate and promenade or repose in splendid isolation.

For some of the wealthiest Americans of the 1880s, isolation was a way of life. On Key West, the island at the tail of the Florida archipelago, a cigar-making industry had sprung up, making the former pirate's nest and whaling station, now home to a U.S. Navy base, the wealthiest city, per capita, in the country. Each year, made of Cuban leaf by Cubans who toiled to the dulcet voice of readers narrating the classics, a hundred million stogies were rolling out of Key West, and the money was rolling in. Local swells could trade boasts with visiting millionaires from up North who came for the warm waters, the superb seafood, and a taste of Caribbean life. Key West was only one mile by four, so land was dear. Streets were narrow, with small lots and the high probability that a *nouveau riche* might live in a splendid Queen Anne next door to a tiny place owned by a cigar maker, wreck salvor, fisherman, or smuggler—"conchs," as they called themselves, after the fierce, tasty mollusks that made up much of their diet. But no matter what its size, the Key West house had to have a porch. Recalling their Bahamian background, owners often painted the trim on conch houses in bright Caribbean shades, a style that made its way onto the gingerbread adorning the porches of the rich folks' mansions.

As Caribbean architecture and Victorian design were flowing together on Key West, a new dwelling form was emerging at another bastion of American recreation—Cape Cod, the sandy peninsula that juts east from Massachusetts. The design owed its name and its basic form to the Anglo-Indian bungalow. The cutline with the picture in *American Architect and Building News* simply read "bungalow," but this two-and-a-half-story house was taller, wider, and more muscular, less concerned with fitting into the land than with looming, albeit amiably, over it—more American, you might say. Its lines blended the eye-pleasing detail of the Queen Anne look with the casually elegant Stick style. The magazine drawing shows a man and a woman standing on the bungalow's deep, wide wraparound porch facing into the waves and wind, looking like a rough for one of Winslow Homer's paintings.

The design had instant appeal. Fabulously appointed bungalows went up by ones and twos on estates in the Adirondacks and other bastions of wealth. Pattern-book architects like Arnold Brunner were soon touting bungalow summer cottages whose verandas—"a particular American feature," Brunner claimed—let occupants commune with nature, a pastime that had become popular after the Civil War and that emerged as a key element of America's version of Arts and Crafts design.

In the second half of the nineteenth century, the porch was a near-ubiquitous fixture on houses at all levels of American society.

The Arts and Crafts movement began in England as a backlash against industrialism and mass production. It was led by John Ruskin and later William Morris, who argued for the primacy of human over machine.

Ruskin was a neurasthenic dilettante, anachronophiliac social theorist, and best-selling author who helped foster the Gothic Revival movement with books like *The Seven Lamps of Architecture* and *Stones of Venice*. In these epic works, he issued edicts along the lines of, "Never encourage the manufacture of any article not absolutely necessary, in the production of which invention has no share. . . . Never demand an exact finish for its own sake, but only for some practical or noble end. . . . Never encourage imitation or copying of any kind except for the sake of preserving records of great works." Ruskin went from being a best-selling author to a crazed scold. Madness slowly engulfed him. At the end, all he could write was his name.

But before Ruskin lost it, his theories animated a generation of English aesthetes. One was William Morris, a bourgeois boy who became an architect, then threw that career path over to become a painter. Unable to find furnishings suitable for a brick house he'd had built, Morris began designing furniture, adopting Flemish painter Jan van Eyck's motto, *Als ik kan* (The best I can). The experience inspired Morris to found a community of craftsmen making high-quality handmade furnishings at affordable prices. Morris & Co. became a carpet-to-chandeliers decorating center; wares included the eponymous Morris easy chair, stained-glass windows, fabrics, rugs, and wallpaper Morris himself designed as part of his belief in "art which is to be made by the people and for the people, as a happiness to the maker and the user." The firm set an august standard for quality and preserved skills on the verge of extinction, but as a business, it was a massive flop. Morris had more success when he founded Kelmscott Press, publisher of fine-art books and handmade paper and bindings. He died in 1896.

With their manifestos and pronouncements, Ruskin and Morris struck a chord. The magazines *House Beautiful, Studio, International Studio,* and others took up the cry they'd raised, kindling excitement in the United Kingdom and the United States and encouraging the emergence of the Arts and Grafts and the Bohemian movements. With their intense but vague ideologies, self-professed "crafters" and bohemians decried modernity and convention, trading heavily in symbol and regarding home design and self-expression with religious fervor. Like Marie Antoinette playing shepherdess, both camps revered the rural retreat. This became the next big thing in housing, as builders and developers realized people would pay to live year-round in bungalow suburbs that offered the illusion of the boho life.

"What is a bungalow?" asked British architect R. A. Briggs, whose designs expanded the bungalow by adding stories and balconies. "Our imagination transports us to India . . . to low, squat, rambling one-storied houses with wide verandahs, latticed windows, flat roofs, and with every conceivable arrangement to keep out the scorching rays of the sun. . . . Or else we think of some rude settlement in our colonies, where the houses or huts built of logs, hewn from the tree and with shingle roofs give us an impression, as it were, of 'roughing it.'"

Americans found this romantic blather as entrancing as had their English counterparts. Along with the notion of the veranda as a respite from the cares of life, what they were hearing about the centrality of the porch was reinforced by the 1892 presidential campaign. Another Republican, Benjamin Harrison, adopted the front-porch strategy—as an incumbent. Having beaten incumbent Grover Cleveland in 1888, Harrison endured the loss of the House to the Democrats in 1890. When he stood for re-election two years later, it was in the midst of populist discontent and strikes. Trying to placate voters, Harrison stayed home in Indianapolis, riding the porch in front of the now-standard manufactured crowds, while Cleveland tried to unseat him. Harrison's image— he was known as "the human iceberg"—may have been more than lemonade and cookies could overcome. This time, the porch magic that had worked for the martyred Garfield didn't take, and Cleveland crushed Harrison in the electoral college, 277 to 145.

After that defeat, the Republicans might have been expected to set aside the front-porch strategy. But four years later, with the country still in conflict, they not only revived the technique, they carried it into the entirely new medium of moving pictures. At a time when Americans were embracing the Arts and Grafts movement and its emphasis on bungalow living, "movies" made the front porch once again the focus of American politics.

The sheer force of faddism propelled the bungalow from its origins as a vacation place into the mainstream of American residential architecture.

CHAPTER ELEVEN

GLORY DAYS

The final presidential election of the 1800s presented Americans with a stark choice and a set of deeply resonant images of the front porch, thanks to the old GOP campaign method. Despite Benjamin Harrison's defeat in 1892 using the "front porch" strategy, the Republicans once again were preparing to set their man on a porch, hoping the strategy could overcome their candidate's personality—and with good reason.

The country was split East from West, progressive from conservative, farmer from urbanite, and the cause was money. The Panic of 1893, with its drain of gold from treasury vaults, had triggered a ruinous depression. Populist Democrats, strongest in the Midwest and West, believed a monetary standard relying on both silver and gold would revive the economy. Bankers and Republicans, who controlled the East, wanted to hew to gold.

Though they held the House and Senate, the Democrats, whose ranks were filled with silver enthusiasts, had turned on their incumbent president. Grover Cleveland opposed the silver standard to the point of engineering the repeal of the Sherman Silver Purchase Act of 1890. Gracelessly booting Cleveland, the silver-bug Democrats had nominated William Jennings Bryan, a fist-pumping, tub-thumping thirty-six-year-old populist. Accepting the nomination, Bryan, who backed unlimited coinage of silver, had thundered, "You shall not crucify mankind upon a cross of gold!" The cry became his theme as he crisscrossed the country by rail, speaking to ever-larger crowds. Darkhaired, vigorous, and animated as only a true believer can be, Bryan would lean out over lectern or railing and let fly that incendiary line, and the adulatory hordes would be his.

GOP candidate William McKinley, on the other hand, was a man so measured of demeanor as to induce snores. His speeches, sonorous, oh-so-reasonable, and calculated not to alienate but to encompass, could put a pick-pocket to sleep.

Tall, handsome, thoughtful, politically savvy, determinedly centrist, and in person a warm and engaging fellow, McKinley was practically James A. Garfield reborn. He'd served honorably in the Civil War, returning to Ohio to become first a lawyer and then a district attorney. Six terms in the House had earned him a reputation as an effective moderate, a coalition builder, and an advocate of high tariffs. He won Ohio's governorship in 1891 and 1893, a springboard to collecting the GOP presidential nomination for 1896.

But at the podium McKinley was distant and lifeless, a man of the establishment. Old-seeming at fifty-three, he was in no way inclined or equipped to joust with the rambunctious, relentless Bryan, Boy Populist from the Prairies.

McKinley had other reasons to dislike the idea of racing from whistle-stop to whistle-stop. Since their two daughters' deaths in childhood, his beloved wife, Ida, had lived in the grip of constant despair. He was reluctant to leave her for any length of time.

But what if the campaign made an asset of McKinley's rootedness, his phlegmatic demeanor, his devotion to hearth and spouse?

Chief handler Mark Hanna and his adjutants could see how their man's mien, with its blend of elements from the genial Garfield and the frosty Harrison, might lend itself to a front-porch campaign, this time abetted by a Republican-controlled media establishment grown far larger and more influential than the press had been fourteen years before.

Goodness knows everybody knew the routine well enough: instead of sending the candidate out to meet the people, the party would let the people—observed by the press—come to meet him. The idea appealed to McKinley, who knew his limitations and wanted to play to his strengths. "When I make speeches, I want to think," he told a campaign manager. "I can't roll them off a megaphone, as Bryan does. Furthermore, we can in traveling greet and meet comparatively few people in the country. Therefore, if every day I say something which I have had time to think over carefully, a large majority of voters will read that statement each day, and in the meantime, I will avoid great fatigue."

So instead of tearing around chasing votes and taking the risk of confirming the suspicion that he was pure-heartedly dull, McKinley stayed put on his porch in Canton, Ohio. His home was close enough to the railroad station that, unlike the Garfield campaign, the railroad men didn't have to build a spur line.

Arrangements were made. Schedules were confirmed. The McKinley front-porch campaign began as soon as the party solons sent him a telegraph reporting that he had the nomination. (In keeping with the statesmanly pose, the candidate didn't sully himself by attending the convention.)

As the summer unfurled, McKinley and his front porch became synonymous. Each day, he would rise like an actor sleeping backstage, dress and eat breakfast, and then pass through the screened door into public life, delivering formal remarks to groups wrangled in like so many herds of prize heifers by Hanna and his elves. Or the candidate might chat with whoever dropped by. "I rang and walked in," an English reporter wrote. "Mr. McKinley was sitting on a rocking chair not ten feet from the door . . . he is gifted with a kindly courtesy that is plainly genuine and completely winning."

It was rope-a-dope, political style. Through the dog days of August and into

September, while Bryan careened around the country, growing hoarse shouting about the cross of gold, McKinley remained *in situ*, a presidential presence amid the wicker and the woodwork, welcoming visitors with lemonade and conversation, urging Americans to quell their regional spats and to support tariff protection that would revive the economy, yadda yadda yadda . . . read the texts, and you'll practically keel over where you sit.

Periodically, the Republican would rise from his shade-graced chair and stroll into the yard to address whatever congregation the Hannites had assembled, while the press, grateful not to be trying to keep up with the peripatetic Democrat, took notes. Though their stories were all the same, they were always printed and always read. A cycle took form that has never abated.

"McKinley's 'front porch' campaign was a very big deal," said Jonathan Auerbach, a professor at the University of Maryland who has written extensively on the 1896 race. "It's the first mass marketing of a presidential candidate in American history. The Republicans know they're outclassed. Bryan is highly respected and an eloquent speaker. Hanna figures out that the best strategy against Bryan is a 'front porch' campaign, which means McKinley stays put at home in Canton, while the party brings in all these delegations to see him. Hanna can do this because the Republicans control the railroads and the media. So they bring in these delegations to visit McKinley. He's sitting on the front porch, they come, and he walks out and addresses them. The reporters love it. They don't have to travel around."

The campaign also traded heavily on Americans' emotional associations with the front porch, wrapping McKinley in the cloak of sentimentality at a time of crisis, when voters wanted to identify with the man they were electing.

"Politically, what is interesting about the front porch campaign is the interface between public and private," said Auerbach. "It's McKinley's house, and he walks out to the front lawn, where public and private meet, creating this nostalgic image of the president not as politician but as family man. It works well."

The 1896 campaign was an epic struggle. Bryan made some 600 stops; he spoke to 5 million people in an election year that saw 6.4 million men vote. McKinley's tally of face-to-face and face-to-crowd encounters was only 750,000, but his captive brigade of reporters delivered a stream of stories that showed millions of readers the candidate in the context of his home, his family, and his small town.

And McKinley had a new tool, one previously unavailable but essential ever after. He was the first presidential candidate to appear in a campaign film, which helped carry him to the White House and cement the image of the porch as an American icon for good and all. Every time you see an ad in which an earnest person sits or stands on a porch and importunes you for your vote, or a utility or soap company shows you a porch as part of its agitprop, you're encountering the ghost of William McKinley.

The porch film came about through the candidate's younger brother, a figure familiar in any family: feckless, reckless, given to marginal schemes that chronically fail, perhaps for the better, since in Abner McKinley's case they included selling bogus railroad bonds and touting a technique for making fake rubber. Billy Carter and Roger Clinton would have found Abner a kindred spirit.

But Abner had had the wit to invest in a film company, American Mutoscope and Biograph, whose other angels included the vaudeville impresario Oscar Hammerstein and former president Benjamin Harrison, who loathed and feared Bryan and the populist hordes. These *machers* and Abner McKinley were unlikely partners, but their partnership led the younger McKinley to observe how enthusiastically audiences responded to the one-reelers being screened in movie houses. He suggested that a film might be made of his brother and circulated to the nickelodeons to reach voters. Hanna and the other GOP operatives mulled the notion. In September 1896, they invited American Mutoscope founder W. K. L. Dickson and camera operator Billy Bitzer to Canton to stage and document a re-enactment of McKinley receiving the news of his nomination earlier in the summer.

With Dickson directing, Bitzer set the camera in the candidate's front yard. The perspective was at a medium distance from the porch, splitting the frame between house and lawn. Dickson explained to McKinley what he wanted to see happen. With the steady-handed Bitzer at the crank to keep the action even and smooth, McKinley hit his marks while the moviemakers filmed a bit of political eye candy entitled *McKinley At Home, Canton, Ohio*.

It's an Indian-summery day. The grass and the foliage on the shrubs and trees are still lush. The shadows are long, but whether from early or late sun, you can't tell. Dressed alike in black suits, McKinley and his secretary, George Cortelyou, stand by the porch, which is in shadow, three low steps up from the lawn. The camera doesn't move, but the men do, looking at the lens as they walk toward it, making no effort to feign nonchalance. They move the way old people, who grew up without constant exposure to photography, used to slow and exaggerate their gestures to help the camera do its job. McKinley pauses and puts on his hat. As Cortelyou looks on, the candidate dons spectacles and squints down at a piece of paper. He examines the sheet, then talks with Cortelyou. McKinley doffs his hat and mops his brow, then looks at the camera. The two walk again, moving out of frame at the right.

It was a mime of the routine McKinley had been doing for months, emerging from his porch like a clockwork figure, making an appearance, departing. Only now the act, once on view only in Canton, could be seen anywhere, anytime someone flipped the switch on a projector. McKinley the Candidate had become a replicable event, taking a giant step toward the commodityhood essential to the creation of movie goddesses, best-selling authors, rock stars, rap moguls, and presidents.

McKinley At Home runs less than a minute; you can see a version of it on the U.S. Library of Congress Web site. However, watching this clip on a small monitor in the privacy of home or office can never match the thrill the audience must have felt when Dickson premiered it the evening of October 12, 1896, in New York City.

Even before the lights went down at the Olympia vaudeville house (owned by Mutoscope investor Oscar Hammerstein), the film was a sensation, previewed in emphatic detail by pro-Republican papers. Reporters who'd attended an advance showing weren't quite sure how to describe this, this, *this . . . thing . . .* in which a candidate running for office by staying at home in one place "appeared" in another place in the form of shapes and shadows flickering on a screen. In their articles, newsmen sounded like the journalistic equivalents of those mythical viewers who, watching a film of an incoming locomotive, reputedly dove out of harm's way, or, seeing a six-shooter pointed at the lens, supposedly ducked for cover.

"Major William McKinley will appear tonight in New York before a great throng of people, which will include members of the Republican National Committee," reported the *Mail and Express,* cautioning that the "candidate" would not be speaking. "The distinguished statesman will make his appearance, apparently on the lawn of his house in Canton, full life size, and in action so perfectly natural, that only the preinformed will know that they are looking upon shadow and not upon substance."

In an illuminating *American Quarterly* article, Auerbach notes that the *Mail and Express* story is a stab at proto-McLuhanism, as the newsman struggles to wrap his brain around the notion of pictures that move and people who are not present seeming to be so. The journalist's own confusion about what is real and what is not is apparent in his descriptions: "The picture thus shown is not flat—in fact it cannot be distinguished as a picture at all—there is no clicking noise to disturb the illusion, and prosaic indeed is the mind that can look upon the rapidly shifting scenes and believe it to be unreal. Major McKinley is likely to get an ovation to-night when he advances to the floodlights."

The film bore out predictions. At the Hammerstein, a full house watched *Stable on Fire, Niagara Upper Rapids,* and other shorts of the sort familiar to frequenters of nickelodeons. Then the projectionist rolled *Empire State Express* (a locomotive running at the camera—mythopoesis time!), footage of a parade staged in McKinley's honor, and finally, the much-ballyhooed, albeit extraordinarily brief, political feature. At the sight of McKinley's image, the crowd burst into shouts and applause. The next day's press accounts drew parallels between the big train charging at the lens and the big man walking past it. Until now, the faces moviegoers had seen on the screen had been those of actors or anonymous workaday subjects. Now a man who would be president, who wanted them in some way to know and trust him, was coming to them, looking at them, walking past them, through this mysterious medium.

Screened repeatedly in New York, Baltimore, Chicago, New Haven, and St. Louis, *McKinley At Home* sent viewers and reviewers into paroxysms. Audiences cheered. Commentators palpitated. Articles on the film tended to use words like "wild," "roar," "frenzied," and "pandemonium." During the show, some viewers, overcome by the simulacrum, called out for the image of the candidate to make a speech.

McKinley's campaign gambit further enshrined the front porch as an icon, thanks to its accidentally exquisite timing. Arriving as Americans were beginning to fall in love with the new medium of film, *McKinley at Home*—short and sweet and unbelievably simple, a template for billions of feet of home movies—drew huzzahs, not only boosting interest in the medium but in McKinley, who enjoyed a bounce in newspaper coverage as more reporters watched more people watch *McKinley at Home.*

"Film was perfectly in keeping with the front porch strategy," Auerbach says. "Every time people saw him walk out from the porch to the front yard, it was new, so it was news." Within a few years, sitting in a movie theater had become as natural an American act as sitting on the porch, but in 1896 Americans were uncalloused enough that Billy Bitzer's Simon-simple short could wield immense power, by keeping the candidate on his porch and in his yard and simultaneously transporting his image around the country.

McKinley won the election, 271 electoral votes to Bryan's 176 and 7,113,734 popular votes to 6,516,722. As president, the Ohioan became a regular in newsreels that circulated among theaters, helping him to get re-elected in 1900.

But on September 5, 1901, in a bitter echo of Garfield's demise, anarchist Leon Czolgosz shot William McKinley at the Pan-American Exposition in Buffalo, New York. McKinley died a few days later, succeeded by Vice President Theodore Roosevelt, who took the oath of office in Buffalo, on the front porch of the Wilcox family's mansion on Delaware Avenue. However, thanks to his brief campaign film, William McKinley lives on, perpetually stepping off his front porch and into history.

"Given the disembodied immediacy of the moving image, McKinley can occupy both spaces at once, so that 'home' comes to stand for the place of reception as well as the image's presumed geographical referent. The vaudeville house turns into home," Auerbach writes. "By choosing to film their candidate in an intimate domestic setting perfectly in keeping with their campaign strategy, and then continuously disseminating this image, the Republicans in conjunction with the Biograph Company and its exhibitors thus helped to redefine traditional public/private dichotomies. Moving from his house across his lawn to greet his audience, McKinley negotiates the space between home and country with the lawn functioning as interface between the two; the candidate's stroll thus serves to domesticate public spectacle by bringing national politics to everyone's collective front porch."

The McKinley campaign's use of the front porch as a political image dovetailed perfectly with developments in American housing at the end of the nineteenth century. Though the porch had been a part of domestic life for decades, it was gaining even more prominence, thanks to the Arts and Crafts movement and the growing affection for the bungalow and the informal style of living that this hybrid house design implied. The bungalow craze had many uncles, but its father was furniture maker Gustav Stickley, who during the 1890s had helped make "Arts and Crafts" a household word.

As a boy, the Wisconsin-born Stickley learned stonecutting from his father, who skipped when Gustav was in his teens. His mother moved the family to northern Pennsylvania, where her brother owned a chair factory. Gustav went to work for his uncle. He liked messing about with wood, and he liked to read, especially John Ruskin's stentorian calls for a return to the values of the medieval guild and the craftsman.

In 1886, Gustav and two of his brothers started making Shaker-style chairs in Binghamton, New York. Using a crude lathe rented from a broom-handle manufacturer, the Stickleys cut components and built and finished each chair by hand—not out of artistic obstinacy, but because they had no alternative.

("The very primitiveness of this equipment made necessary by lack of means, furnished what was really a golden opportunity to break way from the monotony of commercial forms," Stickley later wrote.)

The chairs sold well. Stickley Brothers Co. prospered, but the itchy Gustav left the firm. He jumped jobs several times—at one point, he managed the shops at the state prison in Auburn, New York, where, legend has it, he built a prototype electric chair—before opening another furniture plant in Syracuse. His success with that endeavor allowed him to travel to England in 1898. William Morris was dead, and John Ruskin was mad, but the American craftsman met artisans of like mind, and he saw examples of new furniture with an old attitude. He returned to his factory in Syracuse full of ideas. In autumn 1899, Stickley made ready to start the new century with yet another change. He meant to replicate what he had seen Arts and Crafts mavens doing in England: making furniture that emphasized quality over commerce.

Stickley's company, Craftsman, used the mortise-and-tenon joint, a pains-taking technique that employs precisely cut and placed holes and pegs. The firm produced armchairs, dining and library tables, benches, and other designs. Workers branded the underside of each piece of furniture with an image of a joiner's compass and the motto William Morris had borrowed from van Eyck, *Als ik can*. Craftsman furniture was angular, blocky, solid, and straightforward. Made of honest woods like cherry and oak, it was eminently attractive to Americans sated with the latter Victorian days and their over-the-top interiors crammed with parquetry, marquetry, curvy, swervy ormolu, and dust-magnet bric-a-brac.

In England, Arts and Crafts had been a minor market, but the United States was an enormous and growing country that needed a lot of chairs, tables, and even-armed settles, as sofas were called. Stickley furniture—and Stickley-like furniture, some of it made by Stickley's own brothers—became the rage, and having pursued a path that chose craftsmanship over profit, Gustav Stickley made money hand over fist.

With his revenues, Stickley started a magazine, *The Craftsman* (motto, "The lyf so short the craft so long to lerne"). Each month, he contributed a philosophical column. *The Craftsman* publicized Craftsman furniture, of course, but it also covered crafts of all nations, as well as gardening, education, and city planning. Circulation boomed, and so did furniture sales. On a visit to California, Stickley saw buildings with inflections of the old Spanish missions and their shade-making *portals*. He liked the look enough to start working it into his furniture.

Life itself was Stickley's inspiration. After a fire at his home, he had to refit, so he began to design interiors. They went into the magazine, too. From interiors, *The Craftsman* expanded to exteriors, carrying house designs that readers could purchase. In 1904, Stickley started The Craftsman Home Builder's Club; members had access to plans for building houses. Options included central vacuuming systems and hoists for hauling ashes from the cellar. You could buy your light fixtures and hardware from Craftsman. The magazine showed you how to finish the woodwork. The designs distantly echoed the English Arts and Crafts look—steep roofs, small-paned windows—but the wooden shingles and full front porches were *echt* American.

As Mary Ann Smith notes in *Gustav Stickley: The Craftsman,* Stickley was reversing the route his English confreres had taken. They had been architects who started making furniture when they couldn't find any to suit the houses they'd designed; Stickley went into architecture because he couldn't find a house to match the furniture he made.

The houses Stickley designed weren't, strictly speaking, bungalows, but they would be, since "bungalow" was a term, like "Arts and Crafts," that was about to acquire flexibility of meaning in California, where so many American meanings change.

The next time Stickley went to the Golden State, he found it rampant with what one writer dubbed "bungalow fever." Drawn by the sunshine and sweet air, folks from the rest of the country were flocking to southern California. Housing was in very short supply, and builders like Henry Wilson were ready to accommodate with the design that earned Wilson the nickname "The Bungalow Man"—small, thin-walled, front-porched houses, inexpensive to build and easy on the eye and wallet.

Elsewhere the bungalow might have been a vacation place, but on the West Coast it was an everyday house that filled suburban neighborhoods. Marketing had transformed the little Indian hut into a product; however, thanks to the gift of imagination, the bungalow retained the connotation of living close to the land.

"The bungalow is the renewal in artistic form of the primitive love in a cottage' sentiment that lives in some degree in every human heart," a pattern-book writer gushed. "Architecturally, it is the result of the effort to bring about harmony between the house and its surroundings, to get as close as possible to nature."

Bungalow neighborhoods were usually set at the edge of town to take advantage of lower land prices. Low and horizontal, those neighborhoods made a pleasing visual transition from the right angles and verticality of the urban mass to the undulant countryside, as if providing a note that filled out a chord played on an architectural piano.

Patented January 11th, 1881.

Since the early days of mass media promotion, the porch has had a prominent place in the advertiser's armamentarium.

On his research trips, Stickley saw the entire gamut of California bungalows, from low-priced, mass-built specimens to the elegant custom creations of Charles Sumner Greene and Henry Mather Greene, Pasadena's master designers. The Greene brothers, whose houses were beloved of the shelter magazines, often incorporated Asian elements into their designs. Contemplating the Greene & Greene houses and other designs that mixed the Mission and the bungalow looks, Gustav Stickley saw the future. And then he came home and went to work.

Soon *The Craftsman* was showing its version of the bungalow: an ell, with a porch along the interior of the angle, that looked vaguely western and wholly American. Readers loved it. But Craftsman houses didn't always go bungalow, in look or in language. They tended to be a story and a half, with a dormer or a sleeping porch (one of Stickley's pet touches) at the front of the second floor, above a front porch stretching the width of the façade.

(Besides being sold as an amenity by Stickley, the upstairs porch acquired a halo of healthfulness. In Saranac Lake, New York, physician E. L. Trudeau promoted screened porches as a treatment for tuberculosis; the open air was supposed to fight the disease. Trudeau dubbed his creation the "cure porch." The concept spread west to Denver, where developers built Montclair, a neighborhood of single-story, cure-porch-equipped houses. Less fanciful Denverites called them "tuberculosis houses.")

For country residences, Stickley suggested what he called a cooking porch: ". . . an outside kitchen is most convenient as it affords an outdoor place for such work as washing and ironing, canning, preserving and other tasks which are much less wearisome if done in the open air."

The Craftsman reached many thousands; so did the Building Club. No one knows how many people built houses with the plans they ordered or how many had the Stickley firm build houses for them, since for a year or so the company was in the contracting business. But Craftsman-style houses did exist in enough numbers around the United States to suggest that Gustav Stickley's campaign on behalf of Arts and Crafts–style living, bungaloid or not, had succeeded. He claimed that people spent twenty million dollars building houses from his plans.

Stickley felt his furniture work had led organically to house design and his vision of houses as vessels of family well-being. "Thinking and working along these lines, the houses I planned naturally began to take on certain aspects of country and suburban living—big porches for outdoor work and rest and play, dining porches, sleeping balconies, pergolas and other garden features that would link the interior closely with the outdoor life," he writes. "The next thing that suggested itself was that people, instead of living in houses built merely for speculation, should plan and build and own their own homes— even the people who could afford only a little four- or five-room cottage or bungalow."

By following this path, Stickley put himself close to, if not at, the head of a cast of characters who promoted the bungalow in America. As *The Craftsman* was trumpeting the style, so were pattern-book authors like William Comstock, Henry Saylor, and Frederick T. Hodgson. Architecture and women's magazines praised the bungalow's snug profile and intimations of security. And commentators praised its porch, not only for the visual appeal it contributed but for the way it enhanced family and community life. As Clifford Clark notes, "Here was a house with which middle-class Americans could easily identify."

That sense of identification began with the front porch, which symbolized a potential for living differently, with a sense of adventure and novelty (sound familiar, my fellow SUV owners?). In his book *Bungalows, Camps, and Mountain Homes*, Comstock described the porch as the focus of bungalow household life. As such, he said, porches deserved as much attention to decor as any other room received: "They should be broadly built, furnished with screens, against the wind or sun, and well supplied with easy chairs, hammocks, and all the paraphernalia of an outdoor summer parlor, for here will be gained the object of the bungalow, the utmost benefit of life in the open air."

The craze intensified as writers went into panegyrics over the pleasures of the California bungalow and its porch, embedding them in the national consciousness as emblems of the good life in that storied state. "We were sitting on the porch after a good luncheon, enjoying the warmth of a sunny winter afternoon," writes Charles F. Saunders in *Sunset* magazine. "There was a fragrance of daphne blossoms in the air and the music of humming bees. Beyond the lower end of the garden where the young folks were playing tennis in white flannels, was an orange-grove hanging heavy with its Hesperian fruit, and beyond that, across the green mesa rose the majestic range of the Sierra Madre, its crest white with snow. Now and then the ecstatic note of the meadowlark floated down the air, and on every side mocking-birds were whistling. Automobiles, filled with pleasure-seekers, whirred by on the street, and occasionally a horse-back party of tanned young men and girls bare of arm and head cantered toward the mountains in gaiety and good health."

More caustic scribes hailed the bungalow suburb as an antidote to the dark, dirty city. With coverage like this, the hook was set. Not all Americans could move to Southern California, but the bungalow was moving to them, spreading from its West Coast bastion across the United States.

The architecture profession scorned mass-built bungalows—that is, until designers saw that the style worked so well in so many ways for so many participants in the housing game. The form lent itself to endless interesting variations, as architects tweaked the lines to look Colonial, Moorish, Swiss, Dutch Colonial, Japanese, Mission, or whatever, still keeping the sweet, unassuming front porch and low roofline. Builders could put up bungalows at minimal cost in materials and labor. The design fit with little or no trouble into a wide variety of settings; local or regional forms evolved, like the "Chicago" bungalow, a working-class brick variant. And developers could sell those cute little houses with ease because people were wild to buy them.

After the Victorian era and its corseted strictures, endless rules of behavior, and pickily parsed living spaces, Americans were eager for informality, openness, clean lines, and less muss and fuss. More people than ever lived in or near cities. They longed for the charms of the country that the bungalow conveyed through its naturally finished wooden floors, trim, beams, railings, and balusters, and its orientation to the outdoors, via the porch.

Houses got smaller. The average $3,000 house occupied 1,000 to 1,500 square feet, compared with the 2,000 to 3,000 square feet of its 1880s counterpart. On such compact dwellings, front porches lent a much-needed sense of spaciousness that enhanced their traditional role as a place of greeting, relaxation, and entertainment.

Especially entertainment. With automobiles still few in number, walking was the main means of locomotion, whether to the corner store or the streetcar stop. In the evening, people amused themselves by going out for a stroll or sitting on their porches and watching other people stroll. In bungalow neighborhoods, where economics dictated small lots and shallow setbacks, front porches served as a line of box seats for the passing human show. Anyone who has spent time in the company of Americans of a certain age knows the litany of recollection: the summer nights on the front porch, the conversations of the adults at their end and the uproar of the children at theirs, the rasp and chitter of the bugs, the call-and-response chorus of greeting and counter-greeting exchanged with passersby, the young gentleman caller appraised, the kiss stolen, the last long look into the black sky before turning off the porch light and going to bed. (James Agee later captured this moment in his prose-poem "Knoxville: Summer of 1915," a memoir of a childhood evening when he felt life's bittersweet blend of permanence and transience: "Parents on porches, rock and rock . . .")

But even as the porch was nestling into the American consciousness with such a sense of comfortable permanence, changes were at hand that would lead the country to abandon the porch, neither as suddenly, utterly, nor, necessarily, as a result of the factors you might think.

You might have expected me to mention air conditioning, eventually, but did you know that air conditioning came into being back in 1902, when Willis Carrier installed an experimental cooling system in a Brooklyn publishing plant? After the device not only lowered the air temperature but reduced humidity, Carrier heard from engineers Stuart Cramer and I. H. Hardeman. Both were from the South, and both enthused about the prospects there for Carrier's invention. In 1906, Cramer coined the phrase "air-conditioning"; the same year, Hardeman helped Carrier design and install an air-conditioning system at a Belmont, North Carolina, cotton mill. That example had a revolutionary impact in Southern industries where temperature and humidity were a factor; soon, mills and factories across the region were air conditioned.

Cultural symbolism aside, the South's taste for porches mainly had to do with nature. As U. B. Phillips writes in the first sentence of his classic 1929 study, *Life and Labor in the Old South*, "Let us begin by discussing the weather, for that has been the chief agency in making the South distinctive." As long as they could remember, southerners had been struggling to stay cool; at many antebellum plantations, one of the biggest annual expenses was ice. But after more than 200 years of fighting the heat with dog-runs, breezeways, galleries, piazzas, porticoes, and plain old porches—and in the process developing an elaborate set of social rituals and practices to go with them—the South became an early adopter of one of the phenomena that would all but extinguish life on the porch.

The light bulb went on; if you could cool down cotton and beer, cigars and sugar, bread and rayon, why not humans? Air conditioning began to infiltrate hotels, theaters, and restaurants, and then railway cars. It was only a matter of time and technological development before it reached the home and pulled folks in off the porch.

But before that could happen, the porch had started to disappear for other reasons.

At the peak of its popularity early in the twentieth century, the porch began to shrink, a harbinger of its eventual disappearance from house fronts.

Chapter Twelve

TEETER

If you were to ask what killed the American porch, most people would blame air conditioning or television. Some would indict the social patterns that gestated in the suburbs that spread across the nation after World War II. Others would point to the automobile-induced hyper-speed pace of modern life at large. Each answer is marginally correct, and, like nails of varying size and weight, each can be found in the lid of the coffin into which the porch slipped.

But no single pathology did the porch in. There is strong evidence that, long before a preponderance of American households had the central air, the big color set, two cars in the suburban driveway, and double incomes on the tax return, the porch—at least, the porch as we'd known it for a hundred years—as a center of family life, neighborhood socializing, and community connection, as well as a slice of Americana—had begun its slide into the dustbin of architectural history.

The decline started around the time World War I erupted, but it required thirty years to reach its conclusion.

When Europe got out the guns of August 1914, the bungalow was still wildly popular in America, its porch-oriented style of living firmly entrenched in American culture and headed for an even greater presence. But, like all such phenomena, the bungalow fad was bound to end. Meanwhile, architects working for fashion-forward clients were drawing plans that showed the influence of a new, porchless European aesthetic, along with that of a school of domestic design that took its cues from the bungalow but turned them inward.

The bungalow's eventual fall from favor had its foreshadowing in its foremost proponent's career. Gustav Stickley traveled a particularly American highway to hell, paved, as always, with the best of intentions. Having created a new style in home furnishing, launched a successful magazine, sold mountains of furniture and reams of house plans, and altered the way America looked, Stickley didn't know when to quit.

He moved his operation from Syracuse, New York, to Manhattan, building a twelve-story headquarters at 6 East 39th Street, near Tiffany's, with eight floors of salesrooms, a restaurant, library, lecture hall, offices, and workshops.

Then, recalling how his idol, William Morris, had created a craftsman's guild, but forgetting that the wealthy Englishman had had to subsidize his firm from start to finish, Stickley founded a cooperative. He bought 650 acres near Parsippany, New Jersey, announcing plans for a school and farm. Apprentices would grow their own food, make their own crafts, and construct their own residences as they learned from the master. Stickley got as far as erecting an oversized log cabin with a big screened porch, but after a few years of supplying food for itself and the restaurant at headquarters in Manhattan, Craftsman Farms foundered. Stickley sold the property.

His clunky chairs and tables, with their vast expanses of satin-smooth wood finish, had had a good, long run, but Elsie De Wolfe and other designers were starting to have success with sleek, elegantly painted stuff. Stickley tried a line in that vein, but the hybrid look didn't sell. The Craftsman tower proved to be a money pit. Stickley's pet forum, *The Craftsman* magazine, withered. In 1915, Stickley filed for bankruptcy.

(After that, it was all over but the dying. Stickley went to work for another furniture maker, Simmons Co., then with his brothers. But they fell out, and he returned to Syracuse to live with his daughter and her family in his former home. Ensconced in a third-floor apartment, Stickley spent his days fiddling with finishes; the plumber regularly came to snake pipes that the old man's concoctions had clogged. When Gustav Stickley died in 1942, he left no will. It was no matter; there was nothing to divvy up. But his legacy was immense: the firm his brothers started still makes the mortised and tenoned furniture with that signature electric-chair look. Each September, enthusiasts gather at Craftsman Farms to celebrate Stickley's ideals, and at the start of the twenty-first century, houses in the Craftsman style were all the rage.)

Although the Craftsman furniture look began to fade with the onset of World War I, house buyers were still infatuated with the bungalow. Their enthusiasm persuaded mass merchandisers to adopt the Craftsman approach and produce houses in kit form, with every last rafter and screw included in the package. Purchasers could assemble their homes themselves or hire contractors. Sears, Roebuck, Aladdin, Montgomery Ward, and other companies began selling bungaloid kits.

Each line of assembly-line dwelling had uniform dimensions, but customers could customize the interiors and exteriors, especially the front porches, to achieve a degree of individuality. Considering the houses' diminutive scale and the fact that many of their front doors opened straight into the living room, the porch gained even more importance as an entry and living area, where occupants would greet and often entertain guests or relax and watch the world go by.

The popularity of kit houses convinced mass-market developers that the time was finally right for them to start building bungalows. "Developers take no chances. They're making a tremendous investment in what they're building, and as a result are quite conservative. They'd rather be safely second or third than first. Few of them are innovators or inventors; they're going to try to sell what will sell," said Jeff Limerick, an architect in Boulder, Colorado, who was writing a history of the American house between the two world wars. "The bungalow offered a tremendous design for affordable housing. Most developers produce what will sell—which means what was popular ten to twenty years before."

But the house form that had reached its peak ten years before was just fine with builders who were aiming to capitalize on the postwar boom that was bringing millions of new home buyers off the farm and into the cities and suburbs.

Now that it had reached the mainstream, the bungalow became *the* American house of the 1920s. Even in neighborhoods where there weren't any bungalows, people loved the little houses. In downtown Baltimore, rowhouse façades often had only bare stoops (called "steps") that exposed the living room windows to prying eyes. An artistically inclined grocer, William Oktavec, had the idea to paint scenes on window screens, brightening a house's exterior while shielding occupants' privacy. Painted screens became a local hallmark, and screen painting became a tradition adopted by Oktavec's sons and other Baltimore folk artists. The image patrons requested most often was a rural setting that featured . . . a red bungalow.

The bungalow image seemed to be everywhere, even on the radio, where jazzman Bix Beiderbecke sang of a "bungalow of dreams." When his character Nick Carraway needed housing that fateful summer of' 22, F. Scott Fitzgerald knew his Americana well enough to make sure naïve Nick rented a "weather-beaten cardboard bungalow" next door to Jay Gatsby's mansion. The Hardy Boys and the Bobbsey Twins were always joining their chums at somebody's bungalow for a frolic that was bound to evolve into intrigue.

And the bungalow finally did become an American vacation home on a grand scale—in numbers, anyway. The Rockaway strand on New York City's Atlantic shore filled up with mile upon mile of unheated bungalows catering to the city's proletariat. With the ocean and the subway station only blocks from one another, a family could spend Memorial Day to Labor Day at the seaside on a workingman's wage. Other New Yorkers went west, to the Hudson River Valley and the Catskill Mountains, where bungalow colonies multiplied. Some belonged to unions or fraternal orders, others to entrepreneurs; all charged a modest rent for a vacation house that always included a screened porch where guests ate, played cards, and often slept.

But despite these trappings of permanent acceptance, the bungalow was being consigned to the past. As Gustav Stickley was heading for his hubristic peak, a young Midwestern architect was inventing a new kind of house. Instead of reaching out to the street as Victorian dwellings' madly flung effusions had, or calmly welcoming the world from wide, deep porches in the manner of Craftsman bungalows, Frank Lloyd Wright's designs cast the house as an intimate cavelike setting, withdrawn from the public realm.

Wright's houses, with their low ceilings, massive fireplaces, earth-tone fired tiles, and tactile wood surfaces, offered an emotionally satisfying experience that contrasted with the other coming thing in design—the new European house, whose minimalist façades and purposefully barren rooms reinvented the home as a geometrical grid on which to simplify and purify human experience by purging it of *fin de siècle* excess. Art Deco, the Bauhaus, and the International School would expand on those themes, as practitioners like Le Corbusier, Walter

Gropius, and Mies van der Rohe, determinedly working outside history, brought forth the sleek (some said featureless) and sophisticated (some said soul-killing) look that became Modern-with-a-capital-M architecture.

Another porchless form was coming from the opposite direction, out of the West, where the vernacular design of California had evolved a nonbungalow strain of house that wove together several threads of design, including Spanish colonial, the shacks of pioneers and prospectors, and ranch bunkhouses. This low-profile, low-key dwelling charmed *The American Architect*. "It never put forth any great claims of merit, it never really entered the lists to establish itself as the vogue. Apparently it just grew, naturally, inevitably, a logical result of meeting definite needs in the most direct, workmanlike manner possible with the materials at hand," writes Henry H. Saylor in a 1925 article for the trade magazine. "It borrowed none of the finery of other architectural style; it sounded no blatant note of self advertisement; it never, so far as I know, laid claim to a name, and yet there it stands, a vernacular that is unmistakably a part of the California foothills. . . . Unfortunately, there were few of these ranch houses compared with the multitude of suburban bungalows, and they were usually well off the beaten track where their quiet influence could have little effect on public taste."

But even before the Bauhaus became our house (thank you, Mister Wolfe) and long before the ranch house came into its own, the American home was losing its front porch. I began to suspect this while scanning back issues of architectural and design magazines, and I had those suspicions confirmed in a conversation with Jeff Limerick. Leafing through books from his library as we spoke on the phone, Jeff explained that the shift began to be noticeable after the Armistice.

"The change is a fuzzy one," he said. "You see porches shift position from front to side or rear. The floor plans show the porch shrinking, becoming vestigial. It still offers protection from the elements, but moving into the thirties it becomes smaller and smaller until it's a bump on the face of the house."

Jeff ticked off the designs he was eyeballing: a porchless 1925 Georgian with terrace-like concrete pad at the front, garage integrated into the body of the house, back porch leading into kitchen; Monterey Colonial, old-school Spanish and very conservative, the California equivalent of an East Coast house in the Colonial style, with no porch but with an upstairs balcony ("These are never used," Jeff said. "There are a few Monterey Colonials in Denver that are useless in our climate, a total disaster."); an English Tudor, half-timber and stucco exterior, front porch a skimpy five by seven ("A pretty common design. You couldn't put a chair on this porch to save your life, but it does protect the door a little, and it provides a welcoming gesture to the street"); a French-flavored foursquare box, with vestigial porch—a piece of molding over the door—in the middle of a huge terrace.

"What I see in the houses of this period is a turning away, the beginning of a period in which the house is considered more private and personal," Jeff said. "The porch lost its social function. Once, people would sit on the porch and greet their neighbors as they walked by. But by the time World War I broke out and just after, people didn't care to do that anymore. Their taste went to privacy, and the porch moved around to the side or, increasingly, the back."

One factor pulling people away from the front porch and its engagement with the public realm may have been the backyard's emergence as a more pleasant place to spend time. As John Jakle shows in *The American Small Town: Twentieth Century Place Images,* the backyard of the early 1900s was a holdover from Victorian days, a miniature agricultural-industrial complex whose chthonic nature restricted its use to garden plot, privy, stable, and storage area for fuel and debris.

However, the new century brought indoor sanitation, which erased the need for the outhouse. Architect Andres Duany suggests that one reason designers and builders may have dropped the front porch was to telegraph the fact that a new dwelling's "conveniences" really were convenient. "People would have known that a house with a porch would be old enough to have an outhouse," Duany explains. "But a newly built house with no porch would be signaling that the toilet was inside."

Other developments further sweetened the backyard's appeal. Gas- and oil-powered furnaces got rid of the coal bin and ash heap. The automobile did the same for the buggy, horse, stable, and manure pile. Supermarkets' stocks of canned and fresh produce made the kitchen garden optional.

Suddenly, the backyard began to look like a place where you might want to be, especially as the street out front became more of an artery for motorists than a leisurely avenue for carriages and pedestrians. But folks didn't just want to sit out there on the grass, and so, like an appendage of a mutating organism, the front porch began to shrink, to move to one side of the façade, then to turn the corner and become a side porch, often enclosed in screens and/or glass jalousies that effectively cut occupants off from the street and vice versa. Finally, the porch retreated to the rear of the house, no longer a public place at all but a completely private location, where you might throw a wingding like the one shown in a 1914 advertisement for the Victor Talking Machine Co. In the illustration, a bunch of swells strut their stuff on a posh and secluded veranda, complete with striped awnings, potted palms, and a prominently placed record player. "Dancing to the music of the Victrola is the favorite pastime. The maxixe, hesitation, tango, one-step—you can enjoy all the modern dances in your own home with the Victrola," the copy reads, suggesting that buying one of these spring-driven wonders will transform your back porch into a scene Jay Gatsby would envy.

Along with being sold sophisticated technology with images of the new, improved porch, Americans were growing accustomed to seeing the old familiar porch as a relic of yesteryear, thanks to its presence in Hollywood productions like D. W. Griffith's.

Griffith, a Tennessean, often spun tales about the War between the States. Griffith's first two-reeler, *His Trust* and *His Trust Fulfilled,* takes place at a plantation; throughout, the only house exterior shown is the front porch. Belles and matrons cluster on it to watch Confederate troops march off, and, after the planter runs to join the rebel ranks, Griffith marks the passage of time by showing the porch at the same angle when news comes of the hero's death in battle and when Federals ravage the farm. Pummeling the faithful darkies (persistent figments of Griffith's imagined South—before *Trust*, he'd made eleven one-reelers on Civil War themes), the bluecoats torch the porch, reducing it to a charred skeleton and a symbol of the region as occupied territory. This is the theme Griffith would revisit to electrifying effect in the 1915 *Birth of a Nation*. "This was not just another picture for Griffith," wrote director of photography Billy Bitzer. "He was fighting the old war all over again and, like a true Southerner, trying to win it or at least justify losing it."

Many of *Birth*'s key scenes take place on the Cameron family's front porch: a rousing segment in which the family watches soldiers parade past; the soulful return of Henry B. Walthall as the defeated Little Colonel, Ben Cameron; and the arrival of grim news that Ben reads as his family looks on in dismay. *Birth* is monumental filmmaking disfigured by a hateful message, but the porch scenes glow with humanity that almost neutralizes the stream of racist bile in which they float.

Griffith made the porch a fixture in his films. In *Way Down East,* people stand plaintively on porches trying to borrow money. They read Bibles in reclining chairs. They peer through windows, sleep, churn butter, flirt, break up, and reunite. In *America,* Griffith has Paul Revere riding onto porches to warn that the British are coming. And in *Tumbleweeds,* D. W. bangs all the porch-related gongs that would become standard horse-opera fare: dusty buckaroos jawing outside the saloon, the anxious crowd at the land office, string bands and magicians cavorting on storefront porches.

Other directors played porches for laughs. In *Neighbors,* Buster Keaton stages one of his trademark chases, which ends when his character hides under a pile of laundry, emerging as a ghostly figure that frightens a family of caricature Negroes from their porch. In *Seven Chances,* prototype for many a beleaguered-bachelor comedy, Keaton plays James, who will inherit a fortune if he marries by a deadline. Before the denouement, he gets chased at gunpoint off a country-club porch, importunes his sweetie's mom on her porch, practices his proposal on another porch, and, in a rare cinematic use of the ecclesiastical porch, confronts a mob of would-be brides at the church. And in *The General* (1927), Keaton sends up the Civil War, using porches as rallying points, parade stands, and meet-cute locations—proving that in Hollywood, as everywhere else, history repeats itself as farce.

Political and porch history did repeat itself in the 1920 presidential campaign, though it's still not clear whether the result was more tragedy or farce. Yet another Ohioan, Warren G. Harding, a boosterist newspaperman turned machine pol, had received the Republican nod. The selection of Harding, a handsome and gregarious but, shall we say, intellectually challenged fellow, had been arranged by GOP bosses in the proverbial "smoke-filled room" at the party's convention in Chicago. The ward heelers were determined to retrieve the White House from the Democrats, who'd held it for Woodrow Wilson's two terms. Wilson wasn't running. He'd had a stroke, and his health was shot. Even if he'd wanted to try to stay in office, fury at his campaign for the Versailles Treaty and the League of Nations would have torpedoed his chances, just as opposition to the silver standard had crippled Grover Cleveland in 1896. Wilson's designated heir, Ohio governor James Cox, was running with his predecessor's record wrapped around his neck like a length of anchor chain.

In some ways, 1920 was an updated version of 1896. Instead of the cross of gold, the issue was the League of Nations, which embodied the scary world emerging in the war's aftermath. Wounds from European battlefields still throbbed. The Czar's fall had let slip the djinni of Marxist revolution; U.S. Attorney General A. Mitchell Palmer had begun his eponymous campaign of raids on alleged Reds. White America, which had watched *Birth of a Nation* over and over for five years—the film's warped hagiolatry of nightriders and lynch artists gets credit for reviving the Ku Klux Klan—stood in angry fear of African-Americans. The summer of 1919 had seen twenty-five race riots (which in those days meant whites attacking Blacks), including a spectacularly violent spasm in Washington, D.C.

Beset and belligerent, the country hungered for familiar tropes. The GOP delivered by keeping Harding on the porch of his house in Marion, Ohio, in the manner of the placid martyrs Garfield and McKinley. Republican operatives even transplanted the flagpole from the front yard of the McKinley house to Harding's home. There, the candidate held forth on an expansive porch built to replace one that had collapsed under the weight of well-wishers hailing his 1899 election to the Ohio state senate. As in 1880 and 1896, in 1920 the parades streamed past, the bunting fluttered, the party hacks applauded—and the photographers and cameramen recorded it all for replay in the papers and the newsreels.

These careful gestures were by way of keeping Warren Harding, a handsome knucklehead with a reputation for womanizing and spoonerisms, from being seen coming out of the wrong hotel room, tripping over his tongue, or declaiming anything more than his minimum daily quota of sonorous platitudes, quotidian pieties, and—the salient theme of his campaign—earnest and ungrammatical calls for "a return to normalcy." Historian Frederick Allen Lewis summed up Harding's campaign as one of "mouthing orotund generalizations from his front porch."

Sidelined by history, Woodrow Wilson—trust-busting reformer, ex–Princeton president, wartime president—could only uncork the ultimate derisory remark. He called Harding "bungalow-minded."

However, in a presidential contest that was more about rejecting Wilson and his policies than electing anyone else, Harding swamped Cox and went from his front porch to the White House. Three years later, on the verge of being swamped himself by a series of scandals, Harding suddenly died. He was replaced by his vice president, Calvin Coolidge; a taciturn but canny politician, Coolidge made a point of being photographed on many a front porch but rarely had much to say from them.

Once the Depression hit in earnest, the American housing market went into a decline that didn't end until after World War II.

Chapter Thirteen

TOTTER

Woodrow Wilson's peevish crack about Warren Harding being "bunga-low-minded"—as if to say that the Republican represented the lowest common denominator, made appealing through the combined effects of ballyhoo and self-delusion—summed up the way the little house with the big porch became first a phenomenon and then yesterday's papers, the architectural equivalent of last season's hem length.

We can't discount the element of fashion in the process of decline that over-took the porch. After being the main event of the American façade for a century, the porch had begun to look dowdy and frumpish, like hobble skirts, derbies, horse-drawn trolleys, and iceboxes. We'd entered the era of the roadster and the electrical refrigerator, for goodness sake! The doughboys had been to Paree; the Jazz Age was on. It was time to get modern, and that meant deep-sixing the porch and its baggage: the claustrophobic small-town values, the creaky Babbittic pronouncements, the puny gossip and meanminded judgments, all the confining stuff Sherwood Anderson packed into *Winesburg, Ohio*. In that 1919 collection of short stories (subtitled "The Book of the Grotesque"), Anderson employed the context of the classic small town to reveal uncomfortable truths. He was writing about his own life in Clyde, Ohio, but he also was writing about America through the eyes of George Willard, a young newspaperman struggling to develop the escape velocity that would propel him out of Winesburg. From the book's first sentence, in which a sad little fat man with the false name Wing Biddlebaum paces up and down the "half-decayed veranda" of the old house where he lives in exile from a miserable former life, you know this won't be a Booth Tarkington tale. The porches of *Winesburg* are not happy or sunny places; newspapers may land on them every morning and neighbors wave from them every afternoon. However, these porches are not refuges but redoubts, where characters hunker under siege from their own existences.

This is not to say that the porch suddenly dropped out of use because Sherwood Anderson had a bad time growing up in a small town or because Scott Fitzgerald portrayed the vampiric Buchanans perpetually slurping gin rickeys on the porch of their mansion in West Egg. It took more than a few jabs by literary gentlemen to knock out a national pastime.

In fact, some literary gentlemen liked places where ordinary people sat out on their porches. In the mid-1920s, novelist John dos Passos was hitchhiking around the country. He fetched up in Key West, Florida, which, having run out of cigar money, had descended to an agreeably impoverished condition. There were a few millionaires around, thanks to the railroad Henry Flagler had built, but in general the island town was rundown and raffish. Dos Passos liked it, and he passed the word to his pal, Ernest Hemingway, who came in 1928. Hemingway loved the place; he wrote A Farewell to Arms in an apartment on Simonton Street, then in 1931 bought a big joint built eighty years before by a wealthy wreck salvor. Hemingway's presence lent Key West and its conch houses a literary glow that would attract other writers like Wallace Stevens, Robert Frost, and John Hersey (although, after a 1935 hurricane wrecked Flagler's railroad, the wordsmiths had to arrive by boat).

By then the Depression had the housing industry in a death grip. With no clients, architects waffled to and fro. They designed a host of looks and styles, none remotely as attractive as the bungalow; developers produced only a few of them. Through the thirties, the disastrously slack market and the law of the known commodity kept those builders who did put up houses sticking to the familiar. (One stark set of exceptions: Greenbelt, Maryland, Greendale, Wisconsin, and Greenhills, Ohio, were all federally funded new towns created in 1937 at the behest of President Franklin D. Roosevelt. The architecture in each emulated the Bauhaus and International School, emphasizing plain exteriors, casement windows, and Art Deco curves and swoops. No porches or neo-Victorian furbelows needed apply.)

People who could afford houses usually bought houses with porches, because the only houses they could afford were old, or abused. In places like Palisades, the D.C. neighborhood where I live, a guy like Melvin Snyder—transplanted country boy out of the hollers of West Virginia, gas company worker, motorcycle enthusiast, good with his hands, and willing to tackle a fixer-upper—could buy a nice little bungalow that dated to the early twenties, probably purpose-built as a rental. The last tenants had torn up the screens and stove in the floor on the porch, keeping the price down to four grand in 1934 dollars. The first thing Melvin did was fix up the porch and hang a chain on swings at one end, so he and his wife, Ethel, could enjoy the evening breeze and listen to the streetcars whoosh past behind the houses on the other side of Sherier Place. In neighborhoods across America, that was the commonplace chorus: trolleys, whickering lawnmower and hedge-clipper blades, kids playing tag, neighbors calling out greetings from sidewalk to porch and vice versa, music from living room radios leaking through open windows or even coming straight off porches, where the console stayed under a piece of oilcloth to keep out the moisture.

Sometimes because it was all they could afford, sometimes because they recognized their intrinsic value, Americans were starting to pay attention to old houses. The saving of Monticello and Mount Vernon during the nineteenth century had presaged a grass-roots trend that surfaced in the 1920s. Local and regional organizations such as the Society for the Preservation of Old Dwellings, created to look out for the antebellum houses and piazzas of Charleston, South

Carolina, and the Society for the Preservation of New England Antiquities took up the cause, as did kindred bodies in Savannah, New Orleans, Philadelphia, New York, and other cities.

Developers and politicians derided the activists as little old ladies in tennis shoes, but those little old ladies knew how to work the wires of government. In December of 1933, the U.S. Department of the Interior and the American Institute of Architects (ALA) collaborated to begin the Historic American Buildings Survey, or HABS. HABS had grown out of a series of bleak assumptions put into print by Department of the Interior official Charles E. Peterson, who expected most of the old structures in the country to disappear and thought Americans ought to at least collect a picture and a history of what was before it stopped being.

"The ravages of fire and the natural elements together with the demolition and alterations caused by real estate 'improvement' form an inexorable tide of destruction destined to wipe out the great majority of the buildings which knew the beginning and first flourish of the nation," writes Peterson in his proposal for the program. "If the great number of our antique buildings must disappear through economic causes, they should not pass into unrecorded oblivion." The first HABS project was a ten-week field study that employed 772 architects whom the Depression had put at leisure.

The local interest in preserving historic structures that had spurred HABS into existence was refracted and intensified by federal mandate. ALA chapters helped states create offices to assure that buildings deserving attention didn't come down without having their picture taken. In 1935, the Historic Sites Act established a way to get historic landmark status for structures.

But this modicum of reverence for the past—remember, the original point of HABS was to get pictures of buildings that everyone expected to see demolished—didn't stop Americans from putting the porch into the past tense. Manufacturers continued to shine life back at itself in advertisements for products that once would have been pictured on porches, but no longer were. International Correspondence Schools had a fictional satisfied student declare, "The Proudest Moment of Our Lives Had Come!" when he, his wife, and his daughter could stand in front of the house they had just bought—a terraced-entry bungalow with a vestigial porch off to the right. Paint manufacturers and kit-house makers, whose business depended on being able to recognize changing tastes in residential architecture, got wise. A Devoe Paint and Varnish ad shows two distinguished fellows looking at a bedraggled, porchless façade. One of them is saying, "Jones Must Be Broke." After decades of showing porches in its promotions, Aladdin, the prefabricated-house manufacturer, began to feature angular, flat-fronted Tudoresque façades.

An influential book heightened sympathy for the sharecroppers of the South while causing readers to thank their lucky stars they didn't live anywhere near or in anything like the hovels shown in the photographs Walker Evans made to illustrate James Agee's *Let Us Now Praise Famous Men.* Evans's riveting pictures of the Tengle, Burroughs, and Fields families on the porches of their dog-run shacks elicited groans of guilt and anguish—but they didn't make anyone want to add a front porch. And Agee's sweet but sad 1938 remembrance, "Knoxville: Summer of 1915," evoked the porch life of yesteryear as one might a dead parent: beloved but gone forever.

Movies showed the porch as historical artifact or bastion of cinematic fantasy. With millions out of work, scores of thousands at loose ends, and the nation in a slough of despond, audiences sought the escape that only a night at the movies could deliver—brave tales of earlier days and harder, preferably more uplifting, times, as well as utterly fictional representations of life in a current-day small town—"... that mythical Midwestern town Hollywood keeps somewhere among its sets," as John Updike would later write. "The houses were white, the porches deep, the lawns green, the sidewalks swept, the maples dark and blowzy against the streetlights."

Fans were happy to visit those towns in films like the *Andy Hardy* series that starred Mickey Rooney. Andy lived with his mythical clan in a little town whose inhabitants were a funny bunch. They constantly dropped references to Shakespeare, Sheridan, and Cyrano de Bergerac. The elders spoke in pseudo-aristocratic accents. The kids, who had no accents at all, were able to conceive, rehearse, and produce a costumed musical show in twenty minutes, despite having to take time out to operate push mowers, juggle Indian clubs, jump white picket fences, and loll on front porches, the latter a given as the setting for dramatic encounters, such as the opening of *Andy Hardy Gets Spring Fever,* in which Andy's would-be sweetheart, Polly Benedict (Ann Rutherford) entertains a Navy lieutenant on her family's porch glider, setting off ninety minutes of hijinks.

More serious films also employed the porch to telegraph a sense of Americana—sometimes with grandiosity, as in the pillars of Tara portrayed in *Gone with the Wind,* sometimes with gritty neorealism of the sort John Ford portrayed.

Ford liked one porch so much he used it in both *The Grapes of Wrath* (1939) and *Young Mr. Lincoln* (1940).

In *Grapes,* the porch scene comes once the Joads hit the road, lured west by a flyer advertising fruit-picking jobs in California. After a wretched day's travel, they stop at a campground. Family members join a crowd at the store, whose porch is held up by peeled tree trunks. Connie (Eddie Quillan) leans against a column, strumming his guitar and singing. Preacher (John Carradine) sits on the ground in front of Tom (Henry Fonda), who stands with his back to a sign announcing it costs fifty cents a night to camp. The white placard gives Tom's head and shoulders a square halo. A kerosene lamp shines on men standing on the porch. It also illuminates the store's worn clapboard siding, one board of which sports a deep crack. As folks chat about their prospects, Pa Joad holds up the flyer, saying he and his are headed for the big money. One by one, the other men pull out their copies of the iniquitous sheet, and so does a dream die, only one among many on this story.

The mythical porch at Tara, where Scarlett O'Hara (Vivian Leigh) entranced the Tarleton twins, rekindled fantasies of the Lost Cause and its vanished grandeur. Courtesy of MOMA.

Young Mr. Lincoln's porch scene is upbeat. At midday in a small Indiana town, an exuberant politician standing on the porch of a general store introduces a candidate for town council. Rousing himself from the bench on which he's been reclining, Lincoln (Henry Fonda) rises, and rises, and rises, unfolding like a carpenter's measure to stand at the leftmost porch column. Resting his big right hand on a spot where a branch was lopped, he addresses the crowd with folksy charm. Behind Fonda and beneath his extended arm, you can clearly see that same piece of cracked siding as graces the camp storefront in *Grapes*.

Although they were made late in the thirties, as war was nearing, neither *Grapes nor Lincoln* shied away from presenting a harsh view of life in these United States. Once hostilities broke out, though, patriotic themes prevailed. In the flag-waving category, an early entry was Howard Hawks's *Sergeant York*, in which Gary Cooper played the Tennessee marksman who began the Great War as a pacifist but won a Congressional Medal of Honor for croaking 120 Germans in a single engagement. Knowing his protagonist would have to evolve into a bloody-minded and unrelenting warrior—the real Alvin York dispatched some enemy soldiers with a pickaxe—Hawks had to make him human. The director did so with a meandering but powerful introduction that showed the shootist as a dutiful son, hard-working farmer, and persuasive lover, a rugged American gem observed in a naturalistic setting.

When Alvin comes to court Gracie Williams, the camera looks out across her family's rustic porch toward a backdrop of rolling uplands and buttermilk sky. In the near distance stand a split-rail fence and gnarled tree with an old wagon wheel leaning against its trunk. Alvin, wearing a battered fedora and overalls and carrying his muzzle-loading long rifle, arrives to find Gracie, played by Joan Leslie as saucy and beautifully coiffed but barefoot and clad in homespun, entertaining Alvin's rival, Zeb. After Alvin runs Zeb off, he gazes at Gracie, she seated on a bench and he leaning on the porch railing, as close to one another as hill-country propriety permits. Gracie seems interested but wary; despite his pacifist leanings, her suitor has a reputation as a hell raiser. Alvin exudes the calm serenity of a man who has seen the woman he wants and won't rest until he has her. The props—weather-beaten bucket and bench, splintered porch pillar, rough-sawn floor planks—complement the sequence, as do cuts to Gracie's grandfather in his rocking chair, deep in the shadows. The scene is a diagram of overlapping themes—courtship, competition, male ego, female power, and the yielding of age to youth, all lent gravity by being staged on a porch, that place of negotiation and transition.

Along with providing the touch of Americana that filmmakers sought, the porch also generated a theatrical genre in the late thirties. Set at the backs of houses belonging to sisters, Paul Osborn's *Morning's at Seven* mixed the drama and comedy of ordinary life. The "porch play" had arrived. "In this category of play, almost every set had a porch, because the subject was Middle America, and the playwrights were trying to portray a certain stratum of society," said National Public Radio critic Bob Mondello. "They were mostly about how wholesome everything was, or about how everything was not nearly as wholesome as it appeared." (In 1980, a Broadway production of *Morning's at Seven*, whose cast included Nancy Marchand, won a Tony for Best Revival; the play again returned to Broadway in 2002 and again drew raves, confirming its durability and that of the form. Latter-day users include August Wilson, who set many scenes on front porches in the Pittsburgh neighborhoods where he located his plays.)

In 1939, with the economy starting to recover, the housing market picked up slightly, but it had left the porch behind. Resuming the trend that had stopped when the Depression began, porches shrank, moved to the sides, or around back. Brick "colonial" houses—flat front, pedimented entry door, cosmetic shutters—made their debut. A house might have a screened porch at one side and on the other, a jalousied sunroom that was sometimes called a "Florida" room, in honor of that state's reputation as a locus of leisure, an echo of the old Palladian dependencies that made a house look broader and more substantial.

One American homeowner did cling to the traditional notion of the porch. Midway through his second term in office, president and amateur architect Franklin Roosevelt designed Top Cottage, a Dutch-style country house near his home at Hyde Park, New York. Roosevelt's plan featured a big front porch—handicap-accessible, at the disabled FDR's specification. One afternoon at midsummer 1939, during a state visit by King George and Queen Elizabeth of England, FDR invited his guests to visit him at his newly built cottage. He served the royal couple hot dogs, ham, turkey, and draft beer—a picnic on the porch that, all parties agreed, was the highlight of the trip.

Two months later, Germany invaded Poland.

In his Depression-era photographs of the deep South, Walker Evans captured the particular pain of a people, a region, and a country in the grip of a paralyzing depression.

By the time World War II was over, the porch had been consigned
to the dustbin of American architectural history.

CHAPTER FOURTEEN

FALL

World War II barely touched the physical United States—here a Japanese incendiary balloon, there a German torpedo—but the war so thoroughly penetrated the national consciousness that afterwards nothing was as it had been.

From weaponry to statecraft, politics, race relations, media, manufacturing, popular culture, and individual Americans, the country changed utterly, and few areas changed more utterly than residential architecture. It was as if, to paraphrase Winston Churchill on the benefit of being shot at and missed, the conflict had served to concentrate architects', builders', and consumers' minds, focusing them on a future in which the American house would stand apart from all that had gone before.

Immense pressures drove the search for new places and ways to live. Wartime production had left the Depression in the dust. Fueled by the salaries of war workers and the profits they generated, the economy had galloped to record levels. However, the growth that erased unemployment on the home front involved manufacturing, not housing; in 1944, fewer than 150,000 houses went up. During the war, the issue of how and where Americans would live after the war got modest attention. The German and Japanese surrenders caught planners off-guard.

"Although both consumers and building-material manufacturers in the early 1940s had begun to plan for postwar housing expansion, peace was declared before either business or the public was fully prepared," writes Clifford Clark. In 1945, with 13 million veterans back home or headed there, 3.6 million families lacked a permanent place to live. Hoping for some of the benevolent effect it had obtained in the thirties with the Federal Housing Authority, Congress passed the Serviceman's Readjustment Act—the "GI Bill"—creating a system of Veterans Administration loans that vets could use to buy, build, or rebuild houses.

But what would those houses look like? Though eager for civilian life, veterans were not of a mind to step blindly back into the traditions they'd fought for. The guys ditching their combat boots might have grown up in timeworn inner-city houses with rickety alleyside porches like the one in Norman Rockwell's wryly celebratory "Homecoming GI," but that didn't meant they wanted to spend the rest of their lives in joints like that. Mainly, what GI Joe knew about his future house was that it had to be new. His outlook suited the period's architects, who mainly wanted not to have to refry the beans of accepted style. Everybody was after the same thing: something different.

That was what J. Holocoup Blandings and his wife, Muriel, wanted. Mr. and Mrs. Blandings were the protagonists of Eric Hodgins's best-selling 1946 novel *Mr. Blandings Builds His Dream House,* a satire that began as a short story in *Fortune* magazine and, upon expansion to book length, captured the era's fascination with new houses.

The Blandings are Manhattanites, from the Upper East Side. They've survived the war. He's doing well in the ad game at Banton & Dascomb, and they decide to live upstate, on Bald Mountain. For $11,550, they buy an old farmhouse and some acreage, a hopeful purchase that turns into a comic nightmare. The farmhouse is too decrepit to save; they tear it down and build new, a house that is supposed to resemble the old one but only in spirit, with a sun porch instead of a front porch. Indeed, when a neighbor builds a place visible from the Blandingses', Mrs. B. gets soused and complains about it: "A horrid little house with two rooms and a porch *right on the road*."

Though porchless, the Blandingses' dream house winds up looking a lot like what it replaced, which was the story with much of post-World War II American development. Despite wild flights of architectural fancy in the trade journals, the most popular designs harked back to historical precedents.

The new forms that domestic housing did take bore the fingerprints of Frank Lloyd Wright, whose prewar usonian houses and suburban subdivision plans had anticipated the designs and methods of the postwar housing boom. They also owed much to Cliff May and other West Coast designers, who had synthesized an attractive look from California's pioneer vernacular and Spanish colonial. *The Field Guide to American Architecture* calls this category "neoeclectic." The postwar era called it the "ranch house," reviving the term *The American Architect* had used twenty years before to praise the no-nonsense style, which was about to assume a far more prominent place beside its only real competition, the Cape Cod.

The Cape Cod–style house had come to America with the Pilgrims, and its longstanding appeal was understandable. The design's steep roofs efficiently shed rain and snow, and its minimal mass—with interior entry "porch," room to either side, and upstairs loft—was easy to build, heat, and expand upon. Over the centuries, newer designs overshadowed the doughty little house, but it never went entirely out of fashion. The Cape Cod enjoyed a revival whenever the public's taste tilted toward Colonial, which was, most recently, in the twenties. Now the Cape, with its familiar lines and adaptable interior, beckoned again.

But many would-be purchasers preferred the ranch, also called the "rambler" because it spread across a lot larger than those platted before the war. The ranch evoked magical, marketable California. If you edited the sales spiel, swapping "bungalow" for "ranch," you'd hear what ballyhoo artists had said before World War I: cleaner, healthier, better for parents, better for children, better for the entire family.

The ranch also recalled the bungalow in the extent of its success, but unlike the bungalow the ranch house broke with history, along the prewar/postwar fracture line. Prewar America meant neighborhoods where people walked or took trolleys, where life had a slower pace, and the front porch had a point.

The bungalow was *then*; the ranch house was *now*. It spoke to a country that had spent a decade enduring a depression and then four war-weary years stuck on the porch, counting gasoline ration coupons and dreaming of buying a new car and hitting the road. The main feature on many ranch façades was a carport or garage. If there was a porch—and more often than not there wasn't—it was a shallow, narrow shadow of yesterday's model, more like a bus-stop shelter, a temporary deflector of rain and sleet, than a place of conviviality and community.

The ranch had historic precedents. It came out of Spanish colonial architecture and the make-do houses of later immigrants to the West, a heritage flagged by a best-selling 1946 idea book. *Sunset Western Ranch Houses* showed individual ranches alongside rivers, among mountains, and in the foothills. Crooned the editors, "The history of the Western ranch house is the personal history of many families—those of the soldier of Spain, the Spanish Don, the Mexican politician, the deserter from a British brig-of-war, the merchant from Boston, the fur trader, the American soldier, the adventurer, the pioneer."

Ranch-house avatars like May, who collaborated on the *Sunset* book, had established their reputations with custom designs. These were often built in rural locales where, as with the bangla in precolonial India, the setting could absorb a house, particularly one shaped for it. With their low, horizontal silhouettes, picture windows, and back patios—sometimes fitted with redwood or cedar platforms dubbed "decks" for the nautical feel they conveyed—the first ranch houses reached out to the environment long before "environment" became a commonplace word.

Ranches could be compact because they had large windows, glass walls and doors, and exterior features like decks, patios, and breezeways to lend a maximum sense of connection to the outside. "The ranch house, like both its Victorian and bungalow predecessors, was thus seen as creating a unity with nature," writes Clifford Clark. "But it was a unity that pictured nature as a tamed and open environment."

At last *Sunset* and *House and Garden* and the rest of the shelter press had a design to trill for as they had for the bungalow. Mainstream publications, women's magazines, and architectural journals joined the chorus, hailing the ranch as the right house for American families, an imprimatur that would make the ranch (and its offspring, the split-level) *the* American house design from the forties through the sixties.

We Americans are a suggestible people, able to envision ourselves living on the Pacific coast or on old Cape Cod, when where we really live is in a little box of a house among hundreds, even thousands of others, in a grid of quarter-acre lots as flat and featureless as the baize on a pool table. Fantasy could trump reality in part because both the Cape Cod and the ranch allowed occupants to ignore the scene outside. Postwar housing stressed the interior life, with kitchens and dining rooms that flowed into one another and often out onto the back patio. The ranch in particular drew praise as an exciting new type that rebelled against the oppressive bungalow (which, you'll recall, was sold as a rebellion against the oppressive Victorian styles, which were sold as a rebellion against Gothic Revival, which was sold as a rebellion against Greek Revival, which was based on an actual rebellion, which was inspired by the American Revolution). *Sic semper domibus.*

No matter which style it built, the housing industry had a lot of houses to build. To do so required the application of lessons learned in wartime. Housing was now a product, to be churned out like jeeps, half-tracks, and P-38s, with as little trouble and at as little cost as possible. As they had for the tools of war, builders, manufacturers, trade groups, and government agencies set or expanded standards for materials, fixtures, and household components, such as appliances and kitchen cabinets, as well as layout, room size, and location of services like water, heat, hot water, and electricity.

The template was in place. With enough money, materials, and men, house construction had the potential to go from being an adventure in eyeballing and inexactitude to being an assembly-line mode of manufacturing.

At first, mass production of residential structures occurred in fits and starts, and sometimes in real factories. Converting a Midwestern plant that had made bombers during the war, Lustron built and sold more than 2,500 all-metal Cape Cods; appropriately enough, the U.S. Marine Corps bought nearly a hundred of them in pink, blue, and mint green for its base at Quantico, Virginia. However, most Americans didn't want to live in ammunition boxes. They wanted to live in brick and wood, out in the suburbs, in houses that had to be built in place— quickly, and in enormous numbers.

But most builders didn't work that way. They were too small—in 1949, fewer than one percent of American builders were putting up a hundred or more houses a year—and even when builders were large they didn't think big, until William Levitt provided a role model.

Though he was a straight-no-chaser businessman, Levitt could have been chanting the principles Le Corbusier had articulated in his between-the-wars manifesto, *Towards a New Architecture:* "Architecture has as its first duty, in this period of renewal, that of bringing about a revision of values, a revision of the constituent elements of the house . . . Industry on the grand scale must occupy itself with building and establish the elements of the house on a mass-production basis. We must create the mass-production spirit. The spirit of constructing mass-production houses. The spirit of living in mass-production houses. The spirit of conceiving mass-production houses."

Levitt and his brother, Alfred, had started building before the war. Their first project, a 1934 development on Long Island, featured two country clubs and houses costing as much as $18,500. After Bill mustered out of the Seabees, the

Levitts reversed poles, embracing the old Lower East Side maxim, "Sell to the classes, live with the masses; sell to the masses, live with the classes."

Acquiring expanses of potato field farther out on the island, the brothers built Levittown, a workingman's version of the country-club complex, with community and shopping centers and recreational facilities like swimming pools. Levittown would be a suburban city-state, an affordable haven for families, thousands of which besieged the sales office.

To move the merchandise, the Levitts organized construction crews as if managing an assembly line, achieving such speed and precision that they could complete 180 houses a week, or one every fifteen minutes—ranch or Cape, picture window, open-plan interior, $7,900 per. Guys buying on the GI Bill put no money down and made fifty-six-dollar monthly mortgage payments. Levittown houses sold as fast as the paint on them dried, and as soon as you could say "federally insured mortgage," other builders were adopting Levitt's building methods, financial arrangements, and pricing structure.

Of course, to keep prices low, something had to go, and a lot of things did go: entry vestibules (their erasure countered by low fuel prices, storm doors, and weather-stripping), wide stairwells (houses were either one story or didn't need stairs four feet wide; nobody was carrying coffins down them anymore), basements (too bad about the lost storage space and play room, but no more floods), sleeping porches (so old-fashioned).

Front porches.

Especially front porches.

House buyers still wanted porches, they told pollsters. But they no longer wanted porches out front. Set forward on small lots to leave room for patios at the back, suburbia's tiny houses already felt too close to the street, which was no longer a tree-lined promenade but bare and stark, often an artery for fast traffic. Who wanted to sit on a porch and watch cars whiz past? Plus, even a simple porch cost time, labor, and materials, and it had to look right because it was the first part of the house anyone saw. Builders didn't want to absorb costs for features that didn't make a profit. Buyers didn't want to pay the freight. Bye-bye, front porch. No wonder the threnody Samuel Barber composed in 1947, setting to music James Agee's "Knoxville: Summer of 1915." chimed with such plangent finality. There would always come a day when there'd be no more parents, but now it would have to come without the memory of them as they rocked on the porch.

The side porch had been growing in popularity since the twenties, but many suburban houses sat wide on narrow lots where there was no elbowroom. So the porchifying impulse had to circle to the rear.

The media began to refract that trend, with coverage that emphasized new and front-porchless residential designs. Ignored in the news columns, the porch showed up in the funny papers, portrayed as obsolete and tacky, a haven for hicks and has-beens. Lil' Abner and Snuffy Smith inhabited shacks with extravagantly trashy porches; in *Gasoline Alley*, the likable Skeezix and his friends had much nicer porches, but they were old-fashioned folks, relics of a time gone by.

The real old-fashioned folks who lived in and loved real old-fashioned buildings got a boost in 1949, when the government established the National Trust for Historic Preservation. The Trust was empowered to go beyond the documentary charter of the Historic American Buildings Survey; it had funds to acquire treasures of American architecture and encourage the preservation of lesser gems—although at the time, an old house with a front porch wasn't on anyone's list of buildings to save unless George Washington or Tom Jefferson had slept there.

You still saw porches in the movies. When the boys bloodied into men came home from the war—on the big screen, anyway—they came home to the girl next door in a Queen Anne bungalow with a recessed porch who didn't care that her guy had gotten his hands burned off and needed stainless steel claws to fire his .22 (*The Best Years of Our Lives*). Or they came home to a glamorous doll (Claudette Colbert) gamely willing to endure the privations of rural life with Fred McMurray on a back porch outfitted with a sofa (*The Egg and I*). Or they returned to a big city whose occupants spent half their lives on stoops (*A Tree Grows in Brooklyn*). Veterans could identify with the hero of *My Darling Clementine*, in which Wyatt Earp (Henry Fonda) sits on the porch by the barbershop, the very model of what we imagine a frontier lawman to have been, easygoing and well-balanced, right up to the second he shoots somebody dead. Former GIs less inclined to swagger could connect with freshly demobbed bomber pilot Jimmy Stewart as civilian banker George Bailey, re-evaluating a life spent in Bedford Falls, a town that's really one big front porch, in *It's a Wonderful Life*.

If you edited the sales spiel, swapping "bungalow" for "ranch," you'd hear what ballyhoo artists had said before World War I: cleaner, healthier, better for the family.

(*It's a Wonderful Life,* by the way, hints at another reason the porch went out of fashion even as Hollywood was celebrating it. In a scene that has George flirting wordily with Mary Hatch (Donna Reed) as he walks her home, he blathers on until an old guy reading the paper on the nearest porch gets out of his chair and barks, "Why don't you kiss her instead of talking her to death?" whereupon Mary flees. Memories of such invasive neighborliness no doubt helped convince many a fellow with access to a VA loan to light out for the suburban territories and their flat-fronted, asphalt-sided ranch houses, where there'd be no geezers breathing down his neck from porch-bound forward observation posts.)

The cookie-cutter houses of suburbia didn't hold their shape for long. With the passage of time and the rising of incomes, a *do-it-yourself* movement took shape; the houses of Levittown and the rest of suburbia changed. (In the 1990s, preparing for a fiftieth anniversary celebration, curators of a Levittown retrospective had to search hard to find even one house still in showroom state). As soon as Dad could mix concrete, the backyard acquired a patio and perhaps a sliding glass door. The next step was to add a screened porch. However, it's one thing to build a crappy-looking patio out back where nobody can see it; who'd want to risk making a bad job of a front porch? And besides, neither the ranch façade nor that of the Cape Cod lent itself to retrograde porchification, so the screened porch went on the back of the house.

In some inventive neighborhoods outside Buffalo, New York, the porch impulse expressed itself in an unusual way. Owners of houses with garages began building and installing big sections of screen. Come spring, they'd open the garage door and put the screen in place, then use the bug-free zone like a second living room. The habit persists.

In the South, where residential air conditioning debuted in the years after World War II, the porch went into eclipse in neighborhoods where folks could afford an air conditioner. If they couldn't, the porch was as it had always been—a place of respite and sociability—except when the tremors of the times engulfed, as when nightriders trying to kill Dr. Martin Luther King, Jr. for having the temerity to demand racial equality dynamited his front porch in Montgomery, Alabama.

But even as the South shuddered into the civil rights era, the porch remained a hallowed place there. In *Swinging in Place: Porch Life in Southern Culture,* folklorist Jocelyn Hazelwood Donlon uses her family's life on porches in Louisiana as one of the threads with which she weaves a tapestry that portrays the Southern porch as playground, courtship zone, and literary device. Leaving no angle unprobed, Donlon explains why, despite changing social mores and architectural fashions, never mind the automobile, air conditioning, and television, the porch still resides in the Southern consciousness.

Donlon quotes southerners who say that although their houses may not have front porches, they live their lives as if that is not the case. Others say that though their homes have front porches, they prefer the privacy of the back porch, acknowledging that they may be acting in contrarian contrast to their parents and grandparents, who posted themselves on the front porch as a matter of habit.

Besides showing how strongly the porch still figures in Southern culture and memory, especially as a locus for the telling of tales, tall and otherwise, Donlon parses the porch as a setting for chores, especially garden-related tasks like shelling peas, slicing okra, peeling fruit, and play, from checkers and jacks to counting cars. Her interview subjects remark on the differences between front-porch activities (chatting, card-playing) and those relegated to the back porch (coon- and squirrel-skinning, canning). In the propriety-conscious South, the back porch has never been a place in which to lollygag or loiter; the front porch is more the social setting, even when the activity involved involves labor (like hand-cranking the ice cream freezer).

"The work done on the front porch is much more presentable' than the work accomplished on the back porch," Donlon writes.

Besides assembling a mosaic of oral histories from white and Black southerners to document her conclusions, Donlon analyzes the work of African-American and white writers from the region. Southern characters often confront the world and one another on the porch, a tension that can be between male and female (as in Zora Neale Hurston's *Their Eyes Were Watching God*, where the protagonist's husband bars her from his store's front porch; when he dies, she asserts her control over that very public space, to her neighbors' dismay); white over Black (on a porch in Ernest Gaines's *Catherine Carmier*, dark-skinned Jackson fights his nemesis, Raoul Carmier, a mulatto whose pretense and alienation separate him from the worlds at either end of the racial spectrum); or Black over white (in William Faulkner's *Absalom, Absalom!*, a house slave's haughty demeanor on a porch reminds a character of his white-trash ancestry).

But that's the South of the fictional page. In the real South, the porch isn't always a racial minefield; it can be neutral territory on which whites and Blacks can engage one another, as Donlon shows in the story of her grandmother, Florence Materne Foreman, and the front porch on her house in Lake Charles, Louisiana.

During the turbulence of the civil-rights era, Mrs. Foreman, by virtue of age and tenure the neighborhood's matriarch, caused her porch to be known as a place where neighbor ladies could talk of topics like gardening, cooking, crocheting, funerals, and other social events. One young African-American, Gloria Johnson, like Florence Foreman a widow, had moved home to Lake Charles from Massachusetts. She lived nearby, and began coming often to the Foreman porch. Across twenty years of interaction, she and Mrs. Foreman became close, albeit in a circumscribed way. They rarely visited in the house, and kept conversation at the small-talk level, but theirs was a friendship, forged on the common ground of the porch, the older woman instructing the younger in the household arts and the two comparing the funerary practices of their respective races.

After Mrs. Foreman died and some years went by, Gloria Johnson assumed the role Mrs. Foreman had held, and a cycle set itself in motion again. "Today the Lake Charles neighborhood is entirely black," writes Donlon. "And Gloria Johnson goes from porch to porch serving as the community matriarch."

The impulse to hold onto the old way of out-front living persisted elsewhere in the country, too. Remembering the urban stoops of their youths, some suburbanites sat on the front steps well into the fifties. My neighborhood outside Washington, D.C., filled a traditional grid, with houses on shallow setbacks, sidewalks, and square curbs bordering narrow concrete streetbeds. Not every house had a driveway; few had garages. "In the evening, everybody up and down the street would sit out on the steps," my family's long-time neighbor Pat Lydon told me much later as she reminisced about the mid-fifties. "You'd sit out there and say hello to whoever was walking by with their kids—there were *so* many children—and have a chat. And then all of a sudden no one was out there anymore. They'd gotten television."

The same happened in neighborhoods full of traditional front porches. One minute folks were out there, waving and gabbing, and the next they were gone. What mosquitoes and radio and traffic noise hadn't been able to do, television did, pulling Americans off the porch. Air conditioning took care of the stragglers, although outside the South both window units and central air were far slower to take hold than many people think. But ever so gradually, the porches emptied. Life begets life. In many communities, as life abandoned the front porch, the porch died, succumbing to dry rot, dilapidation, and emptiness. The places where porch life didn't die were those whose inhabitants, whether from poverty or acculturation, couldn't shake the porch-sitting habit.

Hollywood also had trouble jettisoning the porch. After the war's dust settled into the hard peace of the late forties and early fifties, the mirror of the movies began to show Americans how much they and their culture had changed. Hollywood still manufactured comedies and period pieces and melodramas, but more and more often films had a gravity not evident before the war.

You still saw movie families on porches, but now they were troubled families, like the Stark clan in Robert Rossen's *All the King's Men* (1950). In that Oscar-winning account of political corruption and personal downfall, Broderick Crawford, as dictatorial governor Willie Stark, stalks the marble porticoes of his capitol building like a cracker Mussolini, deigning to appear on a humble porch only for a photo opportunity he imbues with a swollen menace that the trappings of home and family cannot disguise, even with a St. Bernard sprawled asleep at his crippled son's feet.

Cinematic porches became embattled, the last redoubt on which armed mother figures defended children by any means necessary. In *The Yearling* (1946),

Jane Wyman as Ma Baxter stands tough on her porch, ready with a double-barreled shotgun to protect her son and home. In Charles Laughton's *Night of the Hunter* (1955), the murderous Reverend Harry Powell (Robert Mitchum), about to kill his runaway stepchildren, encounters Rachel Cooper (Lillian Gish), an apron-clad do-gooder who tells the kids in grandmotherly tones not to worry, then rises from her rocking chair to blow the cackling villain away with a bird gun.

In 1952, Gary Cooper returned to the porch in another role as laconically ironic as he'd played in *Sergeant York*. But in *High Noon*, Fred Zinnemann flips both Cooper's image and the notion of the porch as a safe place and symbol of American character onto their heads. As Marshal Will Kane, who's about to marry Amy Foster (Grace Kelly), Coop must delay his wedding to deal with gunsels who've come to kill him. In a plot often read as a comment on the McCarthy era, Zinnemann portrays Kane as an honorable man under intense pressure, pursued by corrupt enemies and shunned by supposedly upright citizens. No actor has ever shed his cinematic skin as thoroughly as Cooper does. He craw-fishes, he finds his resolve, he loses it, he regains it. Pursued and pursuing, the besieged lawman creeps through a town in which all the cinematic hallmarks of America are transmogrified: every porch is a potential killing zone, every pillar a sight line, every swinging door a death trap. In the end, the exhausted sheriff owes his life to his woman, who steps to a window and does the manly thing for which his fellow townsmen lack the stones.

Zinnemann's allegorical indictment hardly stands alone as an example of how Hollywood played with the image of the porch in the supposedly staid fifties. In 1956 alone, audiences could see it put to unexpected uses in several films: in *Giant*, the last panel in George Steven's triptych of the post-wilderness West, where Bick Benedict (Rock Hudson) and wife Leslie (Elizabeth Taylor) always seem to be standing on or near a porch of their Second Empire mansion scowling at a truculent Jett Rink (James Dean); Elia Kazan's and Tennessee Williams' *Baby Doll* (with Carroll Baker as the woman-child Eli Wallach seduces in a scene that could put you off porch swings for a while); and *Love Me Tender* (in which Elvis Presley makes his film debut as Clint Reno, a good-rockin' Rebel trying to swivel his way through tough times in post-bellum Texas).

In another subtle but telling use of the porch during 1956, John Ford began and ended *The Searchers* reinforcing the idea of the porch as a structure that frames and subdues the wilderness by establishing a boundary of landscape, domesticity, and propriety. At the outset, the doomed Edwards family stands by their roughhewn homestead porch, lit by the dying sun as Ethan Edwards (John Wayne) rides toward them, an angry outlaw carrying stolen gold and a bad attitude. Welcoming her long-absent brother-in-law on the porch, Martha Edwards (Dorothy Jordan) indicates in a glance which Edwards brother she prefers, and *The Searchers* is off and away on its harrowing exercise in violence, sublimation, and Ford's installation of the murderously flawed Ethan among the pantheon of faultless heroes he created in his earlier Westerns. *The Searchers* ends where it begins, with a porch shot. Having rescued his kidnapped niece and returned her home, perhaps against his instincts, Ethan stands alone on another frontier family's porch. He clasps his arm, staring civilization hard in the eye, then, returning to the wilderness whence he came, turns his back on society as the door closes on him.

America was turning its back on the porch, too, as well as on other traces of prewar culture like streetcars, radio dramas, and antique furniture, along with living in the city. Lured by the suburbs, tired of and frightened of the city—which is to say, "Black people," since that was who'd been moving to town since the twenties and thirties—the middle class fled; which is to say "white people fled," since in the 1940s and 1950s America's Black middle class was not only tiny but forced by Jim Crow laws, restrictive deed covenants, and flat-out racism to stay inside the color line by staying inside the city line.

As the suburbs ballooned, urban areas went from white to mixed to Black in about as much time as it took to grow a tomato. Some African-Americans could afford to buy houses and did. Other dwellings became rentals and rooming houses. Landlords usually put in as little on upkeep as they could, so the buildings didn't sink into the ground like the house of Usher, but that wasn't always true. When an area achieved a critical mass of derelict dwellings, the urban renewal juggernaut might roll, and often did. Luckier neighborhoods survived, ramshackle but intact, waiting for those who had the eyes to see their intrinsic value.

Americans' private lives were becoming less public, either conducted indoors, behind heavy draperies, or outdoors and in the backyard, except in one area. Just as the generations lived together less often, old people no longer died at home, and they more and more often were not buried from home. Instead of the deathbed scene in the darkened bedroom and the living room wake that had been the national standard until the thirties, a geriatric American now tended to expire beneath the fluorescent glare of hospital lighting, after which the undertakers came to whisk the corpse away to a rented funerary chamber.

The trend toward using morticians sometimes saved a porch. In towns across the United States, undertakers realized that Victorian mansions—the last houses built deliberately to accommodate the movement of coffins up and down stairs, as well as with servant's quarters and back stairwells—lent themselves to conversion into funeral homes. Those stately houses' bulk imbued a sad occasion with grandeur, and their big porches supplied a handy relief valve for the crowds when a wake proved an especially popular social event.

What mourners sensed intuitively, others put into words. Here and there, amid the postwar passion for the modern, a few voices rose in defense of traditional architecture. At Yale University's architecture school, historian and critic Vincent Scully taught a course on the history of American architecture that covered not only Buildings with a capital B, but lowercase dwellings like beach cottages and workaday nineteenth century houses not usually granted capital-A "Architecture" status because of their quotidian nature. The course was popular; more than one Yalie, architecture major or not, recalls it as the single best classroom experience of those four years.

Scully was an unusual fixture at Yale. A townie who'd grown up in a porch-fronted New Haven row house, he fondly recalled the soft hammer of rain on the roof of the back sleeping porch where he spent all but the coldest nights. He made a ritual of sending his history students into his old neighborhood to examine the harmony of the leaf-shaded sidewalks, picket fences, and front porches on Howe Street, giving the *jeunesse dorée* a chance at understanding the sanctity of ordinary experiences. In his lectures and in books like *American Architecture and Urbanism,* Scully enunciated the premise that architecture, high or low, ought to embody and conserve cultural memory, not try to wall it off with plate glass and plastic panels—an early alarm about the high crimes and misdemeanors committed in the name of modern architecture. Scully would serve as a beacon to several generations of young architects who came up unafraid of history, and who, like Robert Venturi and Robert A. M. Stern, defined the postmodernism that Scully sketched.

But except for Vince Scully's lectures and for day-to-day life in towns too small to notice, the front porch was done for in America. Over. History. The back porch—well, the back porch was, and is, another place, inhabited and used differently and by no means a substitute for its more public sibling. Whether arranged for labor—the modus operandi in the South—or for leisure, as in the suburbs since the fifties—the back porch is a place for communing with family, friends, and acquaintances with the credentials to get past the front door and through the kitchen without being shunted into the nowhere zone of the modern living room. The same is true with side porches. An invisible shield of implied privacy admits the elect but keeps people on the side porch from connecting with passersby on the street.

The porch still showed up in the movies, of course, achieving its apotheosis in 1962. Like Harper Lee's novel, which contains forty-two porch scenes and which served to a remarkable degree as a shooting script for the film, *To Kill a Mockingbird* takes place in Maycomb, the small Alabama town where Scout, Dill, and Jem experience their summer of discovery and terror, mostly on and around porches. In both book and film, each porch scene illuminates a character or advances the narrative, such as when mean old Mrs. DuBose (Ruth White) barks at the children from her porch; when the heroic Atticus Finch (Gregory Peck) gathers his tomboy daughter Scout (Mary Badham) into his arms in a rocking chair on theirs; or at the finale, when Scout shares the porch swing with Arthur "Boo" Radley (a bleached-blond, zombified Robert Duvall, who wouldn't be that scary again until he portrayed Lt. Col. Bob Kilgore in *Apocalypse Now*) as her dad discusses the evening's tumult with Sheriff Heck Tate (Hank Overton), bringing the film to its muted but satisfying conclusion.

In the same way that things would never be the same again in Maycomb, things were never the same again on real porches around the country. When the porch fell from favor, many porches fell apart. Wooden railings and pillars disintegrated. Some owners replaced the mess with metalwork, so that the porch roof seemed to be defying gravity until you got close enough to see that it was riding on a skinny grid of structural steel. Others simply knocked the darned thing down, its condition having declined so much it had become like a diabetic's leg, good only for amputation. Then they either tried to doll up the results as a terrace, or they swept away the debris and installed steps with a platform at the top. More than a few homeowners, like Doug and Lila Lynch, who spent nearly forty years in the house where I live now, enclosed their porches, first with screening and then with jalousies, tempered glass, or even walls, taking what had been outside inside for what appeared to be good. A walk around any neighborhood of a certain age will reveal specimens from each point along this evolutionary spiral. If you see asphalt or asbestos shingles and aluminum siding, look for metal columns and railings and porches that have become something other than porches. This happened because so many people came to see their porches not as elements fully developed and enduring, with a fixed and noble purpose, but as outlines, to be completed as taste and want demanded.

"Porches fill in by stages, not all at once," an architect told Stewart Brand, author of *How Buildings Learn*. "The family puts screens on the porch one summer because of the bugs. Then they see they could glass it in and make it part of the house. But it's cold, so they add a duct from the furnace and some insulation, and now they realize they're going to have to beef up the foundation and the roof."

But as the suburbs expanded, they also aged and entered their next incarnation. With arbitrarily curving streets that had rolled curbs, no sidewalks, and dead ends (cul-de-sacs, please!), and lawns dominated by driveways that led to houses where the garage door or doors dwarfed the doorway, the inhabitants realized they needed something. Something outside that led to the inside. Something that made them feel connected not only to their homes but to the world.

But that connection wasn't going to be the front porch. As the fifties morphed into the sixties and that rumpus-ridden decade began to uncoil, America's suburbs acquired a defensive aspect. Good fences made good neighbors, and you wanted to keep the little ones from roaming too freely, so in went the concrete footings and up went the chain-link. Civil rights activists had stopped being quite so polite and were looking to integrate suburbia—yipes, here come the Negroes!

Another interest group went very public around this time, the one made up of folks who wanted to preserve important and not-so-important American buildings that were threatened by development. Unfortunately, the impetus to renew this crusade grew out of the death of a great building—New York City's Pennsylvania Station—and the replacement of McKim Mead & White's classic palace with what looked like a gigantic roadside trash bin. The subsequent uproar and its repeated echo at the demise of other historic buildings around the country spurred formation of preservation groups like the Victorian Society of America and other era- or type-specific outfits. Municipalities established historic districts, both commercial and residential. Americans began to be more conscious of older structures, including ordinary houses. At colleges and universities, the folklore and material culture departments began to schedule classes on "vernacular architecture," the style of no-style that constitutes so much of the built environment. America was starting to take note, but there was a lot of competition for the country's attention.

The Cold War got hot, missiles headed for Cuba, and here came the bomb shelter—even in my neighborhood, eight miles from the Capitol and therefore well within the Crispy Critter zone that would result from even the most minimal nuclear attack on D.C. Then came LBJ, LSD, Vietnam, Harlem, Watts, and the Motor City, and the sixties became *The Sixties*. No way to delay that trouble coming every day, and it made so much more sense to stay inside and watch the world go to hell on television or sit out in the backyard and not watch the world at all.

In fact, you could watch television and not have to watch the world. Instead, you could tune into a world where everything was sweet and even-tempered and all conflicts were resolved within a thirty- or sixty-minute span, with time out for important messages from our sponsors. Folks on television lived in cute little houses, like the one Andy and Opie and Aunt Bea had in Mayberry— you know, two steps up to the front porch—for two hundred and forty-nine episodes. Starting in October 1960, the show offered an anodyne alternative to the realities of the decade all through the sixties (and forever after in reruns and on videotape). In a later display of television's ability to construct and maintain a separate universe to which fans would flock, we'd have the Waltons, whose front-porched, triple-gabled house on the mountain provided the backdrop for family drama in two hundred and nineteen episodes and six reunion specials.

Another place you still encountered porches was on the page. When published in 1968, John Updike's best-selling *Couples* was as steamy a read as you could borrow from the library. (His soon-to-be-former wife described it as "wading through pubic hair.") But now, at the saltpetric distance of more than thirty years, *Couples* is clearly less a novel of lust and love than one of real estate and residential architecture, mass-production housing versus custom building and renovation, and the question of whether to keep the old porch and enclose it or tear it off entirely.

The story takes place in Tarbox, a seaside Connecticut town where everyone who's anyone sleeps with everyone else. The classless suburbs are closing in, but Tarbox still offers lessons in house-as-class: ". . . the surviving seventeenth-century saltboxes the original Kimballs and Sewells and Tarboxes and Cogswells had set along wobbly pasture lanes . . . the tight brick alleys plotted to house the millworkers imported from Poland; the middle-class pre-Depression domiciles with stubby porches and narrow chimneys and composition sidings the colors of mustard and parsley and graphite and wine . . ."

Lark-smoking protagonist Piet Hanema, a builder and would-be real-estate mogul, makes his first overture to Elizabeth "Foxy" Whitman by tearing away with his bare hands the sheets of plywood covering the doors to the porch on the old beach house that Foxy and her all-but-absent husband Ken have bought. Piet is a real handyman; between meeting the pregnant Foxy and allowing her to fling herself at him, he spills his seed into randy Georgene Thorne on the latter's second-floor sunporch, and occasionally takes a tumble with wife Angela.

The Whitmans pester Piet into redoing their house, at prices to swoon for (twelve thousand for a major overhaul, four for a kitchen, two grand to excavate a basement), and Piet sells Foxy on a porch renovation she hadn't really wanted.

"He had taken a loose piece of rusted screening and crumpled it and showed her the orange dust like pollen in his palm. 'New screen will be one of your least expenses. Alcoa makes nice big panels we can fit into runners along here. And here. Take them down in the fall. In summer this porch is the best room in the house. Grab the breeze.'

'But it makes the living room so dark. I was thinking of having it torn away.'

'Don't tear away free space. You bought the view. Here's where it is.'"

Seeing numerous opportunities laid out before him, Piet begins to work on the Whitman house and on Foxy ("Each change he wrought established more firmly an essential propriety") until, sexually exiled by her scientist husband, she rises to him ("Aren't we in our house? Aren't you building this house for me?") and they begin their affair. The rest of the book is a rondo of fucks and counterfucks, punctuated by history (the Diems' demise and JFK's assassination, the *Thresher*'s sinking, the ascent of Pope John XXIII) and interspersed, always, with talk of houses. Foxy spills the beans to Ken (on the porch, of course). Their marriage implodes, as does the Hanemas'. After Piet dumps his family, his real-estate partner, who wants to concentrate on prefab construction, dumps him. Piet goes full-time into renovation, and hooks up with the similarly dispossessed Foxy. But after they're wed, Piet lets his new father-in-law set him up for a gig handling quality control for military barrack construction. He and Foxy move to Lexington. Updike doesn't say whether their house has a porch. I bet it does.

Decades are funny things. The sixties—excuse me, I mean, *The Sixties*—didn't start until 1963 or so. Maybe they started that November in Dallas, or even earlier, in September 1962, down in Oxford town, when James Meredith tried to register and Ole Miss went off like a cherry bomb in a trash can. The Sixties didn't end until around 1974. Perhaps it happened when Dick Nixon gave his final clenched wave and finally got on the damn helicopter, or maybe it was the next April, when the last Huey spiraled off the Saigon embassy roof with some poor bastard hanging on the skids like a premonition of Francis Ford Coppola's musings.

There's a lot of debate about when the Seventies started, but I think they started sometime in the late sixties when the first guy stood in the sawdust-softened aisle of a lumberyard on the East Coast or in the Midwest, pricing materials for a structure he wanted to build in his backyard.

He'd been looking at *Sunset* and *Southern Living,* thumbing through *Popular Mechanics* and *House and Garden,* and he remembered what he'd seen on a vacation trip to southern California, where they stayed with his wife's cousin and where people appeared to live almost exclusively outside. People in L.A. worked—don't let anybody kid you, the thing they worked hardest at in L.A. was seeming not to work—but at home, Angelenos only went inside to take showers and get a sandwich and a cold one and make some calls.

Always the first to adopt new American modes, southern Californians had long since stopped living in public on the front porch. The caustic arc of the twentieth century had sucked the romance out of what had once been the region's favorite house design, now reduced to a leering reference in a Doors song in which Jim Morrison crooned about his priapic search for "the little girls in their Hollywood bungalows."

So much for Bix Beiderbecke's dreams. No, Californians had turned their backs on reveries about the bungalow and the porch, instead making their backyards fantasias. They had swimming pools. They had Jacuzzis. They had patios.

And Californians had these rigs they called "decks"—platforms, really, but with a nice railing and sometimes built-in seats and planters, a couple of feet off the ground. That is, unless your property fell away from the back of the house, and then you had some real elevation, as if Richard Neutra had reached down from Modern Architect Heaven and waved his wand. You stood on the deck of a California night, the sky like an Eagles song, the air like a caress, feet bare against the redwood planking, and you felt free. Anything could happen. The guy in the aisle at the lumber outlet off the Dan Ryan wanted to feel that way in his backyard, even if he'd never have a pool and even if he'd only get the chance to feel that way during the summer and on a few fleeting days in spring and fall.

But there were problems.

California weather had its moments, but generally speaking it was a dream state, whereas the meteorology at home was brutal, with winters like Stalingrad and summers like Singapore. And Californians built their decks out of tough, dense, long-lasting wood like cedar and redwood, which cost an arm and a leg and maybe the option on a kidney. Pine was cheap, but you couldn't use that; in a couple of years the deck would be compost, warped by the rain and burned by the sun and chewed to bits by termites.

The guy at the lumberyard felt stuck. Then his gaze wandered from the stacks of number-two pine to some peculiar-looking stuff in the wholesale section, where the contractors bought. It was pine, but instead of the usual pale creamy tone it came in a spooky shade of green. He asked the salesman about the green stuff, and he learned it was wood that had been treated to resist rot and insects by pressure-cooking it in a bath of chromated copper arsenate—wicked stuff, man, *arsenic*, y'know? The treehuggers said it caused cancer, but it kept the bugs out and lasted forever.

(Along with the quests for the Holy Grail and the Philosopher's Stone, one of humankind's oldest, most persistent searches has been for a way to keep wood from rotting. Noah protected the Ark from termites with pitch, but not until 1875 did anyone find a better means of treating wood, and that was with petroleum-based creosote. The thick black gunk worked great on railroad ties and harbor pilings, but who wanted a porch that looked and felt and smelled like a dock? In 1900, Karl Wolman, a chemist in Germany, invented a salt-based mix that became popular for industrial uses in that country. In 1933, soon after the National Socialists took over, they began funding R&D into improvements on Wolman salts. Enter Sonti Kamesam, an unlikely hero of the Reich, working far from his native India. The young scientist's hot temper and nationalist politics had alienated his British supervisors, who "suggested" he take a hike. He did—to Germany, where he went to work on the wood preservative project. Kamesam combined copper sulphate and arsenate chromate, dissolved the mixture in water, and forced it into lumber under pressure. Chromated copper arsenate, or CCA, stopped rot the way a Panzer's armor stopped French anti-tank rounds. The Germans adopted CCA to pressure-treat lumber, and eventually it became the state of the preservative art, used to protect telephone poles, fencing, mine timbers, and so forth. A meaner spirit might claim the Nazis were trying to enslave the world with the odious and regrettable deck, but I'm not that kind of man. Later, Kamesam emigrated to the United States, to which the formula for CCA flowed after the war.)

When lumbermen in Mississippi started treating wood with CCA, they buried samples in Delta mud and took them out every few years to see if they'd decomposed. They hadn't, not a bit. After rehearsing with CCA on timbers for phone poles and cooling towers, manufacturers started putting regular lumber into the salt bath in the mid 1950s. The building trades liked to use the stuff for concrete forms and sill plates—the bottom-most piece of wood in a frame house, laid atop the foundation as the basis for the rest of the structure. Demand was steady, but not huge. A lumberyard had to special-order the treated wood from outfits like Koppers or from local mom-and-pop operations that made it in big tanks, the pressure cookers of the gods.

The guy who was thinking of building a deck in his backyard ran his hand over the CCA-treated surface. It felt rough, alien, as if the wood was an animal that had endured something so awful its dorsal hairs stayed up permanently. You wouldn't want to put your bare foot on it. But you could use it for structural elements. He ordered a load, and he spent a couple of weekends installing his deck, a welcome change from the brain games at the office. For flooring he used ordinary pine two-by-sixes. If they rotted, he could replace 'em easily enough. While he was working, his neighbor came over to see what he was doing. The neighbor said he liked what the guy was doing. A lot.

Out of inventiveness and curiosity are markets made. Until then, lumber companies had hardly advertised pressure-treated lumber to the public, instead handling it like a drug for which you needed a prescription. But in the early seventies, some nameless hero at Koppers realized that consumers were buying a lot of pressure-treated wood. If guys were buying the green stuff on their own and using it to build decks, how much more green stuff would they buy, and how many more decks would they build, were somebody to pitch the green stuff at them as the perfect deck material? Think of all those backyards. Think of all those do-it-yourselfers. Think of what it would mean if pressure-treated lumber were required by the building code.

In autumn 1974, Koppers ran a marketing test in the Chicago area, promoting pressure-treated wood to consumers. Sales ballooned. Soon the green stuff was a stock item at lumberyards, and the Age of the Deck had begun. When users bitched about the dorsal-hair feel, as well as the cracking, the splintering, and the cupping to which CCA-treated wood was prone, manufacturers did some experimenting. They realized that if you dried the wood in kilns, you could run it through a mill like ordinary lumber. And charge more.

Decks got smoother, bigger, and more complex. Backyards started to look like adult Jungle Gyms. Ever-larger jerry-rigged 3-D grids rose behind kraal-like stockade walls that went up overnight in eight-foot sections, prefabricated privacy (or was it spite?) fences that made a backyard into a mystery zone (What were they *doing* in there?). Often the mystery was nothing more than the preservation of the species; with young to raise, *Homo suburbanis* experienced a strong need to shield its nest and its hot tub from prying eyes and predators.

The deck became the prime real-world architectural element of the Me Decade. Like leisure suits, Earth Shoes, macramé, waterbeds, and the rest of the era's foibles and fads, it seemed at the time to be a good idea, or at least a new idea. Something different, for God's sake—not the old same same old Cape Cod/ranch house/split level in the suburbs. So many of us wound up with decks and a litany of deck tales to rival Melville and his piazza tales.

A deck was where you started out trying to have a good time and wound up getting a second-degree sunburn.

A deck was what you had somebody build off the back of your new townhouse and which, as soon as all the friends you invited over to check out the new deck were standing on it, collapsed.

A deck was where, when your kid was running around and stubbed the ball of his foot, picking up a splinter big enough to qualify as kindling, you pondered the thought of an entire afternoon at the emergency room and instead plopped him into an Adirondack chair, sat on him, and got the hapless neighbor whose deck had done this awful thing bring you a single-edged razor blade that you sterilized with a match and used to cut the goddamned splinter out.

The deck was a bad idea whose time will really never come. You can't use a deck in the rain. You can't use a deck when it's hot and sunny. When it's cold you have to either go inside or stand around stamping your feet, which makes the beams tremble and causes you to wonder if the lag bolts will hold. Mainly, the deck stands out there like the watch-tower of a suburbanoid stalag, especially in a neighborhood of moderate to high density.

Now, you may have a deck, and you may love it dearly, but I am here to tell you that the deck is the platform shoe of American architecture. As long as people are looking for something new and supposedly glamorous to stick their toes into, platform shoes will walk themselves out of the store. And as long as there are house owners looking for something new and supposedly glamorous to stick onto their dwellings, decks are going to sprout.

But unlike the owner of a platform shoe, who awakens from the febrile state that led to the purchase of the now-loathsome footwear, the owner of a deck can't toss the unwanted object of faded desire into a bag, haul it to Value Village, and be done with it.

There are settings in which the deck functions splendidly, such as the back of a cabin in the Front Range, the side of a bungalow on the outskirts of Mendocino, or aft of the kitchen on a modernist box overlooking Georgica Pond. What makes a deck work is the inverse of the principle that animates the front porch: the fewer there are, the better they are.

But there are entirely too many decks, and most of them, like platform shoes, don't wear well or for very long. The deck seems to the uninitiated to be rakish and devil-may-care, as open to the elements as its nautical namesake. It hints at a languid life that mainly involves sipping summer-colored drinks while wearing snappy sportswear and conversing wittily beneath the blue suburban skies. And because the deck invariably projects off the back of the house, it conveys a sense of private pleasure. You could sunbathe nekkid out there if you wanted.

Or could you?

What about the people behind you? Their deck is the same height as yours, and it's only a few feet away. In fact, when you stop and think about it, most of the houses in the neighborhood have decks just like yours, except for the ones that belong to poor cheap bastards who tried to save some dough by cutting out a few amenities. They figured they'd do the work themselves—it'd be a great weekend project, honey!—only she got pregnant, or he got downsized, or the tranny on the Explorer went. Now, when you pan across the back forty of the development, instead of the smooth and seamless Bath-like curve of casual elegance in the developer's brochures, which showed a sweet smile of tasteful decks stretching to infinity, you see a lopsided grin, punctuated by gaps where the deckless wonders live. The decks of householders bold enough to make the investment bristle with patio furniture, Big Wheels, bicycles, sports gear, planters, polyester flags bearing heraldic images related to dog breeds, pineapples, and sports teams, soccer goals, bug zappers, and urinal-shaped ceramic charcoal ovens.

One key and ludicrous deck accessory is the gigantic umbrella, unfurled to deflect the ultraviolet rays that start hammering down as soon as the sun rises. These are the same umbrellas that, when a thunderstorm whips in, go airborne like canvasback Katyushas, everybody running around trying to hold onto those big bumbershoots before they impale somebody.

Deck owners could prevent that and make their decks work sublimely, if only they'd roof them and turn them into porches. Which brings up the tragically silly flaw inherent in the deck: in all too many of the regions where it has become ubiquitous, the deck isn't usable much of the time without serious adjustment. Otherwise, why would we see the rise of an entire subindustry that specialized in roofing and enclosing decks?

Sure, on a summer evening, you can log an enjoyable hour or two once the sun crosses the theoretical yardarm, provided you live in a mosquito-free zone or you drench yourself in DEET. Spring and fall, before the heat hits, that window of opportunity opens a mite wider. But during the winter—forget it. It's cold, wet, and windy. The snow drifts up, and the steps are slippery. Except for a few meteorologically blessed locations—where, let's face it, you could live in a clapped-out '64 Nova and feel like a natural aristocrat—your basic deck is at its peak of utility for only about three months a year and maybe two hours a day. During this time, if you believe the enviros, that cancerous CCA is also soaking up through the soles of your feet and the palms of your hands.

None of this has stopped Americans from loving their decks, which consistently rank high on National Association of Home Builders surveys of home-buyer preference. For more than twenty years, from the seventies until the nineties, the deck beat out the porch as a favored amenity. It was a deal breaker, a green light/red light kind of thing.

And during much of that time the American porch languished in architectural limbo. No one was building houses with porches, and the porches that had been built were being enclosed or jalousied or torn off or having who-knows-what done to them, thanks to the automobile and the television and the air conditioning and the fickle taste of a public that jumps to grab what's new and shiny and drop what's familiar. We've all seen it all too often. The title of a 1976 article by Pamela West in the journal *Landscape* summed up the situation: "The Rise and Fall of the American Porch."

But something unexpected happened.

The porch looked as if it was going to die off, as if it would join the passenger pigeon and the auk and the outhouse in the Hall of Extinction. Instead, the porch came back.

Not all the way, and not at all the way it used to be, but it came back.

The screened porch, once the butt of hillbilly jokes, gradually regained its popularity.

CHAPTER FIFTEEN

RISE AGAIN

As with its adoption, which began almost four centuries before, and the rejection that started around 1914, the return of the porch in America has been a subtle transformation. In the same way that the porch began to disappear even as it enjoyed its widest popularity, the rebirth of the porch began amid convincing evidence that the porch had become terminally obsolete, doomed to exist as a relic of times gone by until the last vestigial example crumbled of dry rot.

But the porch didn't disappear.

In fact, the porch came back in a variety of subtle and not-so-subtle ways, as well as in variations that continue to evolve. I learned about some of these when I attended the 2001 International Builders Show. Held every February in the Georgia World Congress Center in Atlanta, this gargantuan trade show draws thousands of developers, architects, property brokers, contractors, manufacturers, and housing policy wonks from around the world to its enormous array of everything to do with houses. I joined the hordes wandering this latter-day souk to take the industry's pulse on the porch. My method was a thoroughly unscientific survey, conducted by buttonholing as many people as I could who looked like builders. That wasn't hard. At the show, which the National Association of Home Builders sponsors, pretty much everyone is a builder; if one person isn't, the next is.

I needed to hear from the men and women who put up America's houses not only because they influence trends by deciding what to build. They also reflect trends, because to one degree or another they're giving their customers what those customers want.

The first builders I met, Bob Mohney and Angie King of Saddlebrook, Inc., in Knoxville, Tennessee, had discouraging words to say about the porch.

"We're producing fewer houses with porches," said Bob. "People don't want to dress up their houses. They like the plain front."

He added that clients talk about wanting porches, but when he brings up cost, they demur. Angie agreed.

"Our buyers are mostly empty-nesters, and they want that screened porch—always at the rear, never at the front," she said. "We don't see people getting a front porch unless it's part of the style of the house, like a Victorian. And then it's more of a cosmetic thing. They'll put the rocking chairs out, but nobody sits in them."

But custom builder Gray Wagner, from Sherrill's Ford, North Carolina, said that on the houses he was building near Lake Norman, people were ordering front porches, side porches, back porches, and wraparounds. He said he was getting away from pressure-treated lumber, even lumber itself, and substituting artificial stuff like Trex and polyvinyl chloride that boosts the cost of a porch by forty percent but doesn't need coating or painting.

Thanks to their plainsman-style garb, two Mennonite guys from Ohio stood out from the sportswear-clad crowd. Roy Miller and Dan Miller said they found themselves building plenty of porches.

"Almost every Amish house has a front porch or a side porch," Roy said. "It's a social thing. People visit and chat. It's the focal point, a place where you can unwind." In their area, screened gazebos, set at a distance from the house, were replacing the rear screened porch. A lot of Amish were building prefabricated ranch-style houses with tiny, narrow porches only four feet deep, Dan said.

Jack Babry, from outside Philadelphia, Pennsylvania, said he and his family lived on four acres in a house with a big front porch. "It's a rural setting, and the porch is our exterior family room," he said. "My wife, Susan, *lives* out there. When I was building the house fifteen years ago, the hard part was working on it in the summer and wanting the porch. I knew eventually I'd have one." Jack said he'd noticed that plan books were including more drawings of houses with front porches.

Wes Wegman, from New Orleans, Louisiana, declared that the Big Easy remained strong for the porch. "People in the inner city keep their porches up," he told me. "They still use and decorate them, and we still build front and back porches. Come on down and give me a call and we'll go see some Louisiana porches!"

The porch was also alive and well in the Northwest, according to Niedra North. She'd come to the trade show to represent the Clark County Building Association, out in Washington state. "People like the image," she said. "It takes them back to simplicity, it conjures up the symbol of, 'I want to go there,' and the porch takes them there."

Custom builder Brent Wimpee, of Bowling Green, Kentucky, said he lived in a house with big front and back porches, and so did a lot of his customers. "The porch is definitely coming back, just like the pitched roof," he said, adding that the porches he was building were full-depth, extending at least eight feet. Among his company's remodeling jobs, nearly a third involved porch additions—mostly out back, mostly screened. "I like the look of the houses at Seaside, down in Florida," Brent said, referring to the resort town that marked the debut of the porchophiliac New Urbanist approach to residential architecture and community planning. "I'd like to take that look into the neighborhood." Doug Johnson, from Savoy, Illinois, said eighty percent of the houses in his town had front porches and screened porches. "It's a trend again," he said.

In Bloomington, Minnesota, porches that folks had converted into "four-season rooms," with glass walls, heat, and interior furniture, were being reverse-engineered into variations on their original status, said Craig Pekkenpol.

"Some people are de-enclosing their porches," he said. "Others are going to screens, so they have 'three-season' rooms. There's more of a trend to the front porch than in the past in both new and remodeled houses."

But Prince Georges County, Maryland, outside Washington, D.C., still prefers decks to porches, said contractors Shane Warren and Rob Spies. "Decks are very big," Shane said. "And people are building patios, not back porches."

Homeowners along the mid-Atlantic shore mainly go for unroofed terraces, said Chris Strans and Robert Strans, who work out of Ocean, New Jersey. "Half the houses have porches, half don't," said Chris; when there is a porch, the look is Mediterranean, with arches and columns, he added.

"Where we are, porches are essential," said Rick Fitzer of Savannah, Georgia. "The last home I built had a twenty-five-hundred-square-foot porch that wrapped around all four sides of the house." Rick said he thought the increasing popularity of full-scale porches showed that American builders and their clients were getting over an eighties-vintage crush on what he called "pseudo-porches," structures with a porchlike appearance but no porchological utility because they were too shallow and too narrow.

Three-quarters of the people who buy Ben Larockella's houses in and around Drummond, Delaware, want porches. "They're best-sellers," he said. "Half my clients use them cosmetically, half really use them. People like the feel of a porch. You have a chair or two out there. You can smoke a cigar in peace."

In South Ogden, Utah, the porch has lost popularity, said Lynn Parrish. "It's not as important as it used to be," she said. "But I'd like a wraparound porch myself."

Around the heavily Amish town of Millersburg, Ohio, the porch is a given, said contractor Ruben Yoder. "Most people like porches; they favor screened porches," he said. "The porch is a big asset; you have the family together there. Personally, I wouldn't want a house without a porch. I try to discourage people from building decks, which are totally worthless."

The porch is on the rise again in Napoleon, Michigan, said custom builders Mark and Shawn Murphy. "A house without a porch looks stupid," said Mark.

"Nothing bad has ever happened on a front porch," said Kent Hendricks, an advertising guy from Troy, Alabama, who put a porch on his Greek Revival house and keeps a sofa and chairs out there.

And that was it for the survey. The rest of my foray resulted in scribbles about Norman Rockwell vinyl siding (a licensing deal, like George Foreman cookers—except Mistuh Rockwell, he dead), home elevators ($12,500 installed, and quite nifty, though reminiscent of the claustrophobic elevator scene in the movie *The Producers*), tiny Bobcat 'dozers (I wanted to stick one in my backpack, if my backpack could have held a few tons of industrial steel), PermaPorch (an extruded plastic product that looks, feels, and cuts like wood), the Vita Mix vegetable juicer's excellent soup-making option (on the hunger-inducing veldt that is Georgia World, you take sustenance where you find it), Carlisle Restoration

Lumber (silken-surfaced flooring milled from salvaged beams), and the brilliantly addressed Screen Tight Porch Screening System (headquartered at One Better Way, Georgetown, South Carolina 29440).

By the time I had to catch my train I was hauling about forty pounds of pens, mouse pads, gimme hats, key rings, and brochures. Upon boarding, I strewed the roomette with my loot and began studying.

I read up on Safe Haven (a $3.1 million, 10,000-square-foot steel-and-concrete suburban chateau, featuring a fortified room usable as walk-in closet, disaster shelter, or vault).

I learned about *Creating the Not So Big House*. In a brochure for the sequel to her best-seller, *The Not So Big House,* author Sarah Susanka punctures the pretense of a certain sort of house by turning the phrase "starter castles"; I wished I'd said that.)

I got details on the Live-Work House (a type of mixed-use residence designed by Duany Plater-Zyberk & Co.).

And as I listened to the wheels on the tracks, I thought about how, in the past thirty years, the porch had come back in America.

The return has occurred at the iconic level, to be sure.

The porch is a staple of *New Yorker* artists. At last count, according to the Cartoon Bank, which represents the magazine's artists, George Booth led the league with twenty-five porch-related drawings. (If they put out one of those target-market books with a title like "Porch Cartoons from *The New Yorker*," remember that you read it here first.) The gang of talented idiots at *The Simpsons* has satirized the porch (as in the episode in which Marge has the murderous Itchy and Scratchy bowdlerized into "Porch Pals"). You can hardly watch thirty minutes of television without seeing a porch in a commercial. It's not unusual for the *NBC Evening News* to break for back-to-back ads, each opening with a porch scene, that tout mutual funds, then a blood additive for cancer patients. Porches pop up in ads for International House of Pancakes and utility companies. Burger King regularly runs full-page ads in *USA Today* for its "BK Back-Porch Griller" sandwich.

And in a twofer of resurrected Americana, not a few ads of varying message show an old Black bluesman playing guitar on a porch, perhaps a case of Mammon imitating art. Venerable Piedmont picker John Jackson, who kept his day job as a gravedigger for years after he started enjoying musical success, put out in 1999 what would be his final recording—he died in 2001—*Front Porch Blues,* its back cover illustrated with a picture of the aged bluesman in silhouette, taken on a Takoma Park, Maryland, porch near photographer Tom Radcliffe's studio. The mainstream edition of that image is a Dr Pepper commercial with Garth Brooks and a string band wowing a Rainbow Coalition of hotties on the front porch of a country store.

Since the mid-1990s, shelter magazines, television shows, and newspaper home sections have been running articles about how the porch is coming back, all with effusive asides on how best to decorate the space. The porch is also back in reality, prominently featured in real-estate ads as standard equipment or an option on new houses, as a sought-after feature on old houses in old neighborhoods, and as an addition, even at the front, to houses that never had porches in the first place.

One factor in the return of the porch has been the emergence of a national sensibility regarding old buildings and old ways of living. In the early 1960s, when the suburb reigned as the ideal American residential setting, a few voices began to challenge that template. In a prescient 1961 book, *The Death and Life of Great American Cities,* Jane Jacobs explains how new residential zones prospered at terrible cost to urban centers, how relentless emphasis on new construction erased or eroded the comforting, utilitarian presence of buildings of a certain age and type, and how the suburbs were destined to age badly.

"Each day, several thousand more acres of our countryside are eaten by the bulldozers, covered by pavement, dotted with suburbanites who have killed the thing they thought they came to find," Jacobs writes. "The semisuburbanized and suburbanized messes we create in this way become despised by their own inhabitants tomorrow."

Jacobs, who coined the phrase "eyes upon the street" as shorthand for the human presence a development needs to evolve into a neighborhood, was no Pollyanna. She didn't sanctify the corner grocery or the slum, and she didn't heap simplistic blame on the car as the sole agent of urban despoliation (though she did nail the auto's role in drastically diminishing the quality of pedestrian life).

In making a case for slowing the sprint for the suburbs and renewing cities by gentler means than the carpet-bombing techniques of the day, Jacobs argued eloquently for Americans to consider what they were throwing away—in their architecture and in their way of life—by always grabbing at the box labeled "New and Improved."

Jacobs was not alone. Formally and informally, a preservation movement had been growing, intent on persuading Americans not to trade their architectural and cultural heritage for a mess of pottage with asbestos siding, central air, and a carport. Since the thirties, the federal Historic Architecture and Buildings Survey had been photographing and chronicling old buildings. The National Trust for Historic Preservation was buying up and restoring what buildings it could and encouraging the private sector to do likewise.

But America also preserves by rejecting and ignoring, and that's what happened in the postwar rush from the cities that cost old neighborhoods so dearly in terms of status and population. Because they weren't ranches or Cape Cods or split-levels—in fact, they were anything but, with those big old porches, those vestibules, radiators, fireplaces, and high ceilings, probably built before Woodrow Wilson took office, for God's sake, think of the upkeep!— huge numbers of perfectly serviceable vintage houses sold slowly, or not at all. Something had to happen to them. They became rentals, whether as rooming houses or—especially in college towns—loosely organized households of young adults, of whom, thanks to the enormous birthrates of the late forties and early fifties, there were many.

College towns were important nodes of preservation, as well as conservers and transmitters of porch culture. Many of them dated to the great university-building era that followed the Civil War. Accustomed to the assumption that each fall would bring a new wave of residents, these academical villages developed large stocks of rental housing, much of it dating to the bungalow boom of the early twentieth century.

Although the houses saw heavy wear, the students and their rent checks made the old houses too valuable to tear down. Ratty but rugged, always with the spring-sprung sofa on the porch leaking stuffing and horsehair, college-town rentals made a strong impression on minds formed amid pristine suburban precision. Old houses weren't bad; they were cool. You could sit on the porch with your feet on the railing and a guitar in your lap, stay up all night out there and argue the validity of nonviolent noncooperation, the Gulf of Tonkin Resolution, or the Port Huron Statement. You could haul the speakers out and listen to some Dylan, or those English guys, what were they called, the Beatles. You could stow your dusty, thirsty boots beside the sofa and go inside for some brown rice, seaweed, and a dirty hot dog, then head out for a night in Dinkytown or wherever the genetic material was. College-town neighborhoods and their residential analogues in cities around the country became agar plates for a culture of young people ready for anything except what they'd been handed, which included the inward-turned little boxes of suburbia.

Of course, many students were tourists, only marking time in Scruffyland until it was time to grow up and get with the program; upon graduating, they dutifully headed for the 'burbs and bought split-levels. But suburban living never quite erased that memory of tree-lined blocks of old houses, each with its inhabitants hanging on the porch.

Others headed for the ragged edge, places like the Haight-Ashbury, West Hollywood, the East Village, or Dupont Circle or, if they'd rolled way off the board, Key West, the Central Park—sized island at the far end of Florida, where the rents were cheap, the times were good, and the weather suited your clothes, especially if you were hunting the auras left by dos Passos and Hemingway.

The decade roared into higher gear. Flaming ghettoes full of angry Black folks yelled at the cops and the National Guardsmen from their stoops and porches, and frightened suburban living rooms were full of angry white folks with one eye on the picture window and one watching the news for updates on the riot zones that America's cities had become. From these, respectable adults kept a safe distance, except to work.

But Middle America's adolescent and postadolescent offspring went looking for the poorer quarters. They found they could get a house or an apartment with some people—during the summer, you could get a van with some people and just *go*, like the Brando character in *The Wild One*, which seemed to play every few weeks at the local repertory house—and if you got enough people you didn't have to fork out much yourself. There was usually a dilapidated porch involved, because when it came to renting to people of a certain age and condition and circumstance, only houses of a certain age and condition and circumstance were going to be available. The houses were old, which you knew because they had front porches that lent themselves nicely to parties that were half political rally, half teen club dance. *LIFE* and *Time* magazines wrote about young folks having the times of their lives in communes and group houses, and communes and group houses multiplied.

Fashion flows from the street, and what is architecture but fashion stitched in brick and board? Old houses had texture; they had soul, what the Arabs call *barracca* and the Zen masters call *wabi sabi*, beauty enhanced by use, abuse, and wear. You began to see scrofulous old places as backdrops for fashion shoots, feature articles on rock stars, and album covers. One of the latter comes to mind: a 1969 release by a trio of rock-and-roll princes.

The album, lyrical folk-pop sung sweetly by David Crosby, Stephen Stills, and Graham Nash, came in a deceptively simple package. The outside cover was a medium-distance photo of the trio seated in front of an old wooden house, the inside a close-up of their faces, backlit and winsome, framed by voluminous fur collars. The only graphic information was the group name and the record company logo; otherwise, no song titles, no photo credits, no nothing. The pictures looked like the music and the music sounded like the pictures, as if both had been pulled out of the air, like a true story repeated exactly as somebody had heard it on a porch. Henry Diltz's cover photo was a Bizarro Universe take on the Currier & Ives "American Home" series. Instead of presenting the porch as an ideal, it was an anti-idealization, a slice of nonstandard American pie that was nonetheless utterly American, like Hunter S. Thompson's self-described penchant for sitting naked on the porch of his house in Woody Creek, Colorado, and firing his forty-four Magnum into the mountains.

The Crosby, Stills, and Nash house was decrepit, its window sashes peeling, its clapboard filthy with decades of L.A. smog deposits. Despite a greening touch of palm frond, its porch was slummy and weed-infested, with a crusty mailbox. At the far left, when you held the cover open, you saw a chancrous armchair molting behind a rusted metal drum. Beside the sofa, straddling the fold, a decaying ottoman stood in front of a broken-up door. Through one missing panel peered a ghostly androgyne (the image not a prefiguration of Neil Young, as was thought by those who believed Paul McCartney deceased, but a real picture of recording session drummer Dallas Taylor, inserted with darkroom wizardry).

From the proper angle, the scene's very junkiness made it lovable. A person who'd lived through the thirties and WW II (the Big One) would think, I remember houses like that, and porches like that, and what they smelled like and what it felt like to be stuck on one of them, and thank God for the GI Bill and the suburbs. But to the children of the half-century, Nash and Stills and Crosby looked great in their denim and their suede. You might live at home and have to borrow your mom's Fairlane to get to class at the local land-grant diploma mill (with the requirement that even if you were busy smashing the state, you be home in time for dinner). Maybe you covered your tuition working summers lugging Sheetrock and working weekends making pizza. Whoever you were, you could picture yourself on such a sofa, in the company of such boon companions, outside such a house, at such a moment as the photograph showed—all this, even though it turned out to be only a moment.

Less.

When Henry Diltz shot the picture, the group, then recording the songs that would appear on the album, lacked a moniker. The musicians were thinking of using their last names, as if they were a law or public relations firm, but they hadn't selected a sequence. So when Nash, Crosby, and Stills took a break from recording and went cruising with Diltz for a photo location, no one fretted about who sat or stood where. Someone in the van spotted an old house in West Hollywood that had a sofa on its porch, a pillarless, vestigial thing—really just a roof over a concrete slab, probably a relic of the between-the-wars era when the porch began its disappearing act. But the ratty little house somehow spoke to the musicians. The driver pulled over, and the shoot started. Diltz ran the musicians through a series of poses. They gravitated to the sofa, which had plenty of elbowroom. Stills, a guitar maven, had brought an acoustic; he was idly fretting it when Nash perched on the sofa back, assuming the position all moms yell at their boys to stop doing right now, please. Crosby hoisted his left knee, planting the heel of his cowboy boot in the cushion. Flagrantly long-haired, Crosby and Nash stared at the lens, the earnest Englishman leaning forward, hands clasped, the Yank—Californian, a movie cameraman's son, showbiz in his blood—reclining in lordly manner, a buckskin-jerkin version of Bert Lahr as the Cowardly Lion. The Texas-born Stills, boyish in button-down and v-neck, ears showing, as if he was growing his hair out after a stint with the Guard, was looking off to his left. Diltz squeezed the shutter, and it was on to the next pose.

When the film came back, the consensus was that the frame with Graham perched on the sofa back was the one; as soon as they had the name nailed, Diltz would reshoot with the fellows in the correct order. A week later, when the band's name was officially Crosby, Stills & Nash, Diltz hauled them all back to the location. But the rickety house and its amiable porch were gone, demolished in a blink—"a pile of sticks," Nash said later—so the test shot was all they had, and *Crosby, Stills & Nash*, the album, came out with the singers arrayed in the order Nash, Stills, and Crosby. Over the years, the cognitive dissonance of the name and the photo raised eyebrows, but in the end it didn't matter a lick. The record appeared in the spring of 1969. That summer, at the Woodstock Music and Arts Fair, half a million people watched the trio's debut. Crosby,

Stills & Nash closed Day Three with a seven-song set. An extended, ecstatic "Suite: Judy Blue Eyes" made it into *Woodstock: The Movie,* giving the record belated but massive legs and its song list permanent radio respectability. *Crosby, Stills & Nash* sold by the stack, went gold, double-gold, and mega-gold. The album cover decorated uncounted dorm rooms, living rooms, rec rooms, and bedrooms, the singers' casual pose and lilting music persuading millions of fans that the thing to do was find an old house that had a beat-up sofa on the porch where you could be with your friends, man.

But there were also some scary porches out there, especially in Hollywood Land. By the late sixties, movie makers had finally kicked the sweetness-and-light habit and begun taking American cinema into its hardest-edged incarnation ever. America wasn't sitting amiably on the porch anymore, and neither were the movies.

It had been less than three decades since Henry Fonda had stood tall and honest on the same country-store porch set in his roles as Tom Joad and Abe Lincoln. But come 1967, it was Clyde Barrow and Bonnie Parker that Arthur Penn wanted to meet cute on a porch. In *Bonnie and Clyde,* there's no county council election at hand, and the way to beat the Depression isn't by picking fruit but by stealing. So we see bumptious, weasel-featured Clyde (Warren Beatty) adrift in some tank town. He's loitering at a corner store with intent to commit felony auto, leaning against a porch column stapled with bottle caps, matchstick in his mug and six-shooter in his grip. Up sashays luscious, loose Bonnie (Faye Dunaway), who strokes the gun barrel as if to say, "Hey, big boy, is that a pistol in your fist or are you just glad to see me?"

This was not the porch as we had known it, and it wouldn't be again for some time to come. The porches of *In the Heat of the Night* and *The Sting,* the stoops of *Midnight Cowboy, The French Connection, Mean Streets,* and *The Godfather* (in its many incarnations) showed the liminal space as a place of confrontation and misrepresentation, of threatened and actual violence, and of an America not bound together in glossy happiness at all but fractured and fragmented, able to salvage a semblance of tranquil unity only in passing.

At the start of *Deliverance,* canoeing suburbanites and upland hillbillies meet in a porch scene frightening, exultant, and elegiac all in the same tangled moment. At first tentatively and then with abandon, doomed guitar-picking lawyer Drew Ballinger (Ronnie Cox) and the dimwit boy with the banjo extend their instruments across a vast cultural divide, enveloping themselves and their companions in a storm of gleeful blue-grass you wish would go on forever.

But it doesn't. The last note dies, the smiles vanish, and later, when the canoeists pass beneath the banjo boy on a bridge, he doesn't acknowledge them—the prologue to a sequence of awful events.

Of course, not everyone got a house with some people or a van with some people and joined the Revolution, cutting all ties with the American establishment and spinning off into the ozone, and hardly anyone went canoeing with

Burt Reynolds in the murderous hollers of the Georgia highlands. Even though Vietnam, race, poverty, and all the other issues were tearing at the national fabric, and even though the porches in the movies weren't warm and cozy anymore, for better and for worse, life went on.

For example, the Black Panthers might come to New Haven and incite their acolytes among the Yale student body to rise up on in protest against the trial of Bobby Seale. But even as the tear gas from the resulting demonstrations wafted across campus like a memo from a bill collector, Vince Scully was still teaching the history of American architecture, still pointing out the follies of modernism and still sending the golden youth into New Haven's streets to see what they could see.

In the early seventies, the latest crop of Scullyites included Elizabeth Plater-Zyberk and Andres Duany. Both were born in the umbra of 1950, both dutiful and ambitious. Both with ancestry and upbringing that suggested a degree of foreordainment to their choices of career, they would be rebels with a different cause.

Lizz Plater-Zyberk's parents had come to the United States after the war from Poland. Josaphat Plater-Zyberk, an estate manager's son who'd practiced architecture with his brother until things went rancid for the Jews, had spent the war dodging Nazis. In America, he worked first as a draftsman, then as the staff architect at the Philadelphia Savings Fund Society; on the side, he designed restoration plans for old farmhouses. Maria Plater-Zyberk, née Meysztowicz, had trained in agricultural management; gardening was a mainstay of her life. Family trips frequently involved visits to important architectural sites. Josaphat and Maria and their four children—Lizz was the youngest—lived in Paoli, a railroad suburb. The neighborhood was mostly working-class, truck drivers, mechanics, building engineers, not people advancing up the rungs but holding jobs and raising families in single-family houses and duplexes. Josaphat could walk to the train station—Paoli was on the wrong side of the tracks, with a Black neighborhood across a ravine at one edge—and Maria could walk with the kids to the corner store, where everyone shopped. The children took the train to school. Josaphat and Maria were active in the PTA and helped raise money for the volunteer fire department. No grass grew in the family's shady yard. This made it easy for Lizz, who liked to go with her dad to the office and his farmhouse jobs—she loved the way the old houses looked, both intact and under construction—to organize her siblings into a crew that built miniature towns out of wood scraps. By the time Lizz enrolled at Manhattanville College, she knew she wanted to be an architect. She transferred to Princeton, graduated, and went to Yale for her master's.

Andres Duany spent his childhood in Santiago, Cuba, but he'd been born in Manhattan; his father, also Andres, had had a green card from birth and wanted his offspring to do likewise. The Duanys had been multinational for a long time. In the early 1700s, Ambrose O'Duane, a fortifications engineer, decided to leave his home turf in County Sligo, Ireland. Like many a wild Irish goose, O'Duane landed in Spain, where he learned that the empire needed bastions to defend its New World holdings. O'Duane sailed to Cuba to build forts, and there he stayed, putting down strong roots. Ambrose's son continued the family trade. He begat soldiers and politicians, under whose stewardship "O'Duane" evolved into "Duany," with the patriarch of each generation named "Andres." The family came to own cane farms and mahogany forests outside Santiago, near the Sierra Maestra foothills.

In 1905, with the sugar and lumber markets sagging, the regnant Andres Duany developed a streetcar suburb he dubbed *Vista Allegre*. Happy View spread along a rolling avenue dotted with diamond-shaped squares where statues of poets stood. In 1945, his son, Andres, built forty suburban blocks denser than dad's—flat-roofed and modernist, made of concrete. To build it, Duany's crews used heavy equipment bought surplus from the U.S. military; *Vista Allegre* had taken the easy ground, requiring Andres the Younger to hack *Terraza de la Vista Allegre* from land more montane.

Andres the Youngest and his brother and sister grew up in Santiago until *los barbudos* descended from the Sierra Maestra to put the boot into Fulgencio Batista's dictatorial behind. Believing Fidel and his rebels to be a flash in the political pan, the Duanys decamped to Long Island to await the restoration. Andres, at the age of ten, got a taste of suburban life there and then in Miami, where the family moved when it became clear that Castro was going to be more permanent than expected. Based on frequent drawings of railroad engines and other large machinery, Andres enrolled at Yale to study mechanical engineering, but it turned out what he really wanted was architecture. He finished his under-graduate degree and stayed on for a master's.

Plater-Zyberk and Duany met in studio, scene of the drill that architects call charrette. *Charrette*, the French word for "cart," entered the lexicon at L'Ecole Beaux Arts in Paris during the nineteenth century. When projects were due, attendants would crisscross the studios, pushing carts onto which drawings were to be placed. Few architecture students, French or otherwise, deliver work sooner than required; the run-up to a deadline is a round-the-clock jag that can last more than a week.

The squeak of the cart wheels being to the inmates at L'Ecole as the rumble of tumbrels had been to imprisoned aristocrats in republican Paris, "charrette" acquired a connotation of "brilliant creative output under pressures so huge as to drive ordinary mortals screaming from the room while we the elect resolutely proceed with our work."

On the streets of New Haven, as they followed Scully's instructions to look at the sidewalks, trees, and porches, Plater-Zyberk and Duany saw what their teacher had intended, and more: a harmonious arrangement of elements, yes, but also a way of living that America had forsworn.

In his lectures, Scully explicated the arc of the American city, from village to town, to urban center, to the shrinking core that the suburbs now threatened to erase, unless some new way could be found to house, employ, educate, and entertain Americans. In their fieldwork, Plater-Zyberk and Duany and compatriots saw that New Haven's residential neighborhoods were not just eye-pleasing arrays, but living, breathing organisms, sustaining and being sustained by a variety of life. The stacked flats and duplexes housed the prosperous and the impecunious, the old and the young, adults and children, singles and families, students and workers and retirees, white, black, brown, yellow. Of those who worked, some worked at home; others walked or took public transport to jobs in the city, whether in business offices, factories, or the university's classrooms and laboratories. People sat on the stoops and porches, strolled the sidewalks, patronized the corner stores. Of course, downtown New Haven wasn't a utopia. There was crime; there was traffic; there were pollution and congestion and racial tension. It was a city, with all the attendant problems, but in its flawed reality, architects-to-be Duany and Plater-Zyberk saw possibilities.

Andres graduated first. In 1974 he went to Europe to study, then landed a teaching job at the University of Miami architecture school. Lizz finished her degree and worked for a firm in Italy, returning to Paoli in time for the 1975 recession. She was clerking at a store in the Philadelphia suburbs when Andres called.

The U.S. Navy was closing its base at Key West, Florida, whose Old Town section—a retronym coined to distinguish it from fifties-vintage development at the island's east end—had begun to be a popular tourist spot. As part of a report on the Navy base's fate and its impact on the local setting, Andres had landed a contract to survey Old Town's architecture and planning. The job was literally to take the measure of the place, the frontages, setbacks, sidewalk and street widths, curb heights and turning radii, building masses, and every other physical thing that made Key West *Key West,* and then to translate them to a graphic analysis. He needed a hand. Could Lizz provide it? She could. They went to Key West and started cataloging the housing stock.

The island was as *outré* as ever, with the latest generation of outlaws in whooping residence. Key West had always attracted its share of homosexual residents and visitors—Tennessee Williams had kept a little conch house for himself since 1950, and Truman Capote was a regular around town—and now, with gay liberation in the air, the post-Stonewall crowd felt comfortable cruising Duval Street. But Ernest Hemingway's macho legacy hadn't evaporated. Old Town's residents included Thomas McGuane, who excelled at bonefishing and enjoyed carousing at the Fourth of July restaurant; he'd written a Key West novel called *92 in the Shade* about a would-be bonefishing guide who liked to carouse at the Fourth of July. Jimmy Buffett, a displaced Tennessean who'd quit journalism to see if he could make music in the money business, liked to sit on his porch swing and strum on his six-string; eventually he would write a song about that, and he'd start making money in the music business.

Amid this rich stew, Duany and Plater-Zyberk counted conch houses, measured mansions, and calculated setbacks and street widths. Elsewhere, similar endeavors tried to quantify the quality of life present and past. With the national bicentennial approaching, there was increased interest in how Americans had lived a hundred years before. Books like John Maass's *The Victorian House in America* sold well. Membership in the Victorian Society of America soared.

The era of the Queen Anne house and the bungalow came alive in a best-selling 1974 novel, *Ragtime*. Assembling an intricate, erudite mosaic of America at the start of the twentieth century, author E. L. Doctorow evoked a world in which he blended fiction and fact until each resembled the other. With deceptively simple prose, Doctorow invented a New Rochelle full of lush, shingle-style houses with screen porches, as well as an Atlantic City whose boardwalk was lined with splendorous oceanfront hotel porches like the one at The Breakers. Readers, who bought copies of *Ragtime* by the bale, began to wonder what it would be like to live in a big old house with a porch.

The Arts and Crafts and Craftsman styles, each of which had spent so much time in exile, both underwent rehabilitation. After decades of being derided for looking like the Frankensteins' family furniture, pieces by Gustav Stickley began to sell at auction for stratospheric prices, paid by such enthusiasts as Barbra Streisand. In Parsippany, New Jersey, where Stickley's Craftsman Farms had come to grief and where still stood the only house he ever designed—a 5,000-square-footer made of chestnut logs, with a gigantic enclosed porch—admirers organized a Stickley Day that became an annual event, leading to the creation of the Craftsman Farms Foundation (and, in 1990, to the opening of the house as a museum). Original Stickley designs, made by new manufacturers, started to appear in furniture showrooms. The blocky old style and its accompanying architecture became new again.

The housing market was buzzing. You started to hear the sobriquet "Baby Boomer" in regard to home-buying patterns. Price being a big deal for most first-time purchasers, my g-g-g-generation often had to buy at the bottom of the market, which often meant old places that needed work, usually in prewar neighborhoods thick with porches. Buying an old house was a litmus test for friends and family—either they understood and embraced the stack of Sheetrock in the living room, or they didn't. When you did sign on the dotted line for a house of a certain age, you joined a tribe. You could subscribe to your own newsletter—*Old House Journal*, a hand-typed communiqué that carried the inside dope on plaster restoration, wiring, and such—which had the air of *samizdat* shoved under a refusenik's apartment door in Moscow. (The newsletter's founder, Clem Labine, knew whereof he wrote; in 1967, he and his wife bought an 1882 brownstone in Brooklyn that they resurrected from rooming-house ruin. His family's renovation experience led Labine to start *OHJ* in 1972, supported by an $8,000 nest egg and his wife's work as a writer and producer of the soap opera *Ryan's Hope*. At the start, *OHJ* had five paid subscribers; soon that number was 20,000, and Labine was well on his way to his goal of raising Americans' consciousness about the intrinsic value of old houses.)

At parties, you could titillate horrified suburbanites and thrill the brother- and sisterhood of the Shop-Vac and the pry-bar by stripping your sleeve and showing your scars and saying, "Yep, happened last October 25. You shoulda been there. I was up on a ladder, belt-sander got away from me. Lucky I didn't break my damn neck."

But for every bone-tired renovator who cursed fortune for having dealt him such a great house for so cheap, there were plenty of boomers wanting to pay list for fresh, clean, unused houses, sanitary strips still on the toilet seats. Their avidity drove the market for suburban development into high gear. The asphalt tentacles reached into the countryside, lining it with shopping centers and strip malls, a region where to be carless was to be stateless. Fearing invasion from the cities, counties that could no longer rely on restrictive covenants passed ordinances requiring minimal lots of an acre or more, and the color line became an economic boundary.

America also preserves by rejecting and ignoring, as happened in the postwar rush from the cities that cost old neighborhoods so dearly in terms of status and population.

Design changed, too. Split-levels, ranches, and Cape Cods were passé; that was what we'd grown up in, and if we weren't gonna buy some Addams Family hulk that needed a ton of work like our wacky friend who spent his spare time scraping up old linoleum, pulling wire, and field-testing screwguns—well, then, we wanted to illustrate the length and breadth of our magnificence, and we didn't care if the illustration was true to any particular school of architecture.

On their enormous lots, great pastiches of house style went up, set far apart. They had a castellated look, as if the owners anticipated a return to the Dark Ages and a need for fortified dwellings like the ones that had dotted the Veneto before the *Pax Venetiana*—"tract mansions," in the enviable phrase of stiletto-fingered essayist Henry Allen. There were no porches at the fronts of these beauties, just garage doors like portcullises and out back decks like the surveillance towers in *The Bridge on the River Kwai*. You could stain them to match the stockade-style fence.

In developments where covenants or lack of space limited on-street parking, the need to stow vehicles led to bigger and bigger garages, until practically the whole front of the house was garage, with the entry door barely visible at one side. Critics called them "snout houses" because they suggested the business end of a camel's face.

The jibe showed the extent to which suburbia had become a target of opportunity and an occasion for seeking alternatives. Enough people had had enough of cul-de-sacs, strip malls, and commuting three hours a day between the garage at home and the parking lot at work to fuel a backlash against the style of living that once seemed like the epitome of the American dream.

There were other ways to live.

As they'd seen in New Haven, Lizz Plater-Zyberk and Andres Duany were observing how in Key West the tiny details of intent or accident in a town's or neighborhood's growth influenced not only the way people there lived but the way people there *were*. Gays, straights, workers, hippies, welfare families, trust-funders—sure, Key West had pockets of homogeneity, but across the island representatives of all cadres lived among one another. When houses sat close together and close to the street, with cars parked at the curb to make pedestrians feel buffered from the passing traffic, the sidewalk life touched the porch life. Key West streets were extremely narrow in comparison with those in the suburbs—which had to be wide, public safety officials said, to accommodate fire engines—but the rickety wooden houses didn't seem to burn down any more often than the ones along those expansive boulevards.

Duany and Plater-Zyberk asked themselves, why don't we build places like this anymore? Not long after, Andres asked Lizz to marry him. She said yes.

Around the country, other architects, planners, teachers, writers, and political leaders—people like Stefanos Polyzoides, Peter Calthorpe, Sim Van Der Ryn, John Norquist, Dan Solomon, Elizabeth Moule, Philip Langdon, Anne Tate, Ray Gindroz, Kenneth Jackson, Jonathon Rose, Victor Dover, Christopher Alexander, James Howard Kunstler, to name several—were also asking questions:

Why did we have to keep emptying our cities and filling the countryside with suburbs?

Why did we have to keep segregating ourselves by income and class and race?

Why did everybody have to have a car, two cars, three, and have to spend so much time in them?

Why did we have to keep sprawling across the landscape like a fallen wrestler?

Wasn't there another way to do it?

Each generation of architects has its tribal gatherings, its calendar of conferences and symposia. Through the latter seventies, Duany and Plater-Zyberk and their ilk rode the circuit, hearing one another's tales and nodding, like old-house owners encountering fellow veterans of the DIY wars. But instead of talking radiators and mantles, porch joists and balusters, or beaded tongue-in-groove and ceiling fans, this tribe was talking zero setbacks and narrow frontages, density and public space, multi-use and grandfather clauses. What they had in common wasn't the litany of troubles that came with home ownership but the litany of responsibilities that came with community stewardship. They thought of the way of living and planning and building they had in mind as being anything but of the suburbs: human-scale, with neighborhoods where you could walk to the grocery store, the train station, or the corner store, with people of different incomes and backgrounds and trades all living in the same place, the way they had in Paoli and New Haven and Key West.

And what was the antonym for "suburban," at least as this cadre conceived of that state of existence?

"Urban."

Not the old urban, not urban-decay urban, urban-renewal urban, urban-crisis urban, urban-disaster urban, the tired-out, burned-out, hung-down, brung-down thing the city had become, but "urban" as it once had been and could be again. They resurrected "urban" as the word that once had embodied the vivacity, variety, diversity, and tolerance, as well as the competition, the constant tides of change and opportunity, and the cycles of success, failure, and regeneration that had enabled cities to develop and flourish in the first place.

A new urban.

A new urbanism.

New Urbanism.

The New Urbanists looked backward to sources like *American Vitruvius: An Architect's Handbook of Civic Art,* a 1920s-vintage book by Werner Hegemann and Elbert Peets. *American Vitruvius* became one of the movement's foundation texts, along with Jane Jacobs's *The Death and Life of Great American Cities,* Vincent Scully's *American Architecture and Urbanism,* and Lewis Mumford's *The City in History.* Another prime model was the work of Georges Eugene Haussmann, who, as Emperor Louis-Napoleon's prefect of Paris, dramatically redesigned and expanded that city in the middle of the nineteenth century. But the New Urbanist canon was flexible, and grew constantly. New essays and books began to appear almost daily; the phenomenon seemed to be evolving right before its advocates' eyes.

Along with colleagues at his nonprofit firm in Berkeley, California, Christopher Alexander had been trying to capture the firefly light. Son of a pair of archaeologists, he'd come of age in postwar England, living in neighborhoods around Oxford that were jumbles of academics and blue-collar toilers. Alexander became an architect, teaching at the University of California at Berkeley, designing structures, and philosophizing. The result was a three-volume 1977 exegesis on the nature of building and community. *The Timeless Way of Building,*

A Pattern Language, and *The Oregon Experiment* aimed to identify every single element involved in assembling houses, workplaces, neighborhoods, towns, and cities. The books spouted *Whole Earth Catalog*ish dicta, such as "The suburb is an obsolete and contradictory form of human settlement" and "There is abundant evidence to show that high buildings make people crazy." But they also codified in micrometric detail the tiles that could be used to arrange the mosaic of a place where you actually would want to live. To begin their second volume, *A Pattern Language,* Alexander and cohort synthesized the ten patterns that could be combined in myriad ways to create a porch:

- "Private terrace on the street"
- "Sunny place"
- "Outdoor room"
- "Six-foot balcony"
- "Paths and goals"
- "Ceiling height variety"
- "Columns at the corners"
- "Front door bench"
- "Raised flowers"
- "Different chairs"

It was architecture and town planning as haiku, or the Zen master's slap, and copies began to circulate among the true believers, an additional foundation text to line up beside Hegemann, Peets, Jacobs, and the rest.

Duany and Plater-Zyberk started a firm they called DPZ. He quit teaching at the University of Miami architecture school, and she started teaching there (in 1995 becoming the school's dean). DPZ's first project was a development called Charleston Place, a 110-unit townhouse pod in Boca Raton, Florida.

Learning from Key West—and from Charleston, Savannah, Greenwich Village, and all the other places that worked—DPZ designed Charleston Place as a microcosmically small town of traditionally detailed structures organized around public spaces, with setbacks and frontages calibrated to engineer a social context into what otherwise would have been simply a building development. It worked. The units sold. A community took form. Professional journals took note. Awards were given. Attention was paid. And Robert Davis called.

Davis, who'd inherited eighty acres at the inside curve of the Florida Panhandle, was *avis rarissima*—a developer and an idealist, which is sort of like being a vegetarian butcher. He wanted to turn his birthright into a new kind of town, one that deliberately and consciously wove into its *raison d'etre* the accumulated wisdom of the American small town as it had once been, as Davis saw it recapitulated to a degree in DPZ's design at Charleston Place.

To achieve and heighten that effect at Seaside, as Davis dubbed his experiment, he needed to control the architects and builders who would be designing and constructing its several hundred houses. Obtaining and maintaining control meant writing a strict master plan—the town's genetic code, if you will. To write the rules that would serve as Seaside's DNA, Davis hired DPZ.

Seaside might have been new, but it wasn't urban. The site was twenty miles from Panama City, known chiefly as a point of reference for shady characters in the novels of Elmore Leonard and Ross McDonald. But as Plater-Zyberk and Duany worked and reworked their approach to writing the terms by which the development would define itself, urbanism kept creeping into the conversation. They realized they weren't in the business of designing buildings but planning towns, putting into practice what they'd learned from Scully and other masters like Alan Greenberg, as well as their friends and colleagues.

Plater-Zyberk and Duany began to imagine Seaside as a small town, a neighborhood of neighborhoods, a composition comprising the notes sounded by each house and the chords arising from the precincts in which they stood. The idea wasn't to tell people how to play notes, but what notes to play; the chords and the composition would take care of themselves. Plater-Zyberk and Duany realized they could do that with a building code, the set of specifications by which designers and builders have to play. Conventional suburban developments usually didn't have their own codes. Developers operated within the local regulatory framework, which rarely addressed aesthetics. But if Seaside had its own code, and that code incorporated its own aesthetic, the town would have its own look.

So what should a brand-new Florida resort town look like? Well, it wouldn't be bad if it looked like an old Florida resort town, would it?

Taking out their graphic analysis of Key West's Old Town, Duany and Plater-Zyberk drilled in, mining the data for useful details: building heights, setbacks, frontages. Transferring or adjusting measurements, they made the streets of Seaside narrow, as the streets were in Key West, to keep the neighborhoods intimate. As for the houses, well, the designers didn't fret about architectural specifics except to say all the buildings in Seaside had to reflect the character of the region's architecture by being made of wood. And buildings had to meet certain stipulations regarding windows, roof pitch, overhang, setbacks, and the like.

Oh, and each house had to have a front porch, and a fence.

The fence requirement was a way of setting a boundary on setbacks that tended to crowd the sidewalk, and it made sense. The slight extent to which the pickets defined the border of a property also connected the lot to the sidewalk and the street.

As for the porches—it gets hot in the Florida Panhandle, maybe not Key-West-in-August hot, with the sun feeling as if it's orbiting your skull at a distance of about eighteen inches, but hot enough. Duany and Plater-Zyberk thought it made sense to require porches, not only aesthetically as a nod to Key West's shotguns and conch houses and turreted Victorians, most of which had porches, but practically, as a means of cooling the air coming into the house—even if, in all likelihood, most Seaside houses would have central air conditioning.

DPZ completed the code, and Davis parceled out lots to a variety of builders and architects. Work done, Duany and Plater-Zyberk moved on. Seaside began to take shape.

And a funny thing happened.

The Seaside code turned out to be like the blues, a basic form within which a talented practitioner could improvise endlessly, like R. L. Burnside picking on the porch of a juke joint. The patterns were always familiar but never the same, a note flatted here or bent blue there in an unexpected way that gave the old familiar whole a shimmering newness. Instead of struggling to compose fancy sonatas of postmodernist splendor, designers working at Seaside turned the prescribed riffs over, under, sideways, and down, creating houses that looked simultaneously unexpected and completely familiar, like themselves and like each other, as houses in old neighborhoods often do.

The reviews started to come in. Seaside's visual appeal drew huzzahs, as did its atmosphere. Individual houses elicited praise. But what put the place on the map were the porches. People were wild about 'em. It wasn't unusual for visitors to drive from miles away, park their cars, and walk around Seaside to bask in the ambience, the way the Japanese take placid pleasure in visiting cherry orchards at blossom time. In 1990, *Time* magazine anointed Seaside among its "Best of the Decade" selections.

Plater-Zyberk and Duany took note of the note taken. They had thought of the Seaside porches in literal and practical terms, concentrating on the facts of heat, sun, and shade, but the marketplace had responded to symbolism. The architects had been trading in logic, which reveals what people need; but they had happened onto the accidental magic of giving people what they wanted.

"We thought that the point of requiring porches on the fronts of houses was for environmental reasons—to cool the air coming into the house," Plater-Zyberk said. "We realized after the houses were up that everybody saw the social component of the porch—its status as the important in-between space separating the public realm from the private realm. And we realized that the narrow streets and short front yards that we were imitating also enable you to walk along comfortably because the traffic on the street isn't speeding. You can stop and talk to your neighbors. We began to see a kind of inter-connected complex system with the wisdom of the ages in it."

Simply put, the front porch is too good an idea to be allowed to slip away,
even if the hospitality we display is more theoretical than real.

Chapter Sixteen

REVIVAL

The New Urbanists' rediscovery of the porch had a delicious whiff about it of the law of unintended consequences. In mandating porches at Seaside, DPZ had meant to cool off neotraditional houses, but instead the town planners made the dwellings and their porches the hottest thing going—a trend reflected in the culture at large.

As Seaside's architects were designing porches that appealed to the leisure class, other designers were putting the porch to use as a tool of social engineering in less luxurious settings. Hired to revive a squalorous federally funded public housing project in Newport News, Virginia, another New Urbanist, Raymond Gindroz, remembered Jane Jacobs's adjuration about "eyes upon the street," and designed a renovation plan that put porches on the fronts of formerly faceless units. The porches didn't make residents jump up and get jobs, but they did improve the quality of life, and the humane and human-scale texture that the porches brought to the neighborhood help cut the miasma of anonymity and suspicion that had oozed down those sad streets. The Department of Housing and Urban Development began to look into rewriting its building rules to incorporate more such humanizing approaches into projects it built or managed.

Gindroz, Duany, Plater-Zyberk, and other New Urbanists began to see their vision broaden and acquire detailed form. Growth and building were inevitable; suburban sprawl did not have to be. They would challenge it by planning new towns that carried the spirit of Seaside into the real world, creating what they called TNDs, or "traditional neighborhood developments," that emphasized mixed-use zoning (to bolster diversity), higher density (to reduce sprawl), and reliance on design forms that harkened back to the old-fashioned American neighborhood of sidewalks and front porches. New Urbanist enclaves like Kentlands, outside Washington, D.C., and I'on Village, near Charleston, South Carolina, began to grow. To date, more than two hundred developments in that vein have been started or completed.

Duany, a master panegyrist, went on the road with a slide show that explained the New Urbanist ethos and its applicability to a variety of situations. In spellbinding soliloquies that could go on for hours of witty insight and devastating criticism, he led audiences through the history of urbanism, the rise and decline of the suburbs, and the emergence of the new new thing he and his tribe were pushing. His deft presentations and quick wit won the cause many allies.

In 1993, the Congress of the New Urbanism convened for the first time. Since then, the body has produced *The Charter of the New Urbanism*, a manifesto setting forth the movement's principles and goals, which have expanded and deepened as it has found common ground with the "smart growth" movement. The true believers have acquired more followers. Christopher Alexander's trilogy has become what the *New York Times* has termed "a geek bible." In analyses like Peter Calthorpe's earnest *Next American Metropolis: Ecology, Community and the American Dream*, Philip Langdon's deft *Better Place to Live: Reshaping the American Suburb*, and James Howard Kunstler's bomb-tossing broadside *The Geography of Nowhere: The Rise and Decline of America's Manmade Landscape*, the New Urbanists have made a powerful argument for rethinking residential development. (Kunstler, a masterful writer with eight novels to his credit, has become the movement's Savonarola, adamantly and wittily staking out positions so resplendently dyspeptic that he makes Duany et al seem like a platoon of Casper Milquetoasts). Along with their colleague Jeff Speck, Plater-Zyberk and Duany made headlines with their 2000 book, *Suburban Nation*, an indictment of and prescription for what ails American communities. One oft-aired New Urbanist complaint has been that the movement is about much more than picket fences and front porches.

And they're absolutely right.

But an image whose time has come is a powerful thing. What started at Seaside ballooned at Celebration. That $2.5-billion new town, developed starting in 1991 by the Disney Corporation, embraced some New Urbanist touches, including the porches and the fences and the neotraditional architecture. (With typical Disneyan thoroughness, the company sent an architect on a research tour of the South to photograph and measure porches, storefronts, setbacks, and such in Savannah, Charleston, Key West, and other cities; he compiled his data in a pattern book provided to builders.)

Celebration was a mixed success; the houses sold, and many residents loved the place, but others felt it didn't live up to advance billing, and that the paw of the Big Mouse lay too heavily on the place. There were technical difficulties. Roofs leaked. Pipes had to be replaced. Builders had to redo brickwork, foundations, siding. Disney had promised economic and racial integration, but Celebration turned out overwhelmingly white. Even admirers, like journalists Douglas Frantz and Catherine Collins, who bought a house in Celebration and installed their family in it so they could write a book about the experience, had to admit that the much-touted porch culture never materialized or took the shape of old-time snoopiness and fussbudgetry.

In *Celebration U.S.A.: Living in Disney's Brave New Town*, Frantz and Collins chronicled householders' fears of the "porch police," as the design enforcement authorities were known. But the instant town's porches also had their fans. "Our porches are so close to the street that it makes them like little theater seats," one resident told the authors. "Our movie screen is our front porch. . . . It's a wonderful parade. It's thoroughly entertaining." To Celebration, as to Seaside, outsiders came to drink in the unusual sight of Americans walking around their neighborhoods and sitting on their porches like tame passenger pigeons.

A ripple effect set in. Although builders, developers, and bureaucrats at first pooh-poohed the New Urbanist party line as being out of sync with American tastes, portraying it as a high-end product with a limited market, shelter magazines and newspaper home sections began to run amply illustrated features on the picket fences, porches, narrow streets, and closely set houses of places like Seaside and Celebration, displaying them as if they were game preserves for some rare, endangered, and very lovable species. Even the pointedly modernist shelter magazine *dwell* hailed Prospect New Town, a Colorado development orchestrated by DPZ but whose building codes encouraged quirky postneotraditional designs. In what *dwell* called "America's Coolest Neighborhood," the porches can be cozily familiar or starkly dissonant with the New Urbanist image. Either way, houses in Prospect have porches, and the porches see lots of use.

Although the American housing establishment initially resisted the New Urbanist program, builders and planners began to change their tune. After the 2001 National Association of Home Builders (NAHB) show, which featured a trio of DPZ-designed "live/work" units, the buzz in the biz was that Americans wanted smaller, more utilitarian houses located closer to town, perhaps erected on "in-fill" lots left vacant in previous waves of construction. Mainframe builders like Pulte Corporation and Centex Homes announced plans to build developments in the hearts of cities like Detroit and Dallas.

"Over the next couple of years, in-fill has got to become a way of life," an NAHB spokesman told the *Wall Street Journal*. Reported the *Washington Post*, ". . . as states and counties consider ways of taming sprawl, they are rewriting zoning laws to make it easier to build TNDs and other types of mixed-use, high-density neighborhoods in the suburbs."

The New Urbanist credo had gone from possibility to marketability. In December 2001, Elizabeth Plater-Zyberk and Andres Duany joined Vincent Scully on a dais at the National Building Museum; Duany and Plater-Zyberk were there to accept a $25,000 prize named for their mentor to recognize "exemplary practice, scholarship, or criticism in architecture, landscape design, historic preservation, planning, or urban design." The first recipient of the Scully had been Scully himself; the second, legendary urban planning critic Jane Jacobs. Duany and Plater-Zyberk used the money to take thirty-five members of their firm's staff to Paris for a week, then returned to their mission.

As the New Urbanists were rediscovering the porch, so were American filmgoers and readers. The low art of the late twentieth century exercised no less influence than its antecedent had in the late nineteenth, stirring porch envy in the hearts of Baby Boomers when they watched the aging children of the sixties disport on and around the wraparound of that gorgeous, enormous Low Country cottage in *The Big Chill*. In his bestselling, Pulitzer Prize–winning western tale, *Lonesome Dove,* novelist Larry McMurtry introduced former Texas Rangers August McRae and Woodrow F. Call and their raggle-taggle Hat Creek Ranch outfit by keeping the cowboys mostly on the porch of the wretched Hat Creek bunkhouse for 200-plus pages before finally sending them onto the trail with a herd of purloined Mexican cattle. How many readers, overt or surreptitious, of Robert James Waller's cheesy but wildly popular novel *The Bridges of Madison County* thrilled to the scene of Francesca Johnson drinking lemonade on the porch of her farmhouse in Winterset, Iowa, when manly man photographer Robert Kincaid drives up in his pickup?

But perhaps the most telling example of the porch's comeback as a mass-market icon was a venture by publishing-world highbrows. A 1990 volume that matched old photographs with porch-related passages by Southern writers created a niche market for Algonquin Press of Chapel Hill and its parent firm, Workman Press—and revealed how much more popular the idea of the porch had become. When *Out on the Porch* sold well, Algonquin and Workman started publishing a photo calendar on the same theme. So far every edition has sold out; the annual press run is up to 90,000, and the publisher's main worry is having the quote pipeline dry up. ("We don't assign the photos; we get them from stock houses, which keeps costs down," said editor Shannon Ravenel. "But the literary quotations are getting harder and harder to find. Luckily, the porch is so important to Southern writers that, if we look carefully, we can always find something that works.")

On a less literary level, the phrase "front porch" proved popular on the Internet, where, after all, a home page is the digital equivalent of a liminal space. A mid-2023 query on Google Chrome using "front porch" yielded 31.2 million hits.

But a twenty-dollar book and a myriad of Web site names don't impress the powers of commerce as much as, say, a $325,000 house. When properties in New Urbanist developments began to change hands, they sold at a premium, sometimes more than twenty-five percent above the comparables for conventional houses of the same sort. That got the attention of architects, builders, and developers.

In the go-go nineties, as Baby Boomers were entering their big financial years, something clicked. No longer did so many of the pig-in-the-snake's-belly generation wish to live in splendid suburban isolation, hearing their footsteps echo in the hallways of tract mansions as they walked from the garage to the great room to find their offspring asleep on the sofa in front of Homer trying to strangle Bart. The increasing number of stories about trips to the dermatologist to get precancerous growths frozen off somebody's mug suggested that those glorious days of deck-bound sunbasking might be at an end. And instead of lurking inside one's own personal Xanadu, trying to avoid the ultraviolet rays, it might be nice to live closer to town, maybe even—Holy Regression to the Mean, Batman!—*in* town. (Of course, just as the suburban tide was seeming to ebb, a spate of books and academic studies suggested that maybe the 'burbs weren't so toxic after all—in a few years, we probably can expect a suburban revivalist movement.)

The Boomers looked at old houses with porches and, fondly remembering Andy rocking and chatting with Opie, Barney, and Aunt Bea, said, "Aw, that's cute!" They'd seen Bob and Norm do their thing to all those old houses on PBS. The *Times* was reporting the return of the Adirondack lodge and twig furniture. Articles chronicled old-joint makeovers in magazines like *This Old House, Metropolitan Home, American Homestyle, American Style, Romantic Houses, Victorian Homes, Traditional House Renovation Style* (talk about your tightly targeted market!), *Country Home, Country Journal, Family Handyman, Buildings, Coastal Living, House and Garden,* and a new glossy version of *Old House Journal.* There was even a magazine named *Veranda!*

It seemed that every other week the local paper's "home" section carried a feature about some couple or family or rugged individualist who'd "done" an old house. Hey, honey, remember Tom Hanks and Shelley Long in *The Money Pit,* when the bathtub went through the ceiling and the raccoon leaped onto his face? And that nice couple on *Thirtysomething*—Michael and what was her name, Hope?—every week you could see the unfinished walls in their dining room right there in prime time! A spattering of paint freckles was like a badge of honor. How hard could it be to live through a fixer-upper?

Inevitably, as the old house regained its allure, the porch reacquired its lost cachet. The collective wish for something that had been cast off was too strong to ignore. When mega-painter Julian Schnabel hit the artistic big time in the eighties, he bought a house in the Hamptons—a standard-issue Shingle model in Bridgehampton that he gussied up with a backyard full of sculpture, an eighty-foot swimming pool, and a big wall made of stone. But the real point was the house, which he'd bought for his family, Schnabel told the *New Yorker's* Calvin Tomkins. "I tried to invent a place for my kids so they would have the kind of memories I never had, of screened-in porches and things like that," the art star said.

And so the renovation of ratty old houses in tatty old neighborhoods went from being a fringe activity, if not a financially necessary and crankily contrarian personal statement, undertaken by what Andres Duany calls the "risk-oblivious," to a mainstream fashion.

No longer was it DIY City, with desperate and lonely guys and gals banging away at their brokedown palaces every evening and all weekend for the love of the task and the hope of seeing it come to an end and then fleeing on workdays with their busted knuckles and grit-encrusted eyelids to the clean, well-lighted place of the office for a rest.

Now the contractors' trucks lined up curbside. Tradesmen and laborers paraded. Materials piled up on the porch like matériel in the South of England before D-Day, and yesterday's ruin was tomorrow's showplace, with the vintage wicker arranged just so on the perfect porch, per Martha Stewart's *sotto voce* instructions.

It was not only houses whose porches needed a little or a whole lot of love that got what they required. Houses whose porches had been enclosed suddenly let the sun shine in, and houses that had had their porches amputated got prosthetics that were bigger and better than the originals. At the outer edges of the Outer Banks town of Duck, North Carolina, the dunes came to be dotted with ranks of huge beach houses whose multilevel porches were big enough to stage roller derbies on. Sometimes houses that hadn't had porches at all in the first place got porches.

Porch-oriented image-mongering multiplied in the press and electronic media. From the *Denver Post* to the *Washington Post* and the *New York Times,* along with other taste-making dailies, the word went forth to a new generation of homeowners: Porch good. Porch very very good.

On cable, the HGTV channel aired and re-aired a program entitled "The Porch: America's Window to the World." Porches showed up in television ads for automobiles, pancake restaurants, hospitals, utility companies, sport utility vehicles, and the prochoice movement. In her surprise best-selling book, *The Not So Big House: A Blueprint for the Way We Live Now,* architect Sarah Susanka not only endorses the porch as a means of making that not-so-big house seem not-so-small, she cautions against the impulse that impels many homeowners to do wrong by their porches.

"In a burst of practicality, many people decide during construction to make the porch all-season," Susanka writes. "It seems like such a small change to add windows and doors, but the change will turn a place that would be used and cherished as a protected outdoor space into just another sunny room in a house."

Susanka explains that she well knew the urge, which she felt when she and her family moved to Minnesota, where the summer's clouds of biting insects make it torturous to sit unprotected outdoors. Rather than drench her family in DEET or stay inside, Susanka had the porch screened, and was mighty glad of having done so.

"After just a few weeks of summer, I realized that the porch was the live-in area for the few months of good weather between June and September," she writes. "We ate there, socialized there, watched the thunderstorms and sunsets there. We were outside all the while, separated from nature by only a thin layer of mesh, through which the mosquitoes couldn't penetrate. It very quickly became our favorite room in the house.

"This experience is very different from sitting in a sunroom, which never gives you the impression you are actually outside, despite all the windows. The windows are a definite membrane between inside and outside. Even if you don't live in an area besieged by airborne pests, the experience of sitting on a porch, outside but protected by a section of roof, is delightful. The more sides of the porch open to the great outdoors, the better. One is hardly enough, two is better; three is ideal."

With endorsements like these, the porch started on the path to being a cultural signifier once again. San Francisco painter Bryn Craig made a small splash with a show of soulful paintings on the theme of the American porch; his works captured a series of those small, fleeting moments when the light and the shadows and the mood are just right. Another Northern California artist, the born-again believer Thomas Kinkade, got rich painting canvases of imagined houses that inspired a developer to license the look and build a gated community of real structures in the same semi-Gothic style, an echo of the "Christian home" illustrated in the works of Catharine Beecher. Alabama architect Samuel Mockbee, who designed imaginative low-cost houses for the impoverished residents of Hale County—where Walker Evans had chronicled the hard times and worn porches of thirties-era sharecroppers like the Tingle family—won a MacArthur "genius" grant for creating dwellings that often included whimsical, practical porches made from found materials like fiberglass and old road signs.

Bluegrass singer Dale Ann Bradley had a hit with her second solo album, *Old Southern Porches,* named for its showcase cut, by Leslie Winn Satcher, who composed a deeply felt evocation of a particular place that expanded to become a world of its own. Music and porches have always gone together; vide the Robert Keen/Lyle Lovett classic "This Old Porch," whose oblique yet inescapable sentiments, so vague and yet so specific, always bring a catch to my throat.

As the '90s were ending, "porch music" became something of a *fin de siècle* catchphrase among the pickers and grinners mining a bitter-sweetly melodic vein traceable to Gram Parsons, the flamboyant Alabaman whose late-sixties recordings with The Byrds and The Flying Burrito Brothers had fused country and rock. The movement's Baedeker, a no-nonsense magazine that calls itself *No Depression,* once labeled its letters column the "front porch." *No Depression* has chronicled and helped popularize singers and bands like Ryan Adams, Kasey Chambers, and Lambchop, as well as the string-band revival embodied by the success of the soundtrack to the Coen brothers' Odyssean hick flick, *O Brother Where Art Thou?* A similar musicocultural stream flows with the influence of the jam-happy Grateful Dead and inheritors such as Phish; a band of that ilk called The Recipe, out of West Virginia, dubs its fans "porch people." As a genre, porch music hasn't acquired the status of, say, "beach music" or "surf music"—yet. But give it time.

The porch came back to the funny papers, and it made appearances in books and as part of cutting-edge art. After the horrors of September 11, satirical cartoonist Garry Trudeau—a descendant of "cure porch" inventor E. L.—drew Boopsie, B. D., and other *Doonesbury* characters discussing the attacks on the front porch at their old commune, Walden. Illustrator Jerry Pinckney won awards for and sold many copies of a series of children's books that featured such images as the cast of characters from the tales of Uncle Remus gathered on a worn but homey porch.

Taking a more avant-garde approach, Harlem performance artist Michael Bramwell spent two years on a piece he called *Building Sweeps—Harlem,* in which he methodically swept the hallways and stoops of neighborhood tenements. The *New York Times Magazine* pictured the solemn-faced Bramwell, broom in hand, standing in front of a series of uptown row-house porches. Even foreign publications found opportunities to promote traditional American houses with porches; in a sprawling feature about the Santa Barbara, California, home of actors Paul Hogan and Linda Kozlowski, glossy Brit weekly *Hello!* gushed over their restored farmhouse and its wraparound porch, complete with antique swing shipped west from New England.

In 2001, nearly a hundred and twenty-five years after Benjamin Harrison introduced it and more than a hundred after William McKinley made it a household phrase (and five years after Bob Dole declined to take Peggy Noonan's widely reprinted recommendation that he go home to Kansas and run against Bill Clinton from his front porch), the front-porch campaign made a comeback.

The race was for the Virginia governorship, and the stakes were high. The last governor, James Gilmore, a Republican, had reclaimed the state house for the GOP, but Gilmore had moved on to the U.S. Senate. His would-be inheritor, Mark Earley, was a moderate Republican running against a rich and energetic Democrat, new-technology businessman Mark Warner.

Earley had been Virginia's attorney general, an essential but invisible job. He was earnest and energetic. Earley looked good in a red tie and blue suit, but no one knew who he was. His advisors, like GOP consultant Wayne Johnson, said he needed definition. They wanted to introduce him in a setting that showed his personality and character while he spoke about the issues. That meant home and family. Earley agreed. Someone asked if his house outside Richmond had a porch; it did. The Earleys didn't spend a huge amount of time on the porch, outside of waiting for the school bus, saying hello and goodbye, and putting up Christmas decorations, but they knew what Johnson was after. The game was afoot.

Campaign commercials have come a long way since Billy Bitzer cranked his camera while William McKinley strolled off the porch. Today's political ads are as close to science as art can get. Each is a miniature feature film, with plots and subplots and narrative arcs within narrative arcs, all told in sixty or thirty or even fifteen seconds. The three ads on the schedule would cost the budget-strapped Earley campaign $50,000 apiece.

To direct the commercials, the campaign hired Randy Bond, a veteran filmmaker who divides his time among documentaries, commercials, and network programs. Bond had always liked the porch as a set. That appeal held even when a particular project fell apart, as when Bond and his crew showed up to shoot a commercial for Joe Malone, a Massachusetts Republican who was running a hopeless campaign against Teddy Kennedy. A scout had lined up a fine front porch in Brookline.

"We get there and the owner comes out and asks what we're doing," Bond said. "We say we're here to shoot the ad so-and-so asked about. Who's the candidate, he asks. Malone, we say—the guy who's running against Kennedy. Oh, he says, I can't let you shoot here. This is the house where JFK and Bobby were born. So we had to get our butts off that porch and find another one."

Bond said that shooting commercials for more than twenty years has taught him that on television, the porch screens as Americana, and that few settings convey old-fashioned America as winningly as a wooden porch. "It just feels warm and fuzzy instantly," he said. "They're not as prevalent in California, where we're based, so it's been tough to find a good porch. But the style is coming back."

He'd read the scouting reports on the Earley house, but when he actually saw the porch, he was relieved. "I thought, 'Thank God, it's really nice, a wooden covered porch, very Americana,'" Bond said. "We designed the ads around the porch."

The Earleys' porch wasn't without technical challenges. It was too dark; lights had to be brought in. But otherwise, except for a few minor glitches, the work went well.

The first ad started with Earley and his kids in front of the house. As he talked about issues, they helped Mrs. Earley unload the groceries from the station wagon. The ad wound up with the family going up the steps and across the porch. It ran during the summer, as did an ad with Earley alone, walking toward the camera on the porch, talking about taxes and education. The plan for the third ad was to reintroduce Earley on television after Labor Day, and run with that message until November. But then al Qaeda attacked the Pentagon and the World Trade Center, occasioning drastic changes in campaign ads.

Johnson and cohort wanted to keep showing Earley in the context of family, while bringing in themes of security, safety, home, and tradition. But they didn't want to come across as trying to make political hay out of murderous disaster.

So Bond and his crew shot Earley at the Capitol talking with James Gilmore and John Warner, the state's senators. Then, returning to the house outside Richmond, the team filmed the two youngest Earley children, Anne Harris and Franklin, coming out on the porch, opening a box, and taking out a flagpole kit. The youngsters carefully pounded nails into a column to put the flagpole holder in place, and eventually raised the flag. Some tension arose when it became clear that more takes were needed of the nail-pounding bit.

"That meant the wood had to be filled," Randy Bond said. "Wayne Johnson and I were in there shoving stuff into the hole. First we grabbed some bread and Twinkies off the catering table, but that wasn't any good. Then we shoved some gum in and put Wite-Out on it. We wound up doing the repairs electronically in post-production."

Along with digitally patching the Earleys' porch, the editors at Spectrum Films wove the sequences into a perfect little story about what it felt like to be an American at that time. The ad had a narration, but the kids on their porch with the flag—now, that was the real deal. Unfortunately, by this time the Earley war chest was all but depleted. The ad ran only a few times and only in remote rural markets, not the swing-voting, election-altering precincts of the Washington suburbs, which went heavily enough Democratic that Mark Earley went down in defeat.

The former attorney general was sanguine about that. When I found his home number in the Richmond directory and called him, he said he was proud of reviving the front-porch campaign, and that he wished the flag ad had gotten wider exposure. He'd gone to work for a law firm in Richmond, and he was pondering his prospects.

"I'm going to stay involved in politics," Mark Earley said. "And I'm going to keep spending time on the porch."

Of course, there was bad news about porches, too.

Some porches in Wilson, North Carolina, a once-prosperous town known for its scads of bungalows, many with a signature bluebird cut into the porch trim, became notorious. Wilson's once-bustling tobacco market—back in the day, the New York Stock Exchange had kept an office on the main drag—had fallen on hard times made harder by poorer residents' habit of furnishing their front porches with cast-off interior furniture and refrigerators. Some streets in Wilson looked like the crack hotel in *New Jack City* expanded to a whole neighborhood: people sleeping in their shoes on porches in all kinds of weather and at all hours of the day, sprawled across sofas that looked as if the only thing that would help them was a canister of napalm. Down these mean streets strode hardeyed young bloods carrying boomboxes blaring vicious gangsta rap at maximum volume so all you could really hear of the vocal was the chorus—the heartwarming lyric "Mutha *fuckah!*" bellowed, oh, six or eight times. The solons of Wilson were vexed. Trying to polish their beloved town's appearance, the city council played the health hazard card and passed an ordinance banning the storage or use of appliances and upholstered furniture on porches or other exterior locations. The *Wilson Daily Times* ran a story on the rule that the Associated Press picked up, and pretty soon Wilson's dilemma and its good intentions had taken the town into the hell of late-night talk-show jests and op-ed opinionating. Big-city reporter Rick Bragg came to town and wrote a *New York Times* story that portrayed the regulation as a matter of class and race, as well as an undoing of ancient Southern culture, since the only violators would be poor whites and Blacks for whom porch-setting was a near-vocation. ("It is much easier to disappear inside, to music or videos, if there is not a soft place to sit outside, people here said," Bragg wrote. "It is more important to the poor, because, as entertainment goes, it is about as cheap as it gets. Talking does not cost anything.") The council and the Wilson Appearance Committee cried foul, protesting that they had only emulated college towns like Champaign, Illinois, that had instigated similar bans to fight plagues of sofa-infested porches on student-rented hovels (subsequently, Boulder, Colorado, would try to ban sofas from porches in a bid to deny rambunctious University of Colorado students the chance to burn furniture in the street when the spirit—or spirits—moved them). In Wilson tickets were issued; porches were cleaned up; sofas melted away. In time, the ruckus subsided, and it became possible to have a sofa on your porch in Wilson, as long as you didn't flaunt it.

The porch also made news in Portland, Oregon, where limits on growth and ever-tighter parking restrictions had spurred a surge in the construction of snout houses. In Portland, it was possible to see three-bay snouters that all but erased the houseness from the home to which they were affixed; they looked like chunks of the U-Store Iceberg that had drifted ashore. At Halloween, trick-or-treaters often skipped snout houses because they couldn't find the front doors. But builders and not a few homeowners championed the design. After acrimonious debate, Portland banned the snout house, requiring that on newly constructed dwellings, any garages be placed to the side or back and that house fronts be equipped with some measure of porch—although, being the sensitive folks they are, Portlanders agreed to stop calling snout houses "snout houses," because it hurt the feelings of people who lived in such structures and liked them.

The porch began to show up again in places both expected and unusual. In Montana's Big Sky country, custom builders like Bob Milligan were getting commissions to build houses with humongous porches that had stone fireplaces, elk-antler railings, the whole nine yards. At the other end of the scale, trying to start a program to aid farmers and migrant workers in Pennsylvania, architect Bryan Bell, who'd studied the porch as civic architecture in Vincent Scully's course at Yale, was designing tiny, sometimes portable, prefabricated houses with front and screened side porches where the workers could drop their baskets and stow their shoes and live like humans; the $18,750 units were made to fit into fruit groves and farms as humane temporary housing for pickers, and Bell hoped to expand his business to a national scale.

In Bloomington, Indiana, the Sturbaum brothers, Chris and Ben, who'd taken over a house restoration business their dad had started, developed a reputation for being able to revive ruined or long-vanished porches. At one 1880s stone cottage that once had had a wooden porch, Chris noticed that some long-ago painter had been so sloppy he'd left a perfect outline of the trim that had once graced the porch. "Porch ghosts," thought Chris. Soon he and Ben had recreated the original structure, a job that led to their reprising the project at the 2001 National Folk Life Festival on the Mall in Washington, where many of the hundreds of thousands of visitors paused to watch the brothers Sturbaum and crew build a Potemkin porch against a stage-set house front.

Outside Waco, Texas, governor George Bush and his wife, Laura, built a weekend place with a long, deep wraparound porch. Architect David Heymann designed the house to provide a sheltered outdoor experience in any season for the Bushes, who had told the designer they wanted to sit on the porch and feel as if they were at the end of the world. "The porch is like the brim of a hat," Heymann told the *Austin American Statesman*. "It shades you, but makes it possible for you to have an uninterrupted view of the surrounding landscape."

The long battle between the porch and the deck took a new turn in early 2002, when manufacturers announced that they would phase out chromated copper arsenate as the preservative used to pressure-treat wood. Years of complaint from environmentalists and health researchers, who claim the arsenic compound causes cancer, had proven fatal to Sonti Kamesam's innovation. Eventually, CCA would be history, probably replaced by ACQ, a combination of alkaline, recycled copper, and quat, a fungicide. The new material inevitably would cost more, putting deck fans between the rock of desire and the hard place of expense. While no death knell, the demise of CCA probably presages a drop in the deck's popularity.

The capper of the porch revival came in February 2002, when the judges at the International Builders Show in Atlanta selected the Home of the Year. In designing the 3,400-square-foot house for his own family, Washington, D.C., architect Dale Stewart had forsworn his modernist tendencies to create a house that, except for the open-design interior spaces and high-tech details like modem connections and modern appliances, looks like something from Gustav Stickley's sketch book. Stewart came up with an Arts and Crafts bungalow that could have been the Home of the Year for 1902.

"We see this house as representing where new home design needs to go," *Professional Builder* magazine editor Heather McCune told the *Washington Post*. "We deliberately moved away from bigger twelve-thousand-square-foot homes this year."

Dale Stewart told me the winning house design arose from sharp stylistic differences of the spousal variety. "My wife, Sallie, prefers a traditional-style house. I prefer a more contemporary style," he said. "We realized that, before we started designing, we needed a style that we both could agree to. The Arts and Crafts style provides not only the warmth and richness and comfort she was used to, but the clean, simple detailing I could get behind."

As he worked on the project, Dale, who had liked what he learned about Arts and Crafts when studying architecture at the University of Maryland, realized the hundred-year-old style fit the Zeitgeist.

"The original Arts and Crafts movement was a revolt against the Industrial Revolution that put an emphasis on individual craftsmanship and style," he said. "It seems that today, in the midst of the technological revolution, the Arts and Crafts style is speaking to people's needs again, by offering us a place to go home to, to be in a place where we can slow down and be comfortable. And like the Arts and Crafts movement a hundred years ago, the style also lends itself to modern touches. It can absorb the new technology and put a human face on it, which is what we tried to do with our house."

The Stewarts weren't looking to rile the neighbors in a neighborhood that had been subdivided in 1928. "The houses in it were built between then and the 1960s," Dale told me. "Dutch colonials, Tudors, center-entry colonials, ranches, mid-century designs—the full boat. Our street had everything but a bungalow. Building our house was like filling in a note on the chord."

And although not every house on the block had a porch, the family wanted one. "We liked the idea of a front porch. At our previous house, which was a

Cape Cod, we hadn't had a porch, but we liked to put our Adirondack chairs out in the front yard and read the paper and say hello to the neighbors," Dale said. "Now we love to sit on the porch, which is ten and a half feet deep. The porch wraps slightly around the house; the wrap on the side is six feet deep. There's a side door that opens to the library, a porch swing, and a storage space for firewood. It's a very utilitarian space. It faces northeast, so it gets morning sun, and it's great to be out there from spring through fall."

Another reason for having a porch was that the house was not so small. "We were putting in a house of 3,400 square feet, plus a basement. The basement ceiling is nine feet and the first-floor ceiling is ten feet," Dale explained. "There was a real potential for overpowering the neighborhood. I wanted to break down the massing of the house at the front, to create a horizontality. We put the master bedroom on the first floor so that in old age we don't have to climb stairs, which also reduced the volume of the second floor, so we could step it back. We used the wraparound porch roofline to give the house a long, deep, very horizontal look that lends the house an oblique feeling."

Dale admitted that going the extra distance in building a porch inevitably means reaching deeper into the wallet. "That faux porch you see on some new houses is evidence of builders trying to give a house the aesthetic of a traditional home without spending the money that's needed to have a porch," he said. "The market is there, but not all buyers are willing to spend the $15,000 it takes to make a deep porch. That's not an inexpensive item, but to me it has huge impact on the house and the way you live in it."

What with awards like the one given Dale Stewart's house, and with articles like one in the *New York Times* "House & Home" section touting the bug-free delights of the screened porch in the age of West Nile virus and encephalitis B, as well as the structure's capacity to make a small house seem larger (one featured dwelling measured 1,400 square feet inside, but had 2,200 square feet of porch), the porch had once again gotten huge, and the mainstream housing industry had begun to pay heed. Developers and builders might have had reservations about the New Urbanists and their lofty arias to decorum, but the folks who plat the lots and dig the foundation holes do make it their business to know the melody of one song: dough-re-mi. Americans weren't all flocking to drink the Kool-Aid that Duany and the New Urbanists were pouring, but enough of them were buying houses with front porches to demonstrate palpably that houses with front porches would sell, which meant that you could make money on a front porch.

So after decades of flat-fronted, shadeless entries, developers began building suburban houses that sprouted something like a porch—not a genuine porch, more of a porchlike substance, composed of bits and pieces of roof and column and railing and stoop organized like a *trompe l'oeil* painting to give the maximum appearance of porchness with a minimum of structure.

The design worked, but only on a drive-by, the way that, from a distance, the dots on a billboard congeal in your vision. Up close, these "porches" were travesties, too shallow, narrow, and confining to swing a cat on, never mind lean back in a wicker rocker and hold forth. But people bought them, and jammed them with chairs and umbrellas and Big Wheels, as if by treating these useless spaces like they were useful they might become so.

The next step was the "custom" porch, built at an additional charge onto tract houses sold by outfits like Ryan, Ryland, or Winchester. These structures could be outfitted with lighting systems, ceiling fans, a red roof, and anything else you wanted to pay for. They could be more than six or seven feet deep, too—you could go eight feet, or nine, or more, and feel like Mark Twain summering in Elmira. All you needed was cash.

Dale Stewart's 2002 "Home of the Year," an Arts & Crafts bungalow,
could have been the home of the year in 1902.

Of course, for an American porch really to be an American porch, it has to have some Americans on it. Latter-day porches often honor that principle in the breach. Instead of serving as community-oriented centers of conviviality and welcome, these porches stand, with their perfectly placed rockers and adroitly arranged bibelots, as illustrations of the hospitality folks would extend if only they weren't so busy being busy, and if only being sociable didn't intrude so much on their private lives.

But even if it was as a simulacrum, the porch had returned, and the National Association of Home Builders had the data to prove it. Every few years, NAHB surveys homebuyers to learn what they want and don't want in a house. Among a whole raft of questions, survey subjects are asked to rank amenities like "deck" and "garage" and "carport" and "front porch" according to their desirability. For years, the deck had been leading the front porch; I knew this because I'd made it a point to stay in touch with Gopal Aluwahlia, the NAHB's research chief. The last time I checked in with Aluwahlia, the two main outdoor structures on American houses had reversed polarity; for the first time in twenty years, more people were saying they had to have front porches than rear decks. Maybe the difference was only two percent (twenty-six percent proporch versus twenty-four percent prodeck). Maybe what some people want is the porchlike substance, built to sate the desire for something on the front of the house, or the Pleasantville porch, art-directed to offer a hollow echo of what once was.

But there's hope.

If more houses have porches, more people will have the chance to sit on them. They'll see what's wrong and what's right about the space. Want to see if a porch is big enough? Invite your four largest friends to join you there; if you don't feel as if you're on a crowded elevator, the porch will suffice. The next time a house buyer has a chance to order up a porch, that person may press the builder to make the porch deep enough and wide enough that it can really be used, and that porch will have a chance of moving, as it has on Dale Stewart's award-winning bungalow, from imitation to reality.

I hope that happens, and I hope, if you have the chance to live in a house with a real porch, that you'll take it. You won't regret it, I promise.

I finished the chapter above around noon on a day unusually warm for winter in D.C. The sun was out. The sky was bright. I was stuck for what to write next, so I did what writers usually do in such circumstances. I did something completely different.

When this happens during the summer, I cut the grass or trim the bushes until the words start to flow again. This time I got out my guitar.

The ceiling in my basement office is punitively low, so I carried my Epiphone and Marty's practice amp out to the front porch, where I'd be in the sun. I plugged in and turned on the amp, then began noodling.

As a guitar player, I'm a terrific typist; I know the chords at the bottom of the neck and a few simple melodies, and that's about it. But now and again it pleases me to make noise and that was what I was doing: a little "Sweet Jane," some "Tambourine Man," "Gloria," and the like, interspersed with random crude improvisations.

Except for my fumble-fingered picking, the street was quiet, the curbs almost empty of vehicles—a real change from the old days, when so many of our neighbors were retired folks, enjoying their paid-off houses and their leisure. Palisades had gotten expensive; people had to work to cover those big mortgages. And Palisades had gotten younger; now I had neighbors who only half-jokingly addressed me as "Mister Dolan." It wasn't standoffish, just proper. In time, as it had been for me with my older neighbors when I moved to the 'sades, the first names would come, and then the friendships—and if not friendship, then neighborly cordiality, that pleasant state in which you and the guy next door know one another well enough to say hello from the porch or to invite one another up to sit in a rocker or the glider.

I had accompaniment for my so-called playing. Along the main drag, MacArthur Boulevard, construction crews were cutting and filling trenches to hold fiber-optic lines that someday would connect my neighborhood and the rest of Washington to the Great Web of Infotainment. Their concrete saws and jackhammers and generator trucks served as a quasi-rhythm section.

Planes were headed into and out of National Airport, and with the trees bare the sound of their engines was quite loud. Once, pilots used to fly in and out using the river, a quarter of a mile away, to guide their path. But when the FAA finally cleared National to reopen after the Pentagon and the World Trade Center attacks, the new route sent air traffic straight over my house. Considering how lonely it felt during those months when the only wings over Washington were bomber jet planes riding shotgun in the sky, the roar was comforting.

Mike Johnson, who lives across the street, pulled up in his plumbing truck, walkie-talkie to ear. He gave a wave and headed for his porch, where he sat in the swing and talked on the radio.

I was finding a quasi-groove, working the middle of the neck and wishing, as always, that I really knew how to play. My fingers wandered through a familiar melodic neighborhood, in the vicinity of the riff Beethoven wrote for Schiller's "Ode to Joy." That led me to the Shaker hymn "Simple Gifts," to which a slightly overdriven electric guitar lends a salutary texture; it sounded like the intro to the old CBS Special Reports program played through a Fuzz-Tone. I fiddled with that theme until I couldn't think of anyplace to go other than a melody I'd been trying to figure out for years, one I'd been hearing since childhood at ballgames, school assemblies, and, most notoriously, in the version Jimi Hendrix had detonated at Woodstock.

I started picking at "The Star-Spangled Banner" and by God I got some of the notes right, then some more. I twice played that old pub crawler's anthem through, as far as I could without making a mistake, and as I did I looked around my porch—at the coffin full of sports gear; the resurrected glider, the salvaged carpenter's benches, and the yard-sale wicker furniture; the porch where I'd rocked my newborn son and where I'd last seen my father when he was sentient; the porch that needed a coat of paint on its floor and a good washing. I looked around the porch I'd designed and that had inspired this project, which had taken me into so many nooks and crannies of America, and I realized: I was through with my book.

Author's Notes

Few paragraphs in this book do not show some influence from the *Encyclopedia Britannica*, 15th ed., the *Oxford Classical Dictionary*, 2nd ed., the *Encyclopedia of Southern Culture*, *A Field Guide to American Architecture*, the *Encyclopedia of World History*, and the *Penguin Dictionary of Architecture*.

Individual chapters were shaped by the following influences:

INTRODUCTION: MY PORCH AND WELCOME TO IT

I based this chapter on personal experience of the assassination, persecution, and resurrection of my front porch, with historical asides obtained in conversations with members of the Lynch family and my late friend and neighbor, Melvin Snyder.

CHAPTER ONE: AS AMERICAN AS ANCIENT GREECE . . . AND IMPERIAL ROME

My understanding of the first house came from interviews with Professor Dripps and her book, *The First House*. Background information on Zeno of Citium and the *stoa poikile* of Athens came from the *Oxford Classical Dictionary*, as did the material on Roman farming, siege warfare, and architecture. Robin Francis Rhodes's *Architecture and Meaning on the Athenian Acropolis* provided much illumination. For my analysis of the writings of Vitruvius, I read Morris Hicky Morgan's translation of *De architectura*.

CHAPTER TWO: LOGGIA LOGIC, RENAISSANCE ROOTS

I learned the history of Venice from Garry Wills (*Venice, Lion City*), the *Enyclopedia Britannica*, Roger G. Kennedy (*Architecture, Men, Women, and Money in America*), Jason Goodwin (*Lords of the Horizons*), James S. Ackerman (*Palladio*), Philippe Aries and Georges Duby (*A History of Private Life*), Dana and Michael Facaros (*Venice*), Nikolaus Pevsner (*An Outline of European Architecture*), and firsthand experience during a visit there after my research trip to the Veneto, including an interview with architectural historian Antonio Foscari.

CHAPTER THREE: OUT OF AFRICA . . .

Besides interviewing the pioneering folklorists and material culture I experts John Vlach and Jay Edwards, I read their books and articles. Other timbers that support this chapter are the following: James Deetz's *In Small Things Forgotten*; William Gleason's article on Charles Chesnutt in *American Quarterly*; *The Slave Trade: The Story of the Atlantic Slave Trade 1440–1870*, by Hugh Thomas; and *Drawn From African Dwellings*, by Jean-Paul Bourdier and Trinh T. Minh-ha.

CHAPTER FOUR: . . . OR WAS IT OUT OF INDIA . . .

For the history of the baranda and the bangla, I relied on Anthony King's book, *The Bungalow: The Production of a Global Culture*, as well as Indian history as explicated in the *Encyclopedia Brittannica*.

CHAPTER FIVE: . . . OR OUT OF ITALY?

Along with firsthand research conducted on my April 2001 visit to the Veneto, I depended heavily on Roger G. Kennedy's *Architecture, Men, Women and Money in America, 1600–1860*; Leon Battista Alberti's *Ten Books on Architecture*; Andrea Palladio's *Four Books of Architecture*; Marcus Vitruvius Pollio's *Ten Books on Architecture* (translated by Morris Hickey Morgan); *A History of Private Life*, edited by Philippe Aries and Georges Duby; and Peter Murray's *The Architecture of the Italian Renaissance*. The material presented derives from these sources and from telephone and face-to-face interviews with Carl Gable, Pietro Rigo, Alfonso Vergnano and Catherine Piovene, Luigi di Tomassi, Christian Malinverni, Carla and Giovanna Bianchi-Michiel; Manuela Bedeschi-Bonetti, and Professor Antonio Foscari.

CHAPTER SIX: FROM THE OLD WORLD TO THE NEW

The works of historians Hugh Morrison and Thomas Flexner, as well as research by Jay Edwards, inform my writing here.

CHAPTER SEVEN: GEORGE'S PIAZZA AND TOM'S PORTICO

Along with visits to Mount Vernon and Monticello, I interviewed historian David Konig and archaeologist Dennis Pogue of the Mount Vernon restoration department. The following volumes provided very useful information: the Dalzells' *George Washington's Mount Vernon: At Home in Revolutionary America*; Jack

McLaughlin's *Jefferson and Monticello: Biography of a Builder*; Thomas Flexner's *Washington: The Indispensable Man*; The Mount Vernon Ladies' Association of the Union's *Mount Vernon: A Handbook*.

CHAPTER EIGHT: EARLY DAYS OF AN ICON

I garnered valuable insights into the pattern book from a fascinating history of that genre by Linda Smeins, author of *Building an American Identity: Pattern Book Homes & Communities*; Professor Smeins also granted me a very useful telephone interview. I learned from John Vlach how the shotgun house came to America, as he explained how he painstakingly traced that process in reverse in the course of writing his doctoral dissertation. The *Encyclopedia of Southern Culture* helped me to understand the importance of the porch in that region in the early nineteenth century. To grasp Andrew Jackson Downing's impact on American life, I read his books; likewise for the novels and self-help texts of Catharine Beecher and Harriet Beecher Stowe. Clifford Clark's *The American Family Home 1800–1960* was an invaluable trove of information and analysis, as was Kathryn Kish Sklar's *Catharine Beecher: A Study in American Domesticity*.

CHAPTER NINE: GETTING INTO PRINT

Besides presenting an array of beautifully reproduced prints, Walton Rawls's *The Great Book of Currier & Ives' America* included an illuminating history of that company and its influence. The great historian Shelley Fisher Fishkin told me the story of Mary Ann Cord and Samuel Clemens in a telephone interview just after she'd told it to Ken Burns's camera, and she directed me to her books on Twain. I gleaned information from reprints of pattern books by A. B. Reed and the Palliser brothers.

CHAPTER TEN: UBIQUITY

James Garfield's front-porch campaign came into focus as I read the work of historian Allan Peskin. I learned of Edgar R. Jones's *Those Were the Days* from advertising historian James B. Twitchell in a telephone interview on the porch as brand. I based my thumbnail sketches of John Ruskin and William Morris on material in the *Encyclopedia Britannica*. Mary Ann Smith, author of *Gustav Stickley: The Craftsman*, gave me a telephone interview that deepened my understanding of her book. Along with an extensive interview granted by Professor Jonathan Auerbach and close scrutiny of his article on the McKinley campaign in *American Quarterly*, I studied *McKinley At Home* on the Library of Congress Web site and read Billy Bitzer's posthumously published autobiography and *The American Heritage History of the Confident Years 1865–1916*.

CHAPTER ELEVEN: GLORY DAYS

Along with Anthony King's magnificent *The Bungalow: The Production of a Global Culture,* I read Paul Duchscherer and Douglas Keister's *The Bungalow: America's Arts & Crafts Home.* Richard Guy Wilson's masterful introduction to the catalogue for the exhibit *From Architecture to Object: Masterworks of the American Arts & Crafts Movement* yielded important insights.

CHAPTER TWELVE: TEETER

Frederick Lewis Allen's *Only Yesterday: An Informal History of the 1920's* and Clifford Clark's *The American Family Home* were most useful sources. Interviews with architect and historian Jeff Limerick strongly informed this chapter, as did conversations I had with Andres Duany and Michael Leccese and folklorist Elaine Eff, whose documentary film *The Screen Painters* is a deeply moving introduction to Baltimore's native art form.

CHAPTER THIRTEEN: TOTTER

Bob Mondello explained the front-porch play in a telephone interview. A research trip to the Museum of Modern Art Film Stills Archive confirmed my suspicions about the porch set in *Young Mr. Lincoln* and *The Grapes of Wrath.* I learned much of the contents of this chapter from Clifford Clark's history of the American family home, as well as from review of architecture journals such as *American Architecture* and *Building and Engineering News.*

CHAPTER FOURTEEN: FALL

The history of Levittown appears in many places; I chose to read David Halberstam's fine chronicle in his book, *The Fifties.* Jocelyn Hazelwood Donlon's *Swinging in Place: Porch Life in Southern Culture* was informative and inspirational, as were conversations with Vincent Scully, Elizabeth Plater-Zyberk, and Andres Duany. Huck Devenzio provided the story of Sonti Kamesam and CCA.

CHAPTER FIFTEEN: RISE AGAIN

My trip to the 2001 International Builder's Show yielded the interviews cited. Details on exhibits came from promotional materials and my notes. I obtained the information about the *New Yorker* porch cartoons in an interview with Bodin Suttles of the Cartoon Bank, who kindly provided an informal tally of who has drawn what. Vincent Scully reminisced about the sleeping porches of his youth in a conversation with me at the National Building Museum in

December 2001. H. Lea Lawrence's *A Hemingway Odyssey* provided useful data about Key West. For information about the New Urbanism and their work at Seaside and elsewhere, Andres Duany and Elizabeth Plater-Zyberk granted me extensive interviews, both in person and on the phone; so did James Howard Kunstler. Information on the photo session that yielded the cover of *Crosby, Stills & Nash* came from Henry Diltz, who shot the pictures. I also read *Suburban Nation,* Peter Calthorpe's *The Next American Metropolis,* and *Celebration U.S.A.: Living in Disney's Brave New Town,* by Douglas Frantz and Catherine Collins.

CHAPTER SIXTEEN: REVIVAL

Gopal Aluwahlia of the National Association of Home Builders provided statistical information on the relative popularity of the front porch and the deck. I visited Wilson, North Carolina, to see its beleaguered porches firsthand; LouAnn Munson provided much information, as did Tilghman Henning. Bryan Bell and Bob Milligan told me about their experiences with porches over the phone. (Bob also regaled me with Montana porch tales while we were hanging out in Bariloche, Argentina, for reasons too complicated to mention here.) I met Chris and Ben Sturbaum at the 2001 National Folk Life Festival and later interviewed Chris by phone and e-mail. Dale Stewart, whose house won the 2002 Home of the Year award, told me about his home over the phone, which was also how I learned the details of Mark Earley's front-porch campaign from the candidate himself, as well as from his associates Wayne Johnson and Randy Bond.

BIBLIOGRAPHY

Ackerman, James S., *Palladio*. Baltimore: Penguin, 1972.

Alexander, Christopher et al., *A Pattern Language: Towns, Buildings, Construction*. New York: Oxford, 1977.

Alexander, Christopher et al., *The Timeless Way of Building*. New York: Oxford, 1977.

Allen, Frederick Lewis, *Only Yesterday: An Informal History of the 1920's*. New York: Harper & Row, 1957.

Allen, Henry, *What It Felt Like: Living in the American Century*. New York: Pantheon, 1999.

(American Domestic Architecture) *American Dream Homes*. Cologne: Könemann, 2000.

(American History) Andrist, Ralph K., ed., *The American Heritage History of the Confident Years 1865–1916*. American Heritage/Bonanza, 1987.

(American Photography) *The Social Scene*. Museum of Contemporary Art, 2000.

Anderson, Sherwood, *Winesburg, Ohio*. New York: Penguin, 1992.

Aries, Philippe and Georges Duby, eds., *A History of Private Life*. Cambridge: Belknap, 1987, 1988.

(Arts & Crafts Movement) *From Architecture to Object: Masterworks of the American Arts & Crafts Movement*. New York: Hirschl & Adler, 1989. (Introduction by Richard Guy Wilson.)

Bachelard, Gaston, *The Poetics of Space*. Boston: Beacon, 1958.

Beecher, Catharine, *A Study in American Domesticity*. New York: Norton, 1973.

Beecher, Catharine, and Harriet Beecher Stowe, *American Woman's Home*. Hartford: Stowe-Day Foundation, 1994.

Bitzer, Billy, *His Story*. New York: Farrar Straus Giroux, 1973.

Blumenson, John J.-G., *Identifying American Architecture*. Norton, 1981.

Brinkley, David, *Washington Goes to War*. New York: Knopf, 1988.

Boorstin, Daniel J., *The Americans: The National Experience*. Random House, 1985.

Brooks, David, *BOBO's in Paradise*. New York: Simon & Schuster, 2000.

Burrows, Edwin and Mike Wallace, *Gotham*. New York: Oxford, 1999.

Cahill, Thomas, *How the Irish Saved Civilization*. New York: Doubleday, 1995.

Calthorpe, Peter, *The Next American Metropolis*. New York: Princeton, 1993.

Carley, Rachel, *The Visual Dictionary of American Domestic Architecture*. Owl, 1994.

Caro, Robert A, *The Years of Lyndon Johnson: Master of the Senate*. New York: Knopf, 2002.

Carter, Jimmy, *An Hour Before Daylight: Memories of a Rural Boyhood*. New York: Simon & Schuster, 2001.

(Charleston, S.C.) *Historic Charleston Guidebook.* Junior League of Charleston, 1975.

Churchill, Winston S., *My Early Life: 1874–1904.* New York: Touchstone/S&S, 1958.

Cikovsy, Nikolai Jr. and Franklin Kelly, *Winslow Homer.* National Gallery of Art, 1995.

Clark, Clifford Edward, *The American Family Home 1800–1960.* Chapel Hill: UNC Press, 1986.

Clinton, Catherine, ed., *Fanny Kemble's Journals.* Cambridge: Harvard, 2000.

Cobleigh, Rolfe, *Handy Farm Devices.* New York: Lyons, 1996.

Cohen, Steven A., ed., *The Games We Played: A Celebration of Childhood and Imagination.* New York: Simon & Schuster, 2001.

Connell, John, *Homing Instinct.* New York: McGraw Hill, 1998.

Coppiestone, Trewin, ed., *World Architecture.* New York: Hamlyn, 1973.

Dalzell, Robert F., and Lee Baldwin. *George Washington's Mount Vernon.* New York: Oxford, 1998.

Damasio, Antonio, *The Feeling of What Happens.* New York: Harcourt Brace, 1999.

Davis, Mike, *City of Quartz.* New York: Vintage, 1992.

De Tocqueville, Alexis, *Democracy in America.* New York: Bantam, 2000.

Diner, Hasia R., *Lower East Side Memories.* Princeton: Princeton, 2000.

Doctorow, E. L., *Ragtime.* New York: Random House, 1974.

Donlon, Jocelyn Hazelwood, *Swinging in Place: Porch Life in Southern Culture.* Chapel Hill: UNC Press, 2001.

Downing, A.J., *The Architecture of Country Houses.* New York: Dover, 1969.

Downs, Randolph C., *The Rise of Warren Gamaliel Harding 1865–1950.* Columbus: Ohio State University Press, 1970.

Dripps, R.D., *The First House.* Cambridge: MIT, 1997.

Duany, Andres, Elizabeth Plater-Zyberk, and Jeff Speck, *Suburban Nation: The Rise of Sprawl and the Decline of the American Dream.* New York: North Point, 2000.

Duchscherer, Paul, and Douglas Keister, *The Bungalow: America's Arts & Crafts Home.* New York: Penguin, 1995.

Dunbar, Paul Laurence, *Complete Poems.* New York: Dodd Mead, 1913.

Evans, Walker, *Photographs for the Farm Security Administration 1935–1938.* New York: Da Capo, 1973.

Eyman, Scott, *Print the Legend: The Life and Times of John Ford.* Simon & Schuster, 1999.

Facaros, Dana and Michael, *Venice.* Connecticut: Globe Pequot, 1998.

Faulkner, William, *The Sound and the Fury.* New York: Vintage, 1946.

Ferris, William, and Charles Reagan Wilson, eds., *Encyclopedia of Southern Culture.* Chapel Hill: UNC Press, 1989.

Fishkin, Shelley Fisher, *Lighting Out for the Territory: Reflections on Mark Twain and American Culture.* New York: Oxford, 1997.

Fleming, John, Hugh Honour, and Nikolaus Pevsner, *The Penguin Dictionary of Architecture*. New York: Penguin, 1980.

Flexner, James Thomas, *Washington: The Indispensable Man*. Canada: Little, Brown, 1974.

Fitch, James Marston, *American Building*. Boston: Houghton Mifflin, 1966.

Ford, Richard, *Independence Day*. New York: Vintage Books, 1996.

Frantz, Douglas, and Catherine Collins, *Celebration USA: Living in Disney's Brave New Town*. New York: Henry Holt, 1999.

Fussell, Paul, *Class*. New York: Ballantine, 1983.

Garber, Marjorie, *Sex and Real Estate*. New York: Pantheon, 2000.

Gay, Peter, *Schnitzler's Century: The Making of Middle-Class Culture 1815-1914*. Norton, 2001.

Gladwell, Malcolm, *The Tipping Point*. Little, Brown, 2000.

Gody, Lou, ed., *The WPA Guide to New York City*. New York: The New Press, 1939.

Goodwin, Jason, *Lords of the Horizons: A History of the Ottoman Empire*. Henry Holt, 1998.

Gordon, J.E., *Structures*. Reading: University of Reading, 1978.

Gowans, Alan, *Styles and Types of North American Architecture*. New York: Harper Collins, 1992.

Greenberg, Allan, *George Washington—Architect*. London: Andreas Papadakis, 1999.

Grow, Lawrence, *Classic Old House Plans*. Pittstown: Main Street, 1984.

Gutheim, Frederick, and the National Capital Planning Commission, *Worthy of the Nation*. Washington, D.C.: Smithsonian Institution, 1977.

Hammond, N.G.L., and H.H. Scullard, eds., *The Oxford Classical Dictionary, 2nd ed*. Oxford: Clarendon, 1970.

Hall, B.C., and C.T. Wood, *Big Muddy*. New York: Penguin, 1992.

Halsted, Byron David, *Barns and Outbuildings*. New York: Lyons, 2000.

Hiss, Tony, *The Experience of Place*. New York: Knopf, 1990.

Hodgins, Eric, *Mr. Blandings Builds His Dream House*. New York: Simon & Schuster, 1946.

Howard, Hugh, *The Preservationist's Progress: Architectural Adventures in Conserving Yesterday's Houses*. New York: Farrar Straus Giroux, 1991.

Hume, Ivor Noël, *The Virginia Adventure*. New York: Knopf, 1994.

Hutt, Antony, *North Africa*. London: Scorpion, 1977.

Jackson, Kenneth T., *Crabgrass Frontier*. New York: Oxford, 1985.

Jacobs, Jane, *The Death and Life of Great American Cities*. New York: Vintage, 1992.

(Jefferson Memorial) *AIA Guide to the Architecture of Washington, D.C., 3rd ed*. Baltimore: Johns Hopkins, 1974.

Jepson, Tim, *City Pack—Venice*. New York: Fodor's, 1999.

Johnson, Gerald W., *Mount Vernon—The Story of a Shrine*. New York: Random House, 1991.

Kahn, Renee, and Ellen Meagher, *Preserving Porches*. New York: Henry Holt, 1990.

Kauffman, Henry J., *The American Farmhouse*. New York: Hawthorn, 1975.

Kennedy, Roger G., *Architecture, Men, Women, and Money in America 1600–1860*. New York: Random House, 1985.

Kennedy, Roger G., *Rediscovering America*. Boston: Houghton Mifflin, 1990.

Kidder, Tracy, *House*. Boston: Houghton Mifflin, 1985.

King, Anthony D., *The Bungalow: The Production of a Global Culture*. London: Routledge & Kegan Paul, 1984.

Kunstler, James Howard, *The Geography of Nowhere: The Rise and Decline of America's Man-Made Landscape*. New York: Simon & Schuster, 1993.

Kunstler, James Howard, *Home from Nowhere: Remaking Our Everyday World for the 21st Century*. New York: Simon & Schuster, 1996.

Kunstler, James Howard, *The City in Mind*. New York: Free Press/Simon & Schuster, 2002.

Lawrence, H. Lea, *A Hemingway Odyssey: Special Places in His Life*. Nashville: Cumberland, 1999.

Leccese, Michael, and Kathleen McCormick, eds., *Charter of the New Urbanism*. New York: McGraw Hill, 2000.

Lee, Harper, *To Kill a Mockingbird*. New York: Lippincott, 1960.

Lemann, Nicholas, *The Big Test: The Secret History of the American Meritocracy*. Farrar Straus Giroux, 1999.

Lewis, Sinclair, *Main Street*. New York: Harcourt, Brace, 1920.

Liedtke, Walter, *Vermeer and the Delfi School*. New Haven: Yale University Press, 2001. Lingeman, Richard, *Small Town America: A Narrative History, 1620 to the Present*. New York: GP Putnam's Sons, 1980.

Linsley, Leslie, *Key West Houses*. New York: Rizzoli, 1992.

Maass, John, *The Victorian Home in America*. New York: Dover, 1972.

Macadam, Alta, *Northern Italy*. New York: W.W. Norton, 1985.

McLaughlin, Jack, *Jefferson and Monticello: The Biography of a Builder*. New York: Owl, 1988.

MacDonald, Donald, *Democratic Architecture*. New York: Whitney Library of Design, 1996.

Marshall, Paula, ed., *Better Homes and Gardens Porches & Sunrooms: Tour Guide to Planning and Remodeling*. Des Moines: Better Homes and Gardens Books, 2000.

Martin, Mick, and Marsha Porter, *Video Movie Guide*. New York: Ballantine, 1994.

Massey, James and Shirley Maxwell, *Gothic Revival*. New York: Abbeville, 1994.

McAlester, Virginia and Lee, *A Field Guide to American Houses*. New York: Knopf, 1990.

McGuane, Thomas, *The Bushwhacked Piano*. New York: Simon & Schuster, 1971.

McGuane, Thomas. *Ninety-Two in the Shade*. New York: Farrar Straus & Giroux, 1973.

Melville, Herman, *Billy Budd and Other Tales*. New York: Signet, 1956.

Merlis, Brian, and Oscar Israelowitz, *Welcome Back to Brooklyn*. New York: Israelowitz, 2000.

Meyers, Jeffery, *Hemingway: A Biography*. New York: Harper & Row, 1985.

Miller, Stuart, and Sharon Seitz, *A Tenement Story*. New York: Lower East Side Tenement Museum, 1999.

Morgan, Morris Hicky, trans., *Vitruvius: The Ten Books on Architecture*. New York: Dover, 1960.

Mumford, Lewis, *From the Ground Up*. New York: Harcourt Brace Jovanovich, 1956.

Murray, Peter, *The Architecture of the Italian Renaissance*. New York: Schocken, 1974.

Norquist, John O., *The Wealth of Cities*. Reading: Perseus, 1998.

Nuland, Sherwin B., *How We Die*. New York: Knopf, 1994.

O'Hara, John, *Appointment in Samara*. New York: Random House, 1934.

Olmsted, Roger, and T.H. Watkins, *Here Today*. San Francisco: Chronicle, 1978.

Ordish, George, *The Living American House*. New York: Morrow, 1981.

Owen, David, *The Walls around Us*. New York: Villard, 1991.

(Palladio) *Ville Veneto & Castelli*. Studio Bellemo, 2000.

Palliser, George and Charles, *Palliser's Model Homes*. Felton: Glenwood, 1972.

Palliser, George and Charles, *American Victorian Cottage Homes: Palliser, Palliser & Co.* New York: Dover, 1990.

Panati, Charles, *Extraordinary Origins of Everyday Things*. New York: Harper & Row, 1987.

Peskin, Allan, *Garfield*. Kent: Kent State University Press, 1978.

Pevsner, Nikolaus, *An Outline of European Architecture*. Middlesex: Penguin, 1951.

Pickering, Ernest, *The Homes of America*. New York: Thomas Y. Crowell, 1951.

Pindell, Terry, *A Good Place to Live*. New York: Henry Holt, 1995.

Pollan, Michael, *A Place of My Own*. New York: Random House, 1997.

Price, Reynolds (introduction), *Out on the Porch: An Evocation in Words and Pictures*. Chapel Hill: Algonquin, 1992.

Proctor, John Clagett, *Proctor's Washington*. Washington, D.C.: Washington Star, 1949.

Putnam, Robert D., *Bowling Alone*. New York: Simon & Schuster, 2000.

(Ranch Houses) *Sunset Western Ranch Houses*. Santa Monica: Hennessy & Ingalls, 1999.

Rasmussen, Steen Eiler, *Experiencing Architecture*. Cambridge: MIT, 1989.

Rawlings, Marjorie Kinnan, *The Yearling*. New York: Scribner, 1938.

Rawls, Walton, *The Great Book of Currier & Ives' America*. New York: Abbeville, 1979.

Reed, S.B., *Village & Country Residences*. New York: Lyons, 2000.

Rhodes, Robin Francis, *Architecture and Meaning in the Athenian Acropolis*. New York: Cambridge, 1995.

Rich, Kim, *Johnny's Girl*. New York: Morrow, 1993.

Rifkind, Carole, *A Field Guide to American Architecture*. New York: Bonanza, 1980.

Riis, Jacob A., *Jacob A. Riis*. Paris: Editions Nathan, 1997.

Risebero, Bill, *The Story of Western Architecture*. Cambridge: MIT, 1997.

Robbins, Sally Fennell, *Porch Presence*. New York: Michael Friedman, 1990.

Robinson, C.A., ed., *Selections from Greek and Roman Historians*. New York: Holt, Rinehart and Winston, 1957.

Roquemore, Joseph, *History Goes to the Movies*. New York: Doubleday, 1999.

Roth, Leland, *A Concise History of American Architecture*. New York: Harper & Row, 1979.

Rybczynski, Witold, *Looking Around*. New York: Penguin, 1992.

Rybczynski, Witold, *The Most Beautiful House in the World*. New York: Penguin, 1989.

Rybczynski, Witold, *Home*. New York. Penguin, 1986.

Rybczynski, Witold, *City Life*. New York: Touchstone, 1995.

Santmyer, Helen Hooven, *Ohio Town: A Portrait of Xenia*. New York. Harper & Row, 1984.

Sarris, Andrew, *You Ain't Heard Nothing Yet*. New York: Oxford, 1998.

Scott, Geoffrey, *The Architecture of Humanism*. New York: Doubleday Anchor, 1954.

Sklar, Kathryn Kish, *Catharine Beecher: A Study in American Domesticity*. New York: Norton/Yale, 1973.

Sloane, Eric, *Eric Sloane's America*. New York: Promontory, 1956.

Smeins, Linda E., *Building an American Identity: Pattern Book Homes & Communities 1870–1900*. Alta Mira: Sage, 1999.

Smith, Mary Ann, *Gustav Stickley—The Craftsman*. New York: Syracuse University, 1983.

Sneden, Pvt. Robert Knox, *The Eye of the Storm: A Civil War Odyssey*. New York: Free Press, 2000.

Stageberg, James, *A House of One's Own*. New York: Clarkson Potter, 1991.

Stambler, Irwin, *The Encyclopedia of Pop Rock and Soul*. New York: St. Martin's, 1989.

Steinbeck, John, *The Grapes of Wrath*. New York: Viking, 1939.

Stern, Robert A. M., *Pride of Place: Building the American Dream*. New York: Houghton Mifflin/American Heritage, 1986.

Stilgoe, John R., *Outside Lies Magic*. New York: Walker, 1998.

Susanka, Sarah, *The Not So Big House: A Blueprint for the Way We Really Live*. Newtown CT: Taunton, 1998.

Susanka, Sarah, *The Not So Big House*. Newton: Taunton, 1998.

Susanka, Sarah, *Creating the Not So Big House*. Newton: Taunton, 2000.

Tarkington, Booth, *Penrod*. New York: Doubleday, 1931.

Tatsch, J. Gregory, *Book of Ideas for Porch Design*. Quinlan: Vintage Wood Works, 1994.

Thomas, Hugh, *The Slave Trade: The Story of the Atlantic Slave Trade, 1440–1870.* New York: Touchstone, 1997.

Tunis, Edwin, *Frontier Living.* Cleveland: World, 1961.

Twain, Mark, *The Autobiography of Mark Twain.* New York: Harper & Row, 1959.

Twain, Mark, *Tales, Speeches, Essays, and Sketches.* Penguin, 1994.

Updike, John, *Couples.* Knopf, 1968.

Updike, John, *Pigeon Feathers and Other Stories.* Simon & Schuster, 1962.

Veblen, Thorstein, *The Theory of the Leisure Class.* New York: Modern Library, 2001.

Vlach, John Michael, *The Afro-American Tradition in Decorative Arts.* Athens: Brown Thrasher/University of Georgia, 1990.

Vlach, John Michael, *Back of the Big House: The Architecture of Plantation Slavery.* Chapel Hill: UNC Press, 1993.

Wall, Charles C., *Mount Vernon—A Handbook.* Washington, D.C.: Cognoscenti, 1985.

Wharton, Edith, *The Age of Innocence.* New York: Quality Paperback Book Club, 1993.

Wharton, Edith, *The Buccaneers.* New York: Viking, 1993.

Wills, Garry, *Venice, Lion City: The Religion of Empire.* New York: Simon & Schuster, 2001.

Windham, Kathryn Tucker. *Alabama—One Big Front Porch.* Tuscaloosa: University of Alabama, 1991.

Wolfe, Tom, *From Bauhaus to Our House.* Farrar Straus Giroux, 1981.

Wolfe, Tom, *A Man in Full.* New York: Farrar Straus Giroux, 1998.

Wu, Nelson I., *Chinese and Indian Architecture.* New York: George Braziller, 1963.

Younger, William Lee, *Old Brooklyn.* New York: Dover, 1978.

Additional Sources (NYT—New York Times, WP—Washington Post)

AIA DC Magazine, "The 2000 Washingtonian Residential Design Awards."

Allegood, Jerry, "Wilson Struggling to Understand 5 Slayings." *The News & Observer,* September 30, 2000.

Allen, Henry, "Snapshots of the Soul." *WP,* June 25, 2000.

Ashenburg, Katherine, "Where Long Ago Is Here and Now." *NYT,* September 24, 2000.

Auerbach, Jonathan, "McKinley at Home: How Early American Cinema Made News." American Quarterly, Maddox, Lucy ed. Baltimore: Johns Hopkins, Vol 51, No 4, 1999.

Barker, Karlyn, "Mail-Order Homes Still Standing." *WP,* September 20, 1981.

Barrenche, Raul A., "Puerto Rican Architects Head Home to Greener Pastures." *NYT,* April 20, 2000.

Barta, Patrick, "New American Home Is Smaller, Near City." *Wall Street Journal,* February 27, 2001.

Belfoure, Charles, "Outside Baltimore, a Reach for the Past." *NYT,* December 12, 1999.

Berendt, John, "A Radical Idea to Keep Venice Dry." *NYT,* February 5, 2002.

Berne, Suzanne, "Cooling off on Barbados." *NYT,* October 27, 1996.

Blair, Jason, "Failed Disney Vision: Integrated City." *NYT,* September 23, 2001.

Blumenthal, Ralph, "A Pied-a-Terre Designed by a President." *NYT, June* 14, 2001.

Bragg, Rick, "Comfort vs. Style in Town Clash on Porches." *NYT,* January 2, 1998.

Brock, Fred, "A Never-Say-Old Generation Can't Outrace the Clock Forever." *NYT,* December 3, 2000.

Brooke, James, "A Rare Glimpse inside an Italian Villa in Hartford." *NYT,* April 18, 1985.

Brown, Carolyn Spencer, "A Paradise of Paradox." *WP,* October 29, 2000.

Brown, Patricia Leigh, "A Design Controversy Goes Cozy.com." *NYT,* November 23, 2000.

Brown, Patricia Leigh, "A Carpenter Who Reconstructs the Past." *NYT,* March 26, 1987.

Brown, Patricia Leigh, "For Sale: Everything but the Props." *NYT,* February 10, 2000.

Brown, Patricia Leigh, "Out-Twigging the Neighbors." *NYT,* October 23, 1997.

Brown, Patricia Leigh, "What Price Preservation?" *NYT,* July 23, 1998.

Brozan, Nadine, "Abandoned Houses Are Reborn in Style." *NYT,* November 25, 2001.

Campbell, Robert, "The Nooks and Crannies Nurture Life." *The Boston Globe,* July 27, 2000.

Caputo, Philip, "Lost Keys." *NYT Magazine,* December 15, 1991.

Carvajal, Doreen, "Authentic Vision for Storybooks." *NYT,* August 21, 2001.

Christian, Shirley, "A Corner of New France." *NYT,* September 10, 2000.

Clausing, Jeri, "Aging Well in American Samoa." *NYT,* January 21, 2001.

Cole, Diane, "How Dowdy Old Baltimore Turned Fashionable." *NYT,* July 13, 2001.

Couloumbis, Angela E., "Glen Echo, Where the Past Still Resonates." *WP,* June 22, 1996.

(Chromated copper arsenate) "Wood with Arsenic to Be Phased Out." *Los Angeles Times,* February 13, 2002.

Crossette, Barbara, "Envoys' Homes Evoke Singapore's Past." *NYT,* September 11, 1986.

Cullen, Jenny, "On the Eve of Crocodile Dundee's Return, Paul Hogan, Linda Kozlowski and Their Son Chance Show Us around Their New Californian Home." *Hello!,* August 28, 2001.

Davis, David Brion, "The Enduring Legacy of the South's Civil War Victory." *NYT,* August 26, 2001.

Deane, Daniela, "Baltimore's Past Isn't Etched in Stone." *WP,* June 10, 2000.

Deane, Daniela, "Seeking a Slice of Summer." *WP,* July 8, 2000.

Demenway, Christine, "Mill Town As a Quirk in Progress." *WP,* July 14, 2001.

Dietsch, Deborah K., "Working All the Angles." *WP,* January 14, 1999.

Dietsch, Deborah K., "The Utopia Next Door." *WP Magazine,* August 26, 2001.

Dietsch, Deborah K., "The New Neotraditionalists." *WP,* September 8, 2001.

Dietsch, Deborah K., "A Winning Combination." *WP,* February 14, 2002.

Dorney, Diane, ed., *The Town Paper,* Westhaven Charrette Edition, November 2000.

Dorney, Diane, "New Urbanism Experts Gather in Charleston, S.C." *The Town Paper,* June/July 2001.

Eagleburger, Phillip, "Two Porches, Two Dramas." *AIA DC News,* June/July 2000.

Edwards, Jay, "The Complex Origins of the American Domestic Piazza-Veranda-Gallery." *Material Culture,* William D. Walters, Jr., ed. Vol. 21, No. 2, Summer 1989.

Egan, Timothy, "Sprawl-Weary Los Angeles Builds Up and In." *NYT* March 10, 2002.

Eicher, Diane, "Returning to the Porch." *The Denver Post,* July 31, 1999.

Feuer, Alan, "From the Stoops, Front-Row Seats on the City's Life." *NYT* August 10, 2001.

Fish, H. Bradford, "Instant Homes Break New Ground." *WP,* June 20, 1981.

Fleishman, Sandra, "Green around the Edges." *WP,* April 22, 2000.

Fleishman, Sandra, "New Buyers in D.C. Area Face Dilemma over Length of Commute, House Size." *WP,* June 23, 2001.

Fleishman, Sandra, "Restoration As a Labor of Love." *WP,* July 31, 1999.

Fleishman, Sandra, "Builders' Winning Play: A Royal Flush." *WP,* November 24, 2001.

Fleishman, Sandra, "A Grand Victorian Steps out in Style." *WP,* January 26, 2002.

Foderaro, Lisa W., "Hard Work: Rooming House to Family Home." *NYT,* February 26, 1987.

Frank, Robert H., "Why Living in a Rich Society Makes Us Feel Poor." *NYT Magazine,* October 15, 2000.

Frequently Asked Questions about Preserved Wood. American Wood Preservers Institute, 2000.

Fugard, Lisa, "Doing Nothing is a Fine Art." *NYT,* October 22, 2000.

Galef, David, "The South Has Risen Again. Everywhere." *NYT,* October 19, 1997.

Ginsburg, Steven, "Earley's 'Better Way' Ad." *WP,* October 3, 2001.

Giovannini, Joseph, "Preserving a Survivor of the Clapboard Era." *NYT,* January 12, 1984.

Giovannini, Joseph, "Some Suburban Pioneers in Yonkers Find Creative Ways to Occupy Big Houses." *NYT,* January 3, 1985.

Gladstone, Bernard, "Home Improvement." *NYT,* March 12, 1987.

Gleason, William, "Chesnutt's Piazza Tales: Architecture, Race, and Memory in the Conjure Stories." *American Quarterly,* Lucy Maddox, ed. Baltimore: Johns Hopkins University Press, Vol. 51, No. 4, 1999.

Goldberg, Carey, "Under Sail through the Grenadines." *NYT,* December 20, 1998.

Greene, Elaine, "Parsippany Home of Gustav Stickley Opening this Weekend." *NYT,* April 26, 1990.

Groer, Annie, "How a House in Falls Church Survived Life in the Movies." *WP,* January 13, 2000.

Groer, Annie, "The Whole Kit and Kaboodle." *WP,* February 7, 2002.

Halbfinger, David M., "Homesteaders Are Nearly Homeowners." *NYT,* May 31, 1998.

Hamilton, William L., "A Porch, a Chair, No Care." *NYT,* July 4, 1996.

Hamilton, William L., "A Writer Rebuilds a Home Called Childhood." ATT, July 13, 2000.

Hansen, Barbara Braun, "The 'New' Old Neighborhood." *Geico Direct,* Fall 2001.

Haskell, Molly, "In the Land of Self-Invention, You Can Always Start Over." *NYT,* September 9, 2001.

Hass, Nancy, "A Strange House and Its Strange Story." ATT, March 2, 2000.

Heavens, Alan J., "Behind the Stone, Modern Miracles of Efficiency." *WP,* July 22, 2000.

Hertzberg, Hendrik, "Two Little Words." *The New Yorker,* July 15, 2002.

Home Gallery Collection. Aired Associates Home Plan Gallery, Inc., 2000.

Homeplans. Frank Betz Associates, Inc., Vol 23.

Iovine, Julie V., "Not Just a Roof, but Roots for a Season." *NYT,* October 26, 2000.

Jacobs, Karrie, "Something Happened." *Dwell,* April 2002.

Johnson, Kirk, "Artful Echoes, in Parks and Porches." *NYT,* September 2, 2001.

Jones, Charisse, "Seeing Black History in Four Hidden Homes." *NYT,* April 22, 1996.

Kennedy, Shawn, "Seeing Bedford-Stuyvesant Brownstones." *NYT,* October 18, 1990.

Kessler, Glenn, and Sarah Schafer, "A Check this Summer, and Then . . ." *WP,* June 24, 2001.

Kimmelman, Michael, "Flags, Mom and Apple Pie through Altered Eyes." *NYT,* November 2, 2001.

Kinzer, Stephen, "Quiet, Please: Chicago Is Reading, the Same Book at the Same Time." *NYT,* August 28, 2001.

Langdon, Philip, "The American House: What We're Buying and Building." *The Atlantic,* September 1984.

Lane, Anthony, "Art for Love's Sake." *The New Yorker,* August 14, 2000.

Latham, Aaron, "Fine Company on a Desert Isle." *NYT,* December 20, 1998.

Lehmann-Haupt, Christopher, "Sales Pitches That Put the M (for Mega) in Madison Ave." *NYT,* January 3, 2001.

Leland, John, "After Worst of Times, Building for the Best." *NYT,* October 12, 2000.

Leland, John, "Subdivided and Licensed, There's No Place Like Art." *NYT,* October 4, 2001.

Lelen, Kenneth, "Elements of Style: Builders Find Neo-Traditional Designs Have Their Limits." *WP,* June 22, 1996.

Levine, Carol, "Taking on the 'Impossible' House: Three Renovations in Progress." *NYT,* July 11, 1985.

Lewis, Roger K., "'New Urbanist' Charter Returns to Old-Fashioned Architectural Ideals." *WP,* June 15, 1996.

Lilliefors, James, "Writers' Blocks." *WP,* December 15, 1996.

Louie, Elaine, "Mom Gets a Place in the Woods." *NYT,* September 27, 2001.

Lubow, Arthur, "Rem Koolhaas Builds." *NYT Magazine,* July 9, 2000.

Marcus, Frances Frank, "Bargains under Tropical Skies." *NYT,* October 22, 2000.

Marcus, Frances Frank, "Leaving the Hammock Behind." *NYT,* October 27, 1996.

Marling, Karal Ann, "Nice Front Porches, along with the 'Porch Police.'" *NYT,* September 6, 1999.

Mason, Katrina, "Big House Little House." *WP,* January 13, 2001.

Mason, Katrina, "Porches Are on the Upswing." *WP,* August 5, 2000.

Mayer, Caroline E., "In VA, a Dream of Development." *WP,* June 22, 1996.

Meyer, Eugene, "Where Porches Are King." *WP,* December 8, 2001.

Moriarty, Ann Marie, "Hot Tin Roofs." *WP,* September 28, 2000.

Moses, Jennifer, "Blending in Quickly in Margaritaville." *NYT,* November 25, 2001.

Muschamp, Herbert, "Mies Dreams with Windows: Two Shows Retrace a Life's Work." *NYT,* June 22, 2001.

Myers, Steve, "Wilson Tires Cited Most Often, Records Show." *The News & Observer,* September 29, 2000.

Navarro, Mireya, "What's Doing in Key West." *NYT,* October 27, 1996.

Nesmith, Lynn, "Leave the Porch Light On." *Southern Living,* February 2000.

(New Urbanism) "On Certification." *New Urban Post,* August 2001.

Niebuhr, Gustav, "What's Doing in Jackson Hole." *NYT,* February 11, 2001.

O'Keefe, Karen, "Growth and Growing Pains Celebrated at CNU IX." *The Town Paper,* August/September 2001.

Owens, Mitchell, "'Palm Beach Story' Part 2: The Bungalow." *NYT,* June 29, 2000.

Owens, Mitchell, "Sixty-Room Elephant Trumpets Again." *NYT,* June 6, 1996.

Page, Tim, "The Powerful Echo of Silents." *WP,* November 19, 2000.

Peterson, Iver, "Some Perched in Ivory Tower Gain Rosier View of Suburbs." *NYT,* December 5, 1999.

Pollan, Michael, "Town-Building Is No Mickey Mouse Operation." *NYT Magazine,* December 14, 1997.

Richard, Paul, "From the Collection: Washington's Prized Possessions." *WP,* June 24, 2001.

Roger, Marie Francis, *International Home Plans.* Drummond Designs, Inc., 2000.

Rogers, Patricia Dane, "A Fine Catch." *WP,* July 13, 2000.

Rogers, Patricia Dane, "Porches Designed." *WP,* June 29, 2000.

Rogers, Patricia Dane, "The Porch." *WP,* July 3, 1997.

Rogers, Patricia Dane, "Enduring Appeal." *WP,* October II, 2001.

Rohter, Larry, "Former Slave Havens in Brazil Gaining Rights." *NYT,* January 23, 2001.

Rozhon, Tracie, "Be It Ever Less Humble: American Homes Get Bigger." *NYT,* October 22, 2000.

Rozhon, Tracie, "Between Living Room and Lawn." *NYT,* July 4, 2002.

Sacks, Andrew, "Photograph: Mackinac Island, Mich." *NYT,* June 29, 1997.

Salant, Katherine, "By the Book: Building a Smaller House Can Provide Bigger Rewards." *WP,* November II, 2000.

Shaman, Diana, "Eight Brownstones Rehabilitated in Harlem." *NYT,* July 12, 1991.

Sidorsky, Robert, "On Nevis, Escape for Golfers." *NYT,* December 20, 1998.

Siegal, Nina, "At Poe's Door, a Hint of Nevermore." *NYT,* July 19, 2000.

Solomon, Deborah, "The Downtowning of Uptown." *NYT Magazine,* August 19, 2001.

Span, Paula, "Best Seller Dreams." *WP Magazine,* February 4, 2001.

Spano, Susan, "Puerto Rico, Beyond the Mountains." *NYT,* October 27, 1996.

Squier, Prudence, "Inside Out." *WP,* September 23, 1999.

Stanley, Alessandra, "New Frontiers in Comfort." *NYT,* December 6, 1998.

Star, Alexander, "What Feelings Feel Like." *NYT Magazine,* May 7, 2000, p31.

Steinhauer, Jennifer, "The Back Porch As Assembly Line." *NYT,* December 24, 1996.

Stewart, Mark, "For Old Greenbelt, Bonding Is by Design." *WP,* February 9, 2002.

Straight, Susan, "A Door Closes on the Past." *WP,* February 23, 2002.

Strauss, Neil, "Among the Big Winners at Grammys: Alicia Keys, 'O Brother' and U2." *NYT,* February 28, 2002.

Tanaka, Karen, prod., "The Art of Working." *WP Magazine,* October 3, 1999, p20.

Thompson, Ginger, "Reaping What Was Sown on the Old Plantation." *NYT,* June 22, 2000.

Tomkins, Calvin, "Schnabel in Lights." *The New Yorker,* March 19, 2001.

van Ryzin, Jeanne Clair. "The House That Bush Built." *Austin American Statesman,* January 18, 2001.

Varoli, John, "A Little Levittown on the Neva." *NYT,* July 13, 2000.

Veale, Scott, "Drinking Gin with the Dead." *NYT Book Review,* September 10, 2000.

Verhovek, Sam Howe, "From Ashes: Hope Comes to a Block in the South Bronx." *NYT,* November 10, 1987.

Weber, Bruce, "From Dugout to 'Short Porch' to Top Tier: It's Simply Historic." *NYT,* October 31, 2001.

Weeks, Linton, "City Limits." *WP,* September 7, 1999.

Weiner, Tim, "What's Doing in Los Cabos." *NYT,* October 22, 2000.

Wentzel, Michael, "Baltimore Folk-Art Form: Painted Window Screens." *NYT*, August 12, 1982.

Whoriskey, Peter, "The Quandary Next Door." *WP*, February 6, 2001.

Whoriskey, Peter, "A Puzzle for Preservationists." *WP*, December 13, 2001.

Wilford, John Noble, "Inches Underground, Secrets of Northern Slave Life." *NYT*, July 27, 1999.

Wilkes, Kevin, "Building a Grand Verandah." *Fine Home Building*, Newton, Connecticut: Taunton. No 3132, July 2000.

Wise, Anne, "Public Art and New Urbanism: A Look at the Village of Cheshire." *The Town Paper*, February 2001.

Yazigi, Monique P., "Storming the Last Civilized Sandbox." *NYT*, May 25, 2000.

ACKNOWLEDGMENTS

To everyone who, whether voluntarily or after shameless pandering and/or insidious hectoring, proffered personal experience, historical information, wild-eyed notions, reasonable concepts, and the like, as well as hospitality, travel directions, invitations to set a spell and talk, floor space, meals, and/or encouragement in any form, I send thanks, and thanks, and more thanks, particularly to Alex Heard, whose innocent telephone call sent me on this mission; Jane Dystel and her merry band, particularly the protean Miriam Goderich; the exquisitely accurate Virginia Beck; the extraordinarily deft LeAnna Weller Smith; Becky Koh, who saw the possibilities; Bill Holland and Marianne LaRoche; Judge David Hughes; Joel Achenbach; Michael Leccese and Kathleen McCormick; Pat McNees; Andres Duany and Elizabeth Plater-Zyberk; Jeff Limerick; the Brownell family, especially Barbara; Dennis Melamed; Jason Wilt; Antonio Foscari; Mary Lee Eggart; Robin Dripps; the Piovene and Bianchi-Michiel families; Regina Washington; Joseph Lewis and Tom Lewis; Raymond Einhorn; Robin Marantz Henig; Lucy Rowland; the fabulous Konig brothers; Huck DeVenzio, Tilghman Herring; LouAnn Munson; my sister, in spirit and blood, Maureen Dolan Rosen; Michael and Polly Johnson; Henry Diltz; Tom Radcliffe; Nelida Ruiz; Chris O'Toole; Marguerite Lavin; William Guy; John O'Toole; Larry Pilot; Alan Aiches; Glenn Pearson; Andrew Ferguson; James Howard Kunstler; Eddie Dean; David and Mary Alex Dill; Steve Dryden; Joel Embry; Rebecca Cooper and Doug Dupin; Michael Pittarelli; Peggy Eastman; Luigi di Tomassi; Penny Trams; Elaine Eff; Brian Powers; Sam Myers and Mary Helen Boone; Melvin Snyder; Anne Marie and Ed Resor, Robert Safran, and Abdul Wahab; Kathy and Paul Warren; Patti Francis and Sean Griffin; Mark Burnett; Gopal Aluwahlia; Mary Ellen McFerran; Thomas V. Hynes; Chuck Naylor; Pat Lydon; William Gleason; Frank Turner Sr. and Jr.; Shelley Fisher Fishkin; Michael Zack; Jonathan Auerbach; Herman Belz and Kristin Belz; Julie and Mark Oxley, Nick Carson, and Peter Grina; Else and Dan Moskowitz; Marina Moskowitz; Penny Pagano; Lenny Cassuto; Mary Corliss; Terry Geeskend; Dawn Bonner; Rob Fowler; Brown-Foreman Distillers Corp.; Shannon Ravenel; and Christian Malinverni. If I left anyone out, I apologize from the bottom of my forgetful heart.

For superb work as a field assistant, finagler of arrangements, interpreter, and translator, I thank the indomitable Nadia Bettin.

For sharing their epochal insights into the African origins of the American porch, I thank John Vlach and Jay Edwards.

For copyediting above and beyond the call of friendship, I thank Alice Leccese Powers and Steve Brown who, in their time of recovery from dire illness, attended to my needs when it should have been vice versa.

ACKNOWLEDGMENTS

For editorial guidance of Nordenesque precision that enabled me to hoist the contents of this volume to a level I never imagined I could achieve, I thank Ann Treistman.

For their often puzzled encouragement as I made my irregular way in the working life, I thank my late parents, Joan and Austin Dolan.

For the so-called career that led to and underwrote a substantial portion of the work that resulted in this exercise, I owe much to my late patron, the mad genius David Swit, and to the great Sam Gilston, both of whom taught me to find out *what it means*; as well as to the relentless Jack Shafer, who goaded me in a decade of writing better/longer/deeper for *Washington City Paper*; to Brian Breger and Jon Goodman, my genially demanding mentors in script writing; and to my friend and neighbor, Michael Rosenfeld, who unlocked the door to the editing suite.

Finally, I owe debts even Bruce Springsteen couldn't pay to my beautiful and tenacious wife, real-estate partner, and unindicted coconspirator, Eileen O'Toole, and to our son, the formidable Marty Dolan, for their patient and occasionally even eager engagement (on Eileen's part, as an extrapolation on twenty years of coping with her-husband-the-writer; on Marty's, during a research foray to the Veneto that saw him dragooned into serving as best boy, key grip, gaffer, camera/sound tech, and sometime Sancho Panza) with an endeavor that came to engulf our lives. Now we can sit out on the porch and relax, at least until the next deadline. I love you.

As a postscript, I apologize to those whose porch stories and porches didn't make it into this volume. My apologies also go to anyone disappointed that *The American Porch* isn't a variant on Kramer's coffee-table book. (I vow that, if the market dictates, I'll subject the porch to a visual treatment worthy of any veranda's coffee table, or any coffee house's veranda.)

CREDITS

Images in text: p. 2 Aaron Belz; p. 6 Eileen O'Toole; p. 12, 17 Sean Griffin; p. 26 Mary Lee Eggart, after a print by Franz Post; p. 36 George Chinnery; p. 62 (top) Historic American Buildings Survey, (bottom) Max L. Hill III; p. 79 courtesy U.S. Bureau of Engraving and Printing; p. 82 Dan Grogan; p. 86, 93 from *The Architecture of Country Houses*, by Andrews Jackson Downing; p. 100, "Home from the Brook," Currier & Ives, courtesy of the Museum of the City of New York; p. 106, courtesy of the Stowe-Day Foundation; p. 114 Marty Dolan; p. 121 from Palliser's Model Homes 1878; p. 151 "Gone With the Wind" still courtesy of Museum of Modern Art Film Stills Archive; p. 153 Walker Evans, for the U.S. Dept. of Agriculture Farm Security Administration; p. 210 Michael Moran Photography, New York, New York, courtesy of CORE.

All other photographs, unless otherwise indicated, are by the author.

"This Old Porch" Words and music by Lyle Lovett and Robert Earl Keen, Jr. Copyright @ 1986 Michael H. Goldsen, Inc., Lyle Lovett Music and Keen Edge Music. All rights for Lyle Lovett Music controlled and administered by Michael H. Goldsen, Inc. All rights for Keen Edge Music administered by BMG Rights Management (US) LLC International Copyright Secured. All rights reserved. Reprinted by permission of Hal Leonard LLC.

ABOUT THE AUTHOR

Michael Dolan is a writer, a former editor for *American History* magazine, and a musician. He also consults for documentary television productions and book manuscripts. Dolan's articles have appeared in the *New Republic*, the *New Yorker*, *Smithsonian*, *Outside*, and the *New York Times Magazine*, among others. From 1983 to 1995, he and his wife renovated a 1920s home near the Potomac River, including the replacement of an old front porch with one of Dolan's own design. This project inspired his book, *The American Porch*. Dolan's porch now hosts occasional rehearsals by his band, the Powerful House Ways & Means Committee. He lives in Washington, D.C., his hometown.

OPEN ROAD

INTEGRATED MEDIA

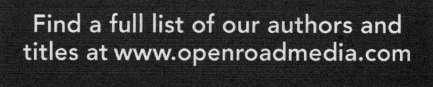

Find a full list of our authors and titles at www.openroadmedia.com

FOLLOW US
@OpenRoadMedia